Operational Risk

A Guide to Basel II Capital Requirements, Models, and Analysis

ANNA S. CHERNOBAI
SVETLOZAR T. RACHEV
FRANK J. FABOZZI

BICENTENNIAL
1807
WILEY
2007
BICENTENNIAL

John Wiley & Sons, Inc.

Published by John Wiley & Sons, Inc., Hoboken, New Jersey.
Published simultaneously in Canada.

Wiley Bicentennial Logo: Richard J. Pacifico

For general information on our other products and services or for technical support, please contact our Customer Care Department within the United States at (800) 762-2974, outside the United States at (317) 572-3993 or fax (317) 572-4002.

Wiley also publishes its books in a variety of electronic formats. Some content that appears in print may not be available in electronic books. For more information about Wiley products, visit our Web site at www.wiley.com.

ISBN: 978-0-471-78051-9

Printed in the United States of America.

10 9 8 7 6 5 4 3 2 1

Contents

Preface

The field of risk management has it origins in the insurance industry. In the 1980s, risk management in manufacturing firms took hold with the adoption of total quality management. It was not until the 1990s that the field of risk management received greater recognition for its importance in financial and nonfinancial corporations. In 1993, for example, GE Capital designated a *chief risk officer* (CRO), James Lam, charged with the responsibility of managing all aspects of the firm's risks, including back-office operations. Today, most major firms have as part of their corporate executive staff an individual with the title of CRO who in some cases have a direct line reporting to the board of directors.

As further evidence of the growing importance of the field of risk management, today there are designations that can be earned to identify risk management specialists, just as with accountants (CPAs) and asset managers (CFAs). For example, the Global Association of Risk Professionals (GARP), founded in 1996 and with roughly 58,000 members from more than 100 countries, awards the Financial Risk Management (FRM) certificate upon the completion of a series of examinations. Universities offer not only courses on risk management, but also degrees in the area of financial engineering, with risk management being a major part of the curriculum. The number of books published each year on various aspects of risk management continues to grow. The interest in risk management by the general public is evidenced by the appearance of Peter Bernstein's book in 1996, *Against the Gods: The Remarkable Story of Risk*, on the bestseller list in North America and Europe and subsequently translated into 11 languages. Each year at least one new journal appears dedicated to some aspect of risk management.

Often in financial institutions when there is a discussion of risk managment, the two major risks identified are credit risk and market risk. Risks not attributable to either of these two risks are labeled *other risks* and, unfortunately, do not receive the same level of attention as credit risk and market risk. As we explain in Chapter 1, a number of prominent financial institutions have been shaken by losses in excess of $1 billion each in the past couple of decades. Even worse, many of these failures resulted in bankruptcies. None of these losses, however, were due to credit risk or market risk. Rather, they were attributable to *operation risk*, one of the risks that has been historically lumped into other risks. The irony is that operational risk, which is at the core of these high-profile failures, appears to be, at least in part, a byproduct of the recent rapid technological innovation, revolutionary advances in information network, financial deregulation, and globalization.

The banking system has faced the painful reality that it is not sufficiently prepared to handle operational risk. Many banks now share the opinion of Roger Ferguson (who served as the vice chairman of the board of governors of the Federal Reserve System from 2001 to 2006), who said in 2003, "In an increasingly technologically driven banking system, operational risks have become an even larger share of total risk. Frankly, at some banks, they are probably the dominant risk."

As a drastic countermeasure, the Basel Committee for Banking Supervision introduced an amendment to the Basel Capital Accord to support operational risk with regulatory capital and outlined several measurement approaches in 2001. The implementation of the Basel II Capital Accord is expected to begin in January 2007 for all internationally active banks (with a few exceptions and some transitional adjustments).

This brings us to the purpose of this book. With the Basel II deadline approaching, risk managers are overwhelmed with gathering and absorbing the literature related to operational risk modeling and management. In this book, we have summarized all important empirical studies based on real operational loss data (a good number of which have not yet been published in journals) and have further supplemented them with discussions of relevant theoretical background, with the intention of providing the reader with a comprehensive and up-to-date package of practical tools for modeling operational risk. We believe the contents of this book will relieve the risk manager of the burden of collecting, reading, and assessing the literature on operational risk measurement and its implications.

In the first two chapters of this book, we review major operational loss-related banking failures and discuss the concept and specifics of operational risk. Chapter 3 is devoted to the discussion of the three pillars of the Base II Capital Accord and Chapter 4 explains the main challenges that exist in modeling operational risk. Throughout the rest of the book, Chapters 5 to 13, we concentrate on addressing these challenges one by one and discussing the proposed solutions.

We require minimum quantitative background from the reader and have tried to maintain a balanced discussion of the quantitative and practical sides of the topic. All chapters are self-explanatory, and whenever possible, important statistical concepts are illustrated with examples. The chapters after Chapter 4 have a distinct structure: They begin with a summary of the essential statistical and mathematical tools relevant to the topic covered in the chapter, followed by a discussion of the implementation of these tools in practice with real data as reported in empirical studies. At the end of every chapter, we provide an extensive list of references for further reading.

The target audience of our book is expected to be broad, consisting of practitioners, students, and academics who are willing to learn about operational risk and its recent developments. The book can also serve as a test for graduate seminars and specialized MBA courses. The wide range of topics coverd in this book will equip the reader with an essential understanding of the statistics of operational risk and the challenges in their real-world implementation.

We would like to acknowledge the support received in the preparation of this book. Anna Chernobai's research was supported by various sources of assistance from Syracuse University, University of California at Santa Barbara, and University of Karlsruhe. Svetlozar Rachev's research was supported by grants from the Division of Mathematical, Life and Physical Sciences, College of Letters and Science, University of California at Santa Barbara, and the Deutschen Forschungsgemeinschaft.

Anna S. Chernobai
Svetlozar T. Rachev
Frank J. Fabozzi

About the Authors

Anna S. Chernobai is an Assistant Professor of Finance in the Martin J. Whitman School of Management at Syracuse University, New York. She earned her Ph.D. in statistics and applied probability in 2006 from the University of California at Santa Barbara. Her doctorate thesis focused on statistical modeling of operational risk in financial institutions. Professor Chernobai also holds a master's degree in economics and finance from the Warwick Business School, the University of Warwick, and a master's degree in economics from the University of California at Santa Barbara.

Svetlozar (Zari) T. Rachev completed his Ph.D. in 1979 from Moscow State (Lomonosov) University, and his Doctor of Science Degree in 1986 from Steklov Mathematical Institute in Moscow. Currently he is Chair-Professor in Statistics, Econometrics and Mathematical Finance at the University of Karlsruhe in the School of Economics and Business Engineering. He is also Professor Emeritus at the University of California, Santa Barbara, in the Department of Statistics and Applied Probablity. He has published seven monographs, eight handbooks and special-edited volumes, and more than 250 research articles. Professor Rachev is cofounder of Bravo Risk Management Group specializing in financial risk-management software. Bravo Group was recently acquired by FinAnalytica, for which he currently serves as Chief-Scientist.

Frank J. Fabozzi is Professor in the Practice of Finance in the School of Management at Yale University. Prior to joining the Yale faculty, he was a Visiting Professor of Finance in the Sloan School of Management at MIT. Professor Fabozzi is a Fellow of the International Center for Finance at Yale University and on the advisory council for the Department of Operation Research and Financial Engineering at Princeton University. He is the editor of the *Journal of Portfolio Management* and an associate editor of the the *Journal of Fixed Income*. He earned a doctorate in economics from the City University of New York in 1972. In 2002, Professor Fabozzi was inducted into the Fixed Income Analysts Society's Hall of Fame. He earned the designation of Chartered Financial Analyst and Certified Public Accountant. He has authored and edited numerous books in finance.

CHAPTER 1

Operational Risk Is Not Just "Other" Risks

Until very recently, it has been believed that banks are exposed to two main risks. In the order of importance, they are *credit risk* (counterparty failure) and *market risk* (loss due to changes in market indicators, such as equity prices, interest rates, and exchange rates). Operational risk has been regarded as a mere part of "other" risks.

Operational risk is not a new concept for banks. Operational losses have been reflected in banks' balance sheets for many decades. They occur in the banking industry every day. Operational risk affects the soundness and operating efficiency of all banking activities and all business units.

Most of the losses are relatively small in magnitude—the fact that these losses are frequent makes them predictable and often preventable. Examples of such operational losses include losses resulting from accidental accounting errors, minor credit card fraud, or equipment failures. Operational risk-related events that are often more severe in the magnitude of incurred loss include tax noncompliance, unauthorized trading activities, major internal fraudulent activities, business disruptions due to natural disasters, and vandalism.

Until around the 1990s, the latter events have been infrequent, and even if they did occur, banks were capable of sustaining the losses without major consequences. This is quite understandable because the operations within the banking industry until roughly 20 years ago have been subject to numerous restrictions, keeping trading volumes relatively modest, and diversity of operations limited. Therefore, the significance of operational risk (whose impact is positively correlated with income size and dispersion of business units) has been perceived as minor, with limited effect on management's decision-making and capital allocation when compared to credit risk and market risk. However, serious changes in the global financial markets in the last 20 years or so have caused noticeable shifts in banks' risk profiles.

EFFECTS OF GLOBALIZATION AND DEREGULATION: INCREASED RISK EXPOSURES

In the course of the last two decades, the global financial industry has been highlighted by several pronounced trends, which have been in response to increased investors' appetites. The global financial system has been characterized by globalization and deregulation, accelerated technological innovation and revolutionary advances in the information network, and an increase in the scope of financial services and products. Globalization and financial deregulation have been working to effectively put together the world's dispersed financial markets into a unified complex network.

An example from Asia is the Japanese "Big Bang" financial deregulation reform, launched in 1998 by then Prime Minister Ryutaro Hashimoto, as a response to a prolonged economic stagnation that started with the burst of the bubble economy in late 1989 to early 1990. Financial reform was aimed at the liberalization of banking, insurance, and stock exchange markets and boosting the competition of the Japanese financial market relative to the European and American markets, and to regain the status of one of the world's major financial centers.

As for the United States, an example is the Financial Services Act of 1999. The bill repealed the 1933 Glass-Steagall Act's restrictions on bank and securities firm affiliations and allowed affiliations among financial service companies, including banks, registered investment companies, securities firms, and insurance companies—formerly prohibited under the Bank Holdings Act of 1956. It also called for the expansion of the range of financial services allowed by banks.

Several reforms have taken place in Europe. In October 1986, the London Stock Exchange underwent a radical change in organization, the *Big Bang* (a title later adopted for the Japanese financial reform). It eliminated fixed commissions on security trades and allowed securities firms to act as brokers and dealers. It also introduced automated screen-based trading, enabling the movement away from the traditional market floor. Another prominent example is the formation and expansion of the European Union, and adoption of a single currency, the euro. The purpose of the union is to relax financial barriers and break down trading constraints, and achieve integration on cultural, economic, and political levels. In Eastern Europe, the collapse of the Soviet regime in the early 1990s created a massive new market for capital flows.

Financial globalization due to financial liberalization has caused players in the financial and business sectors across the world economies to be subject to an unprecedented degree of competition, from both domestic and foreign counterparts. Liberalized trade has given customers and investors choices and opportunities they did not have before. This has resulted in the development of new financial products, instruments, and services. Securitization has turned otherwise illiquid instruments into tradeable commodities. Privatization has turned thousands of former state enterprises into private ventures and competitors for risk capital. New derivative instruments have been offered to provide for powerful hedging tools against various market and credit-related risks.

Financial deregulation has coincided with (or, perhaps, in many cases has triggered) a number of remarkable technological innovations including the development of the Internet, leading to revolutionized banking activities such as online banking, growth of e-commerce, and e-mail services. An immediate consequence of this development is a breakthrough in the means and speed at which the financial information is obtained and shared by investors, calling for a higher degree of transparency and market disclosure about banks' business practices.

As a side-effect of these global financial trends and policies, outsourcing, expansion of the scope of financial services, and large-scale mergers and acquisitions (M&A) have become more frequent around the globe. These, in turn, inevitably result in an elevated exposure of the financial institutions to various sources of risk. As a simple example, increased use of computer-based banking services is vulnerable to viruses and computer failures, and credit card fraud. When business units expand, this requires additional employees—this may increase the number of errors committed and increase the hazard of fraudulent activities.

Newly developed and optimized financial products (such as derivatives and securitized products) now provide better protection against market risk and credit risk. Furthermore, previously nonexistent or insignificant risk factors have become a large (or larger) part of the complex risk profiles of financial institutions. Yet some of these risks have not been adequately addressed. Without exaggeration, operational risk is the most striking of all, and has been the subject of heated discussions among risk managers, regulators, and academics in the last few years. As Roger W. Ferguson, Vice Chairman of the Board of Governors of the Federal Reserve System, stated, "In an increasingly technologically driven banking system, operational risks have become an even larger share of total risk. Frankly, at some banks, they are probably the dominant risk."[1]   Major banks share the same view. As an example, a report by the HSBC Group (2004) states that "... regulators are increasingly focusing on operational risk ... This extends

---

[1]From the 108th session on The New Basel Capital Accord Proposal, Hearing before the Committee on Banking, Housing and Urban Affairs, United States Senate, 2003.

to operational risk the principle of supporting credit and market risk with capital, since arguably it is operational risk that potentially poses the greatest risk."[2]

Another important impact of globalization is the effect of culture. Culture is an important basis for trust. Internal control practices that prove effective in Asia may fail in Europe or the United States. Using an example from van den Brink (2002), while it is common in Europe and North America to give one staff member the code of the safe and another staff member the key, the same procedure in Indonesia would be perceived by senior management as being mistrusted. Or, as another example, in Japan it is uncommon to say no to or argue with senior management. As we will see later in this chapter, many large-scale operational losses are a result of misuse of trust and responsibility.

Sophisticated instruments and techniques have been developed to manage low- and medium-magnitude losses that are due to market-related and credit-related financial risks. However, recent experiences from the financial market suggest that cash-flow fluctuations of a larger scale, which are more likely to be incurred by the institution/bank's operation practices rather than market or credit risk related factors, have not been well-managed.[3] To support this view, in 1999 the Basel Committee pointed out "the growing realisation of *risks other than credit and market risks* which have been at the heart of some important banking problems in recent years."[4]

EXAMPLES OF HIGH-MAGNITUDE OPERATIONAL LOSSES

The world financial system has been shaken by a number of banking failures over the last 20 years, and the risks that particularly internationally active banks have had to deal with have become more complex and challenging. More than 100 operational losses exceeding $100 million in value each, and a number of losses exceeding $1 billion, have impacted financial firms globally since the end of 1980s.[5] There is no question that the cause is

---

[2]HSBC Operational Risk Consultancy group was founded in 1990, and is a division of HSBC Insurance Brokers.
[3]See King (2001).
[4]See BIS (1999, p. 15.), with reference to the BIS survey.
[5]According to de Fontnouvelle, DeJesus-Rueff, Jordan, and Rosengren (2003), large, internationally active banks typically experience between 50 and 80 losses exceeding $1 million per year.

unrelated to market or credit risks, which we noted earlier are the two major risk factors that banks had been believed to face. Such large-scale losses have resulted in bankruptcies, mergers, or substantial equity price declines of a large number of highly recognized financial institutions. Here are a few examples of such losses that occurred in the 1990s.[6]

Orange County, 1994, United States

On December 6, 1994, a prosperous district in California, Orange County, surprised the markets by declaring bankruptcy. The treasurer, Robert Citron, was entrusted with a $7.5 billion commingled portfolio managed on behalf of the county schools, cities, districts, and the county itself. Investors perceived Citron as a financial wizard who could deliver high returns on their funds during a period of low short-term interest rates by investing in mortgage derivative products that had a substantial exposure to interest rate changes (i.e., securities with a high effective duration). The portfolio performed well when interest rates were declining; however, when rates increased in early 1994, the portfolio blew up. Losses reaching $1.7 billion, forcing Orange County into bankruptcy.

Citron either did not understand the interest rate exposure of his portfolio because he was unacquainted with the risk/return of the securities in the portfolio or he ignored the magnitude of the risk exposure, believing he could correctly forecast the direction of interest rates. In any case, there were no systems in place to monitor the portfolio's exposure to changes in interest rates. Orange County illustrates combination of lack of expert risk oversight and incompetence.[7]

Barings Bank, 1995, United Kingdom

In February 1995, Barings Bank declared bankruptcy. Barings Bank was the United Kingdom's oldest merchant bank, founded in 1762. Nick Leeson, who was appointed the general manager of the Barings Futures subsidiary in Singapore in 1993, was assigned to exploit low-risk arbitrage opportunities

---

[6] Other well-known examples from the financial industry include losses incurred by Bank of Credit and Commerce International (1991, fraud), Bankers Trust (1994, fraud), NatWest Markets (1997, error, incompetence), and Nomura Securities (1997, fraud). Some individual case studies are discussed in Cruz (2002), Adams and Frantz (1993), Beaty & Gwynne (1993), FDIC (1995), Shirreff, (1997), Crouhy, Galai, and Mark (2001), as well as daily periodicals and various Internet sites.

[7] For a more detailed description of the Orange County fiasco, see Jorion (1998), Jorion and Roper (1995), and Irving (1995).

that would leverage price differences in similar equity derivatives on the Singapore Money Exchange (SIMEX) and the Osaka exchange markets. However, due to a lack of higher supervision, he was was given control over both the trading and back-office functions. He began taking much riskier positions by trading different amounts on contracts of different types on the two exchanges. The derivatives contracts on the Singapore and the Japanese foreign exchange markets were highly dependent on the market conditions in 1993 to 1994.

When the market became volatile, losses in Leeson's trading account began to accumulate, forcing him to increase his bets in an attempt to recover losses. He created a special secret account to keep track of his losses, account 88888. This account had originally been set up to cover up a mistake made by an inexperienced member of the trading team, which led to a loss of £20,000. Leeson then used this account to cover his mounting trading losses.

Finally, the Nikkei index dropped sharply after the January 17, 1995, Kobe earthquake in Japan, and the losses exceeded $1 billion. The fraud was only exposed when Nick Leeson failed to show up at work at his Singapore office in February 1995; he was attempting to flee from Kuala Lumpur to England in order to escape the tough Far Eastern justice system. The bank was unable to sustain the loss and announced bankruptcy. Here is an extract from Leeson's book *Rogue Trader* (1997, pp. 2–3), about his last trading day:

> *I knew I'd still lost millions of pounds, but I didn't know how many. I was too frightened to find out—the numbers scared me to death. . . . I'd gone in trying to reduce the position and ended up buying another 4,000 contracts. . . . Traders looked at me and knew I'd done an amazing volume of trade; they marvelled at the sheer amount of business I'd got through. They wondered whether I was dealing for myself or for clients, and whether I'd hedged, protected my position. But they knew—as the whole of Asia did—that I'd built up an exposure to over £11 billion worth of Japanese shares. They were doing their sums and they reckoned I was well long: it was hard to conceal it when you stand for over 40 percent of the Singapore market. The rest of the market had smelled what Barings back in London were completely ignoring: that I was in so deep there was no way out.*

A month later, in March 1995, the bank was purchased by the Dutch Bank ING for £1 sterling! In November 1995 Nick Leeson was sentenced to 6.5 years in a Singaporean jail. This is another example of the dramatic consequences of internal fraud, unauthorized trading, and poor internal surveillance and control.[8]

Daiwa Bank, 1995, New York

On July 13, 1995, the executive vice president of Japan's Daiwa Bank's New York branch, Toshihide Iguchi, confessed (in a 30-page letter to the president of Daiwa Bank in Japan) that he had lost around $1.1 billion trading U.S. Treasury bonds. At the time of the incident, Daiwa was one of Japan's top 10 banks and one of the world's top 20 banks in terms of asset size. An astonishing part of the incident is that Iguchi's illegal trading had been taking place over an 11-year period. Daiwa's New York branch managed the custody of the U.S. Treasury bonds that it bought, as well as those that it bought on behalf of its customers, via a sub-custody account held at Bankers Trust. Through this account, interest on the bonds was collected and dispersed, and bonds were transferred or sold according to the wishes of either customers or the bank's own managers.

When Iguchi lost a few hundred thousand dollars in his trading activities, he began selling off bonds in the Bankers Trust subcustody account to pay off his losses, falsifying Bankers Trust account statements so that they would not indicate that the securities had been sold. Throughout the 11 years he forged about 30,000 trading slips and other documents. When customers needed to be paid interest on bonds that had been sold without their knowledge, Iguchi would settle their accounts by selling off more securities and further altering more records. In total, Iguchi sold off roughly $377 million of Daiwa's customers' securities and $733 million of Daiwa's own investment securities to cover his trading losses. Shortly after the incident came to surface in November 1995, the Federal Reserve ordered Daiwa Bank to end all of its U.S. operations within 90 days; by January 1996 Daiwa agreed to sell most of its U.S. assets of $3.3 billion to Sumitomo Bank and to sell off its 15 U.S. offices.

In December 1996, Iguchi was sentenced to four years in prison and fined $2.6 million. The scandal led to Standard & Poors downgrading Daiwa from A to BBB and to Japan's Ministry of Finance imposing restrictions on the bank's activities for a year. In September 2000, a Japanese court in Osaka ordered 11 current and former Daiwa board members and top

---

[8]Detailed reports on the case include "Not Just One Man—Barings" by L. Chew, Bank of England (1995a), Bank of England (1995b), and Koernert (1996). A number of books have been written about the case: Rawnsley (1995), Fay (1997), Gapper and Denton (1996), Leeson (1997), and Leeson and Tyrrell (2005). The case was turned into a movie, *Rogue Trader*, released in June 1999.

executives to pay the bank $775 million as a compensation to shareholders' damages. This is yet another example of internal fraud and illegal trading.[9]

Allied Irish Banks, 2002, Ireland

On February 6, 2002, Allied Irish Banks (AIB), Ireland's second-biggest bank, discovered a large-scale and what the bank described as a "complex and very determined fraud" in its Baltimore-based subsidiary Allfirst. Total losses to AIB/Allfirst are estimated to have exceeded $700 million. A report stated that around 1997, John Rusnak, a trader, had lost a large amount of money on a misplaced proprietary trading strategy, repeatedly falsifying bank statements in an attempt to recoup losses. Rusnack did this by writing nonexistent options and booking the fictitious premium income as revenue, thereby getting himself into a loop of accruing even bigger losses. One weekend he failed to show up at work on Monday morning. As a result of his disappearance, the details of his fraudulent activities came to light. Rusnak, a U.S. citizen, was nicknamed a second Nick Leeson, and entered the league of the infamous rogue traders, together with Toshihide Iguchi. He was sentenced to 7.5 years in federal prison, and was barred for life from working in any financial services company. Amazingly, this case demonstrates how the lessons from Barings Bank's collapse of almost a decade earlier had not been properly learned.[10]

The Enron Scandal, 2001, United States

The collapse of Enron Corporation has been the largest bankruptcy in U.S. history. The Enron Corporation was one of the world's largest energy commodities and services companies. Enron was formed in July 1985 in Houston, Texas, by a merger of Houston Natural Gas and InterNorth of Omaha, Nebraska. Initially a natural gas pipeline company, Enron quickly entered the energy futures as energy markets were deregulated. It entered the European energy market in 1995.

On January 25, 2001, the stock price of Enron had reached its peak at $81.39 per share, and began to drop. Just two days earlier, on January 23, Enron's CEO since 1985, Kenneth Lay, resigned. By the middle of August 2001, it fell to $43. At the same time, the new CEO, Jeffrey Skilling, quit his

---

[9]More on Daiwa's case can be found in FDIC (1995) and Lectric Law Library (1995). A 1997 interview with Iguchi appeared in *Time* magazine (1997). Iguchi also wrote a memoir from prison titled *The Confession*.

[10]Detailed case studies on AIB can be found in Leith (2002) and various Internet sources.

new job after six months, for "purely personal" reasons. In November the price per share fell below $10, and Enron announced $600 million in losses from 1997 to 2000. On December 2, when the share price finally hit zero, Enron filed for bankruptcy protection, making it the largest bankruptcy case in U.S. history. In the middle of January, Enron's stock was formally delisted from the New York Stock Exchange.

The board of directors of Enron blamed the failure on poor information from the accountants and the management. An investigation into the case conducted by the Securities and Exchange Commission in 2002 suggested that Enron may have overstated its assets by up to $24 billion due to poor accounting practices.

A number of financial institutions were involved in the Enron case. Arthur Andersen, which was Enron's auditing firm for 16 years, was charged with obstruction of justice for destroying some of the Enron's documents in order to protect the firm, while on notice of a federal investigation, and were ordered to cease auditing publicly traded companies on August 31, 2002. Their losses due to the case were estimated at over $750 million. Merill Lynch has been accused of a conspiracy to help Enron hide its true state of financial affairs, and estimated its losses due to the involvement at over $80 million. Other banks involved in the scandal include NatWest (losses over $20 million), Citibank, JPMorgan Chase & Co., and Salomon Smith Barney, among others, were accused of lending Enron billions of dollars with the full knowledge that Enron was not reporting these loans as debt on its balance sheet. This is an example of losses due to legal liability in combination with fraudulent activities.[11]

MasterCard International, 2005, United States

In June 2005, MasterCard International Inc. in the United States announced that the names, banks, and account numbers of up to 40 million credit card holders were feared to have been accessed by an unauthorized user. It was revealed that a computer virus captured customer data for the purpose of fraud and may have affected holders of all brands of credit cards. This was one in a series of recent incidents involving security failures and external fraud. In the same month, Citigroup said United Parcel Service lost computer tapes with sensitive information from 3.9 million customers of CitiFinancial, a unit that provides personal and home loans. As of 2006, the final impact (and possible losses) have not been estimated yet.

---

[11]Reviews of the Enron scandal include books such as Eichenwald (2005), Swartz and Watkins (2003), Bryce (2002), Fox (2003), McLean and Elkind (2003). Daily periodicals are a good source of updates on the issue.

Terrorist Attack, September 11, 2001, New York and Worldwide

On September 11, 2001, the heart of the U.S. financial center, New York's World Trade Center, and the Pentagon became the targets of large-scale terrorist attacks. On the morning of September 11, two American Airlines jets were hijacked and used to crash into the Twin Towers of the World Trade Center, causing them to collapse about an hour later. Two other airlines were hijacked and one hit Pentagon; the other crashed in Pennsylvania. This dramatic unprecedented incident (referred to as *9/11*), apart from its devastating civilian loss (for example, Cantor Fitzgerald alone lost 700 of its employees), resulted in tremendous property loss. The Bank of New York's losses alone were estimated at $140 million. The financial losses due to 9/11 have been reported to be the costliest insured property loss in history, with current estimates of $40 billion to 70 billion. Other consequences have been business disruptions of the affected financial service companies, and a tremendous economic and political impact worldwide. This is a striking example of the damage to physical assets, business disruptions, and losses inflicted by external causes.

OPERATIONAL LOSSES IN THE HEDGE FUND INDUSTRY

In the financial industry, banks are not the only ones concerned with operational risk. In recent years, numerous hedge fund failures have been linked to operational risk. Approximately $600 billion is invested in 6,000 or so hedge funds worldwide. In hedge funds, operational risk is defined as "risks associated with supporting the operating environment of the fund; the operating environment includes middle- and back-office functions such as trade processing, accounting, administration, valuation and reporting."[12]

In 2002, Capco (the Capital Markets Company) studied the causes of hedge-fund failures based on 20 years of data on hedgefund failures. The results of the study showed that approximately 50% of the failures were due to operational risk, 38% to investment risk, 6% to business risks, and 6% to multiple risk sources.

The most common operational losses that caused the failures follow:[13]

- Misrepresentation of fund investments (creating or causing the generation of reports and valuations with false and misleading information)

---

[12]See Kundro and Feffer (2003a).
[13]See Kundro and Feffer (2003a) and Kundro and Feffer (2003b) for more details of the study.

- Misappropriation of investor funds (investment managers who knowingly move money out of the fund for personal use, either as an outright theft or to cover preexisting trading losses)
- Unauthorized trading (making investments outside of the stated fund strategy or changing the investment style of the fund without the approval of investors)
- Inadequate resources (technology, processes, or personnel that are not able to properly handle operating volumes or the types of investments and activities that the fund engages in)

These four sources, according to the study, account for 41%, 30%, 14%, and 6% of all hedge fund failures, respectively.

Table 1.1 lists examples of prominent hedge funds that have had enforcement action taken against them in 2005, with a brief description of the alleged misdemeanors.

TABLE 1.1 Examples of hedge fund failures due to operational risk

Hedge Fund Name	Country	Amount	Alleged Misdemeanor
KL Group LLC	U.S.	$81 million	Sending false account statements to investors showing similar gains while suffering tremendous trading losses since 1999
Phoenix Kapitaldienst	Germany	$800 million	Manipulating account statements, feigning assets
Vision Fund LP/DEN Ventures	U.S.	$22.8 million	Falsifying investment returns and taking unearned incentive payments based on inflated results and extracting capital for personal use since 2002
Ardent Domestic/Ardent Research	U.S.	$37 million	Diverting funds to invest them in illiquid securities of entities in which they had a stake and made loans to, entities in which principals had an interest
Portus Alternative Asset Management	Canada	$590 million	Unconventional sales and compliance practices as well as allocation of assets and promises of principal-backed guarantees

Source: Banga (2005, p. 3). Reprinted with permission from EDHEC Risk and Asset Management Research Centre.

SUMMARY OF KEY CONCEPTS

- Financial institutions bear various operational losses on the daily basis. Examples are losses resulting from employee errors, internal and external fraud, equipment failures, business disruptions due to natural disasters, and vandalism.
- Operational risk affects the operational efficiency in all business units.
- Until recently, credit risk and market risk have been perceived as the two biggest sources of risk for financial institutions. Operational risk has been regarded as a mere part of "other" risks.
- The weight of operational risk in banks' risk profiles has been elevated substantially as a side effect of financial deregulation and globalization policies.
- Serious banking failures in the last 20 years have demonstrated serious dangers of operational risk. More than 100 operational losses exceeding $100 million in value each and a number of losses exceeding $1 billion have occurred globally since the end of 1980s. Operational risk is also the source of approximately 50% of all hedge-fund failures. The task of managing operational risk has moved from being a minor issue to becoming a matter of survivability of financial institutions.

REFERENCES

Adams, J. R., and Frantz, D. (1993), *A Full Service Bank: How BCCI Stole Billions Around the World*, Simon & Schuster, United Kingdom.

Banga, D. (2005), "Operational Risk and Hedge Fund Failures," *EDHEC Risk and Asset Management Research Centre*.

Bank of England (1995a), "Report of the Banking Supervision. Inquiry into the Circumstances of the Collapse of Barings," *Bank of England, Her Majesty's Stationery Office, London.*

Bank of England (1995b), "The Bank of England Report into the Collapse of Barings Bank," http://www.numa.com/ref/barings/bar00.htm.

Beaty, J., and Gwynne, S. C. (1993), *The Outlaw Bank: A Wild Ride into the Secret Heart of BCCI*, Random House Inc, Beard Books, United Kingdom.

BIS (1999), "A New Capital Adequacy Framework," http://www.bis.org.

Bryce, R. (2002), *Pipe Dreams: Greed, Ego, and the Death of Enron*, PublicAffairs, New York.

Chew, L., "Not Just One Man—Barings," *IFCI Risk Institute report*, http://riskinstitute.ch/137550.htm.

Crouhy, M., Galai, D., and Mark, R. (2001), *Risk Management*, McGraw-Hill, New York.

Cruz, M. G. (2002), *Modeling, Measuring and Hedging Operational Risk*, John Wiley & Sons, New York, Chichester.

de Fontnouvelle, P., DeJesus-Rueff, V., Jordan, J., and Rosengren, E. (2003), Using Loss Data to Quantify Operational Risk, Technical report, Federal Reserve Bank of Boston.

Eichenwald, K. (2005), *Conspiracy of Fools: A True Story*, Broadway Books, New York.

Fay, S. (1997), *The Collapse of Barings*, 1st ed., W. W. Norton & Company, New York.

FDIC (1995), "Regulators terminate the U.S. operations of Daiwa Bank, Japan," http://www.fdic.gov.

Fox, L. (2003), *Enron: The Rise and Fall*, John Wiley & Sons, Hoboken, New Jersey.

Gapper, J., and Denton, N. (1996), *All That Glitters: The Fall of Barings*, Hamish Hamilton, London.

Irving, R. (1995), "County in Crisis," *Risk*, Issue? pp. 27–33.

Jorion, P. (1998), "Orange County Case: Using Value-at-Risk to Control Financial Risk," http://www.gsm.uci.edu/~jorion/oc/case.html.

Jorion, P., and Roper, R. (1995), *Big Bets Gone Bad: Derivatives and Bankruptcy in Orange County*, Academic Press, San Diego.

King, J. L. (2001), *Operational Risk: Measurement and Modelling*, John Wiley & Sons, New York.

Koernert, J. (1996), "The Collapse of Barings 1995. Financial Derivatives, Banking Crises and Contagion Effects," *Freiberg Working Papers 96/2*.

Kundro, C., and Feffer, S. (2003a), "Understanding and Mitigating Operational Risk in Hedge Fund Investments," *A Capco White Paper*.

Kundro, C., and Feffer, S. (2003b), "Valuation Issues and Operational Risk in Hedge Funds," *A Capco White Paper* 10.

Lectric Law Library (1995), *11/95 Criminal Complaint & Indictment Against Daiwa Bank*, http://www.lectlaw.com/files/cas60.htm.

Leeson, N. (1997), *Rogue Trader*, Time Warner, New York.

Leeson, N., and Tyrrell, I. (2005), *Back from the Brink: Coping with Stress*, Virgin Books, London.

Leith, W. (2002), "How to Lose a Billion," *The Guardian: Business. October 26 2002 issue.*

McLean, B., and Elkind, P. (2003), *Smartest Guys in the Room: The Amazing Rise and Scandalous Fall of Enron*, Penguin Books, New York.

Rawnsley, J. (1995), *Going for Broke: Nick Leeson and the Collapse of Barings Bank*, HarperCollins, New York.

Shirreff, D. (1997), "Lessons from NatWest," *Euromoney*.

Swartz, M., and Watkins, S. (2003), *Power Failure: The Inside Story of the Collapse of Enron*, Random House, New York.

Time Magazine (1997), "I Didn't Set Out to Rob a Bank," *Time Magazine* (6).

van den Brink, J. (2002), *Operational Risk: The New Challenge for Banks*, Palgrave, London.

CHAPTER 2

Operational Risk: Definition, Classification, and Its Place among Other Risks

I n Chapter 1 we provided a few examples of operational loss events, with the intention of giving the reader a feel for what operational risk is all about. We have assumed that the reader is familiar with the notions of credit and market risks, and we mentioned that operational risk has been loosely defined as part of "other" risks. In this chapter, we formalize the notion of operational risk and the place it takes among other financial risks.

WHAT IS RISK?

In finance risk is the fundamental element that affects financial behavior. There is no unique or uniform definition of risk, but this is not surprising: the definition depends on the context and the purpose for which one wishes to formulate the concept of risk. Broadly speaking, there are two ways to define risk:

1. Risk is a measure of uncertainty.
2. Risk is a measure to capture the potential of sustaining a loss.

The first definition, which is common in the economics literature, postulates that risk is a measure of uncertainty about the future outcomes, or, in other words, is a measure of dispersion of actual from expected future results. For example, in the context of an investment, risk is the volatility of expected future cash flows (measured, for example, by the standard deviation). Because of this uncertainty and because fluctuations in the underlying value may occur in either negative or positive direction, risk defined in this way does not exclude the possibility of positive outcomes. Hence, risk is not necessarily perceived as a negative concept.

The second definition suggests that risk has negative consequences. Risk is perceived as the probability of a negative deviation or sustaining a loss. More formally, risk is "a condition in which there is a possibility of an adverse deviation from a desired outcome that is expected or hoped for"[1] and "an expression of the danger that the effective future outcome will deviate from the expected or planned outcome in a negative way."[2] For example, insurance companies face the risk of having to pay out large claims to the insured, and banks are exposed to the risk of bearing losses due to adverse movements in market conditions (i.e., market risk) or losses due to inability of a counterparty or a borrower to perform on an obligation (i.e., credit risk).

In discussions of operational risk, the second definition is more appropriate. Of course, it is not entirely impossible that operational risk results in a gain for a bank. Examples may include certain employee errors. However, such outcomes are generally ignored for the purpose of operational risk modeling. We do not treat this case in this book.

DEFINITION OF OPERATIONAL RISK

We now need to distinguish operational risk from other categories of financial risk. Operational risk is, in large part, a firm-specific and nonsystematic risk.[3] Early publications of the Bank of International Settlements (BIS) defined operational risk as follows:[4]

- Other risks
- "Any risk not categorized as market and credit risk"
- "The risk of loss arising from various types of human or technical errors"

Other definitions proposed in the literature include:

- Risk "arising from human and technical errors and accidents"[5]

---

[1] See Vaughan and Vaughan (2003).
[2] See Geiger (1999).
[3] However, operational risk is not entirely idiosyncratic. Later in this chapter we will discuss a study that investigated the effect of macroeconomic factors on operational risk in banks.
[4] See BIS (1998).
[5] See Jorion (2000).

- "A measure of the link between a firm's business activities and the variation in its business results"[6]
- "The risk associated with operating a business"[7]

The formal definition that is currently widely accepted was initially proposed by the British Bankers Association (2001) and adopted by the BIS in January 2001. Operational risk was defined as

> *the risk of direct or indirect loss resulting from inadequate or failed internal processes, people or systems or from external events.*

The industry responded to this definition with criticism regarding the lack of a clear definition of *direct* and *indirect* losses. A refined definition of operational risk dropped the two terms, hence finalizing the definition of operational risk as

> *Operational risk is the risk of loss resulting from inadequate or failed internal processes, people or systems, or from external events.*
> (BIS (2001b, p. 2))

This definition includes legal risk, but excludes strategic and reputational risk (these will be defined soon). The definition is "causal-based," providing a breakdown of operational risk into four categories based on its sources: (1) people, (2) processes, (3) systems, and (4) external factors. According to Barclays Bank, the major sources of operational risk include operational process reliability, IT security, outsourcing of operations, dependence on key suppliers, implementation of strategic change, integration of acquisitions, fraud, error, customer service quality, regulatory compliance, recruitment, training and retention of staff, and social and environmental impacts.[8]

Large banks and financial institutions sometimes prefer to use their own definition of operational risk. For example, Deutsche Bank defines operational risk as

> *potential for incurring losses in relation to employees, contractual specifications and documentation, technology, infrastructure failure and disasters, external influences and customer relationships.*[9]

---

[6]See King (2001).
[7]See Crouhy, Galai, and Mark (2001).
[8]See Barclays Bank Annual Report 2004, Form 20-F/A.
[9]Deutsche Bank 2005 Annual Report, p. 45.

The Bank of Tokyo-Mitsubishi defines operational risk as

the risk of incurring losses that might be caused by negligence of proper operational processing, or by incidents or misconduct by either officers or staffs.[10]

In October 2003, the U.S. Securities and Exchange Commission (SEC) defined operational risk as

the risk of loss due to the breakdown of controls within the firm including, but not limited to, unidentified limit excesses, unauthorized trading, fraud in trading or in back office functions, inexperienced personnel, and unstable and easily accessed computer systems.[11]

OPERATIONAL RISK EXPOSURE INDICATORS

The probability of an operational risk event occurring increases with a larger number of personnel (due to increased possibility of committing an error) and with a greater transaction volume. The following are examples of operational risk exposure indicators include:[12]

- Gross income
- Volume of trades or new deals
- Value of assets under management
- Value of transactions
- Number of transactions
- Number of employees
- Employees' years of experience
- Capital structure (debt-to-equity ratio)
- Historical operational losses
- Historical insurance claims for operational losses

For example, larger banks are more likely to have larger operational losses. Shih, Samad-Khan, and Medapa (2000) measured the dependence between a bank size and operational loss amounts. They found that, on

[10]Bank of Tokyo-Mitsubishi Financial Performance, Form 20-F (2005), p. 124.
[11]"Supervised Investment Bank Holding Companies," SEC (2003), p. 62914.
[12]Examples of operational risk exposure indicators are given in BIS (2001a, Annex 4), Haubenstock (2003), and Allen, Boudoukh, and Saunders (2004).

average, for every unit increase in a bank size, operational losses are predicted to increase by roughly a fourth root of that.[13]

CLASSIFICATION OF OPERATIONAL RISK

Operational risk can be classified according to the following:

- The nature of the loss: internally inflicted or externally inflicted
- The impact of the loss: direct losses or indirect losses
- The degree of expectancy: expected or unexpected
- Risk type, event type, and loss type
- The magnitude (or severity) of loss and frequency of loss

We discuss each one in the following subsections.

Internal versus External Operational Losses

Operational losses can be internally inflicted or can result from external sources. Internally inflicted sources include most of the losses caused by human, process, and technology failures, such as those due to human errors, internal fraud, unauthorized trading, injuries, business delays due to computer failures or telecommunication problems. External sources include man-made incidents such as external fraud, theft, computer hacking, terrorist activities, and natural disasters such as damage to physical assets due to hurricanes, floods, and fires.

Many of the internal operational failures can be prevented with appropriate internal management practices; for example, tightened controls and management of the personnel can help prevent some employee errors and internal fraud, and improved telecommunication networks can help prevent some technological failures.

External losses are very difficult to prevent. However, it is possible to design insurance or other hedging strategies to reduce or possibly eliminate externally inflicted losses.

Direct versus Indirect Operational Losses

Direct losses are the losses that directly arise from the associated events. For example, an incompetent currency trader can result in a loss for the bank

---

[13]This means that when they regressed log-losses on a bank's log-size, the estimated coefficient was approximately 0.25. In a different study, Chapelle, Crama, Hübner, and Peters (2005) estimated the coefficient to be 0.15.

TABLE 2.1 Direct loss types and their definitions according to the Basel II capital accord

Loss Type	Contents
Write-downs	Direct reduction in value of assets due to theft, fraud, unauthorized activity, or market and credit losses arising as a result of operational events
Loss of recourse	Payments or disbursements made to incorrect parties and not recovered
Restitution	Payments to clients of principal and/or interest by way of restitution, or the cost of any other form of compensation paid to clients
Legal liability	Judgements, settlements, and other legal costs
Regulatory and compliance	Taxation penalties, fines, or the direct cost of any other penalties, such as license revocations
Loss of or damage to assets	Direct reduction in value of physical assets, including certificates, due to an accident, such as neglect, accident, fire, and earthquake

Source: BIS (2001a, p. 23), with modifications. Permission to use this table was obtained from the Basel Committee on Banking Supervision. The original table is available free of charge from the BIS website (www.BIS.org).

due to adverse exchange rate movements. As another example, mistakenly charging a client $50,000 instead of $150,000 results in the loss for the bank in the amount of $100,000. The Basel II Capital Accord (the subject of Chapter 3) sets guidelines regarding the estimation of the regulatory capital charge by banks based only on direct losses. Table 2.1 identifies the Basel II Capital Accord's categories and definitions of direct operational losses.

Indirect losses are generally opportunity costs and the losses associated with the costs of fixing an operational risk problem such as near-miss losses, latent losses, or contingent losses. We now discuss near-miss losses.

Near-miss losses (or near-misses) are the estimated losses from those events that could potentially occur but were successfully prevented. The rationale behind including near-misses into internal databases is as follows: the definition of *risk* should not be solely based on the past history of actual events but instead should be a forward-looking concept and include both actual and potential events that could result in material losses. The mere fact that a loss was prevented in the past (be it by luck or by conscious managerial action) does not guarantee that it will be prevented in the future. Therefore, near-misses signal flaws in a bank's internal system and should be accounted for in internal models. It is also possible to view near-misses from quite the opposite perspective: the ability to prevent these losses before they happen demonstrates the bank's effective operational risk management practices. Therefore, the losses that would result had these events taken place should not be included in the internal databases.

Muermann and Oktem (2002, p. 30) define near-miss as

an event, a sequence of events, or an observation of unusual occurrences that possesses the potential of improving a systems operability by reducing the risk of upsets some of which could eventually cause serious damage.

They assert that internal operational risk measurement models must include adequate management of near-misses.

Muermann and Oktem propose developing a pyramid-type three-level structure for the near-miss management system:

1. Corporate level
2. Branch level
3. Individual level

At the corporate level within every bank, they propose establishing a Near-Miss Management Strategic Committee whose primary functions would include the following:

- Establishing guidelines for corporate and site near-miss structures
- Developing criteria for classification of near-misses
- Establishing prioritizing procedures for each near-miss class
- Auditing the near-miss system
- Integrating quality and other management tools into near-miss management practice
- Identifying gaps in the near-miss management structure based on analysis of incidents with higher damage (beyond near-misses) and taking corrective actions
- Developing guidelines for training site management and employees on near-miss system.

At the branch level, they propose establishing a Near-Miss Management Council for every business unit. The key responsibilities of the council would include the following:

- Adapting criteria set by Near-Miss Management Strategic Committee to the branch practices
- Monitoring site near-miss practices
- Promoting the program
- Ensuring availability of necessary resources for analysis and corrective action, especially for high priority near-misses

- Periodically analyzing reported near-misses for further improvement of the system
- Training employees on Near-Miss implementation

Finally, a successful near-miss management system relies on the individual actions by managers, supervisors, and employees. Appropriate training is necessary to recognize operational issues before they become a major problem and develop into operational losses for the bank.

Expected versus Unexpected Operational Losses

Some operational losses are expected; some are not. The expected losses are generally those that occur on a regular (such as every day) basis, such as minor employee errors and minor credit card fraud. Unexpected losses are those losses that generally cannot be easily foreseen, such as terrorist attacks, natural disasters, and large-scale internal fraud.

Operational Risk Type, Event Type, and Loss Type

Confusion arises in the operational risk literature because of the distinction between risk type (or hazard type), event type, and loss type. When banks record their operational loss data, it is crucial to record it separately according to event type and loss type, and correctly identify the risk type.[14] The distinction between the three is comparable to cause and the effect:[15]

- *Hazard* constitutes one or more factors that increase the probability of occurrence of an event.
- *Event* is a single incident that leads directly to one or more effects (e.g., losses).
- *Loss* constitutes the amount of financial damage resulting from an event.

Thus, hazard potentially leads to events, and events are the cause of loss. Therefore, an event is the effect of a hazard while loss is the effect of an event.

Figure 2.1 illustrates the mechanism of operational loss occurrence. The following example, adopted from Mori & Harada (2001), further illustrates how the correct identification of the "event type" is critical in determining whether a loss of a particular *loss type* is attributed to market, credit, or operational risk:

- A reduction in the value of a bond due to a change in the market price

---

[14]See the discussion of this issue in Mori and Harada (2001) and Alvarez (2002).
[15]See Mori and Harada (2001).

Examples of hazard types:

- Inadequate employee management
- Obsolete computer systems
- Inexperienced personnel
- Large transaction volumes
- Diversity and cultural differences
- Unfavorable climate conditions or geographical location
- Other

Examples of event types:

- Internal fraud(e.g., unauthorized trading, forgery, theft)
- External fraud (e.g.,credit card fraud)
- Diversity/discrimination events
- Improper business and market practices
- Failed/inaccurate reporting
- System failure
- Natural disasters
- Other

Loss type categories:

- Write-downs
- Loss of recourse
- Restitution
- Legal liability
- Regulatory and compliance (e.g., fines and taxation penalties)
- Loss of or damage to physical assets
- Other

FIGURE 2.1   The process of operational loss occurrence.
Source: Mori and Harada (2001, p. 3), with modifications. Reprinted with permission of the Bank of Japan. The information is based on material copyrighted by the Bank of Japan and has been modified at our own responsibility.

- A reduction in the value of a bond due to the bankruptcy of the issuer
- A reduction in the value of a bond due to a delivery failure

In this example, the write-down of the bond (the loss type) belongs to the scope of market risk, credit risk, and operational risk, respectively. Accurate documentation of operational risk by the type of hazard, event, and loss is also essential for understanding of operational risk.

The Basel II Capital Accord classifies operational risk into seven event-type groups (see Table 2.2) and six operational-loss types (see Table 2.1).

Operational Loss Severity and Frequency

We have already stated that expected losses generally refer to the losses of low severity (or magnitude) and high frequency. Generalizing this idea, operational losses can be broadly classified into four main groups:

1. Low frequency/low severity
2. High frequency/low severity
3. High frequency/high severity
4. Low frequency/high severity

The idea is illustrated in the top half of Figure 2.2.

TABLE 2.2 Operational-event types and their descriptions according to the Basel II capital accord

Event Types and Descriptions According to Basel II	
Event Type	Definition and Categories
1. Internal fraud	Acts intended to defraud, misappropriate property or circumvent regulations, the law or company policy, which involves at least one internal party. *Categories*: unauthorized activity and theft and fraud.
2. External fraud	Acts of a type intended to defraud, misappropriate property or circumvent the law, by a third party. *Categories*: (1) theft and fraud and (2) systems security.
3. Employment practices and workplace safety	Acts inconsistent with employment, health or safety laws or agreements, from payment of personal injury claims, or from diversity/discrimination events. *Categories*: (1) employee relations, (2) safe environment, and (3) diversity and discrimination.
4. Clients, products and business practices	Unintentional or negligent failure to meet a professional obligation to specific clients (including fiduciary and suitability requirements), or from the nature or design of a product. *Categories*: (1) suitability, disclosure, and fiduciary, (2) improper business or market practices, (3) product flaws, (4) selection, sponsorship, and exposure, and (5) advisory activities.
5. Damage to physical assets	Loss or damage to physical assets from natural disaster or other events. *Categories*: Disasters and other events.
6. Business disruption and system failures	Disruption of business or system failures. *Categories*: systems.
7. Execution, delivery and process management	Failed transaction processing or process management, from relations with trade counterparties and vendors. *Categories*: (1) transaction capture, execution, and maintenance, (2) monitoring and reporting, (3) customer intake and documentation, (4) customer/client account management, (5) trade counterparties, and (6) vendors and suppliers.

Source: BIS (2001b, pp. 21-23). Permission to use this table was obtained from the Basel Committee on Banking Supervision. The original table is available free of charge from the BIS website (www.BIS.org).

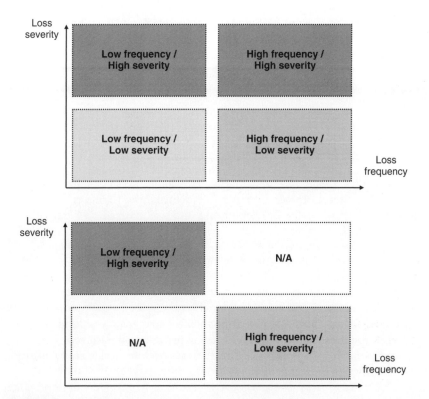

FIGURE 2.2 Classification of operational risk by frequency and severity: unrealistic view (top) and realistic view (bottom).

According to Samad-Khan (2005), the third group is implausible.[16] Recently, the financial industry also agreed that the first group is not feasible. Therefore, the two remaining categories of operational losses that the financial industry needs to focus on are "high frequency/low severity" and "low severity/high frequency" losses. The idea is illustrated in the bottom half of Figure 2.2

The losses of high frequency/low severity are relatively unimportant for an institution and can often be prevented. What poses the greatest

---

[16]More precisely, Samad-Khan (2005) suggests classifying each of the frequency and severity of operational losses into three groups: low, medium, and high. This creates a 3 × 3 matrix of all possible frequency/severity combinations. He states that "medium frequency/high severity," "high frequency/medium severity," and "high frequency/high severity" losses are unrealistic.

damage is the low frequency/high severity losses. Banks must be particularly attentive to these losses as these cause the greatest financial consequences to the institution, including potential bankruptcy.[17] Just a few of such events may result in bankruptcy or a significant decline in the value of the bank. Therefore, it is critical for banks to be able to capture such losses in their internal risk models.

TOPOLOGY OF FINANCIAL RISKS

Until recently, credit risk and market risk have been considered the two largest contributors to banks' risks. We describe the topology of financial risks, primarily using the BIS definitions, and summarize it in Figure 2.3.[18]

- *Credit risk*: The potential that a bank borrower or counterparty will fail to meet its obligations in accordance with agreed terms.
- *Market risk*: The risk of losses (in on- and off-balance sheet positions) arising from movements in market prices, including interest rates, exchange rates, and equity values. It is the risk of the potential change in the value of a portfolio of financial instruments resulting from the movement of market rates, underlying prices and volatilities. The major components of market risk are the interest rate risk, equity position risk, foreign exchange risk, and commodity risk.
- *Operational risk*: The risk of loss resulting from inadequate or failed internal processes, people or systems or from external events. As already mentioned, operational risk includes legal risks, which includes, but is not limited to, exposure to fines, penalties, or punitive damages resulting from supervisory actions, as well as private settlements.
- *Liquidity risk*: The risk of inability to fund increases in assets and meet obligations as they come due, such as inability to raise money in the long-term or short-term debt capital markets, or an inability to access the repurchase and securities lending markets.[19]

---

[17] The events that incur such losses are often called the *tail events*. We will discuss tail events in later chapters of this book.

[18] Slightly different variations of classifications of financial risks were suggested by Crouhy, Galai, and Mark (2001), van Greuning and Bratanovic (2003), Tapiero (2004), and Frost (2004).

[19] An alternative definition by Crouhy, Galai, and Mark (2001) says that liquidity risk is the risk that the institution will not be able to execute a transaction at the prevailing market price because there is, temporarily, no appetite for the deal on the "other side" of the market.

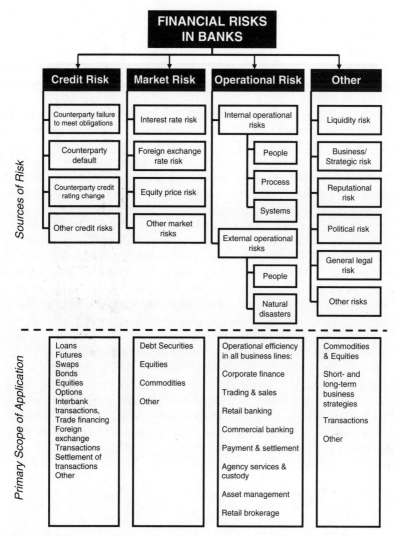

FIGURE 2.3 Topology of financial risks in banks.

- *Business and strategic risk*: The risk that a bank would have to modify the line of behavior and activity in order to cope with changes in the economic and financial environment in which it operates. For example, a new competitor can change the business paradigm, or new strategic initiatives (such as development of a new business line or reengineering an existing business line, for example, e-banking) can expose bank to strategic risk.[20] Many strategic risks involve timing issues, such as the inability to keep up with rapid technological changes and the increasing use of the Internet.[21]

- *Reputational risk*: The potential that negative publicity regarding an institution's business practices, whether true or not, will cause a decline in the customer base, costly litigation, or revenue reductions.[22] This definition suggests that reputational risk takes the form of an indirect, rather than direct, loss resulting from a bank's past business practices. Reputational risk generally includes the risks associated with customers (i.e., the risk of failure to meet customers' expectations). According to the BIS (2000), reputational risk includes risks related to customer data and privacy protection, e-banking and e-mail services, timely and proper information disclosure, and so on. Therefore, banks with a large private banking sector and e-banking activities are especially vulnerable to reputational risk.[23]

- *Political risk*: The risk of an adverse impact on bank's activities due to changes in country and/or regional political or economic pressures, such as monetary controls. Changes in political policies may adversely affect the ability of clients or counterparties located in that country or region to obtain foreign exchange or credit and, therefore, to perform their obligations to the bank.

- *General legal risk*: The risk that a bank would have to modify its activities due to changes in the country's legal system or law enforcements. Examples include a potential impact of a change in the tax code. In the United States, examples include compliance with the Bank Secrecy Act, the Patriot Act, and anti-money laundering regulations: noncompliance may result in high penalties and fines and lawsuits against the banks' directors and officers.[24]

---

[20]See Crouhy, Galai, and Mark (2001).

[21]See BIS (2000).

[22]The Board of Governors of the Federal Reserve System (1995).

[23]Perry and de Fontnouvelle (2005, p. 6) suggest several ways in which reputational risk can result in material losses for a bank:

- Loss of current or future customers
- Loss of employees or managers within the organization, an increase in hiring costs, or staff downtime
- Reduction in current or future business partners
- Increased costs of financial funding via credit or equity markets
- Increased costs due to government regulation, fines, or other penalties

[24]For more details, see "Bank Secrecy Act/Anti-Money Laundering Manual" of July 2006 by the Federal Financial Institutions Examination Council.

TABLE 2.3 Ratio of operational risk economic capital to overall economic capital and to minimum regulatory capital in the 2000 BIS loss data collection exercise

	Median	Mean	Minimum	25th percentile	75th percentile	Maximum
Operational risk capital/Overall economic capital	0.150	0.149	0.009	0.086	0.197	0.351
Operational risk capital/Minimum regulatory capital	0.128	0.153	0.009	0.074	0.170	0.876

Source: BIS (2001b, p. 26). Permission to use this table was obtained from the Basel Committee on Banking Supervision. The original table is available free of charge from the BIS website (www.BIS.org).

CAPITAL ALLOCATION FOR OPERATIONAL, MARKET, AND CREDIT RISKS

The primary role of a capital charge imposed by bank regulators is to serve as a buffer to protect against the damage resulting from risk. It can also be seen as a form of self-insurance tool.

A clear distinction should be made between two types of risk capital, economic capital and regulatory capital. *Economic capital* is defined as the amount of capital market forces dictate for risk in a bank. *Regulatory capital* is the amount of capital necessary to provide adequate coverage of banks' exposures to financial risks. A one-year *minimum regulatory capital* (MRC) is calculated as 8% of reported risk-weighted assets for the year in question.

Large, internationally active banks allocate roughly $2 billion to $7 billion to operational risk.[25] According to Jorion (2000), current estimates suggest that the allocation of total financial risk of a bank is roughly 60% to credit risk, 15% to market risk and liquidity risk, and 25% to operational risk. However, Cruz (2002) suggests an allocation of 50% credit risk, 15% market risk and liquidity risk, and 35% operational risk, while Crouhy, Galai, and Mark (2001) suggest an allocation of 70%, 10%, and 20% to credit risk, market risk and liquidity risk, and operational risk, respectively. According to the BIS (2001a), the portion of economic capital allocated to operational risk ranges from 15% to 25%. A 2000 Loss Data Collection Exercise carried out by the Risk Management Group of the BIS revealed the

[25]See de Fontnouvelle, DeJesus-Rueff, Jordan, and Rosengren (2003).

overall allocation of minimum regulatory/economic capital to operational risk across 41 banks shown in Table 2.3.

IMPACT OF OPERATIONAL RISK ON THE MARKET VALUE OF BANK EQUITY

As stated earlier in this chapter, losses due to operational risk can be direct and indirect. Some studies of operational risk have addressed the assessment of the indirect impact of operational risk on the market value of a bank's equity. In particular, several studies explored reputational risk caused by operational loss events, and its impact on the market value of a bank. Reputational damage inflicted on a bank as a result of an operational loss can be viewed as an indirect operational loss. Perry and de Fontnouvelle (2005) argue that, from the point of view of shareholders, operational loss announcements convey negative information about the bank's internal activities and signal direct adverse effect on the future cash flows generated by the bank. Therefore, the bank's stock price will be directly affected by such an announcement.[26]

For example, Cummins, Lewis, and Wei (2004) examine the effect of the announcements of large operational loss events on the market value of a financial firm. They argue that announcements of large operational loss events (i.e., losses that exceed $10 million) have a statistically significant adverse effect on the stock price. They found statistically significant evidence that the material damage to the firm value exceeded the amount of actual operational loss, which in turn implies that there is reputational damage to the firm due to an announcement of a large operational loss. Furthermore, they showed that firms with stronger growth opportunities suffer greater losses in the market value due to operational loss announcements.

In a similar study, Perry and de Fontnouvelle (2005) measure the reputational consequences of operational loss announcements on the value of a bank. Their study revealed that announcements of operational losses of all loss types resulted in a statistically significant decline in the firm's market value. Furthermore, for internal fraud events, the announcements resulted in a material loss amount that is, on average, three times larger than the initial operational loss that was announced. This means that, on average, the market capitalization of a bank that makes an internal fraud announcement is reduced by three times its announced loss. They also showed that the market reacts more to internal fraud events for banks with strong shareholder rights than for banks with weak shareholder rights.

---

[26]Related studies include Palmrose, Richardson, and Scholtz (2004), Karpoff and Lott (1993), and Murphy, Shrieves, and Tibbs (2004).

EFFECTS OF MACROECONOMIC ENVIRONMENT ON OPERATIONAL RISK

Although a large portion of operational risk is endogenous to an institution, it may also be affected by the macroeconomic environment. In a related empirical study, Allen and Bali (2004) investigate the effect of cyclical pattern in macroeconomic environment on operational risk which they defined as the residual risk after credit risk and market risk are accounted for.

Allen and Bali found evidence of comovements in the parameters of the operational risk distribution with changes in the macroeconomic environment. The macroeconomic variables included general U.S. macroeconomic variables (such as GDP and unemployment rate), foreign exchange rates, equity market indices, consumer price indices, interest rates, money supply figures, and some regulatory variables to account for major regulatory changes. They showed that operational risk is strongly correlated with each of these macroeconomic variables. For example, operational risk tends to increase in recessions, during stock market booms, when interest rates drop, and during periods of high unemployment.

SUMMARY OF KEY CONCEPTS

- Operational risk in banks is formally defined as the risk of loss resulting from inadequate or failed internal processes, people or systems or external events. This definition identifies operational risk as coming from four major causes: processes, human, systems, and external factors.
- Operational risk can be classified according to several principles: nature of the loss (internally inflicted or externally inflicted), direct losses or indirect losses, degree of expectancy (expected or unexpected), risk type, event type or loss type, and by the magnitude (or severity) of loss and the frequency of loss.
- Operational risk is one of the top three banking risk categories, credit risk and market risk being the other two risk categories. Other risks include liquidity risk, reputational risk, political risk, and general legal risk.
- Current estimates of banks' capital allocation share for operational risk stand between 15% and 25% of total economic capital, with the shares for market and credit risks being around 15% and 60%, respectively.
- Operational risk can be the cause of reputational risk, a risk that can occur when the market reaction to an operational loss event results in reduction in the market value of a bank that is greater than the amount of the initial loss. Empirical evidence suggests that large operational

loss announcements result in a statistically significant decrease in equity returns.
▪ Macroeconomic factors strongly affect operational risk: operational risk tends to increase in recessions and times of stock market booms.

REFERENCES

Allen, L., and Bali, T. (2004), Cyclicality in Catastrophic and Operational Risk Measurements, Technical report, Baruch College.
Allen, L., Boudoukh, J., and Saunders, A. (2004), *Understanding Market, Credit, and Operational Risk: The Value-at-Risk Approach*, Blackwell Publishing, Oxford.
Alvarez, G. (2002), "Operational Risk Event Classification," http://www.garp.com.
BBA/ISDA/RMA (2000), "Operational Risk Management—The Next Frontier," *Journal of Lending and Risk Management*, March, pp. 38–44.
BIS (1998), "Overview to the Amendment to the Capital Accord to Incorporate Market Risks," http://www.bis.org.
BIS (2000), "Electronic Banking Group Initiatives and White Papers," http://www.bis.org.
BIS (2001a), "Consultative Document: Operational Risk," www.BIS.org.
BIS (2001b), "Working Paper on the Regulatory Treatment of Operational Risk," www.BIS.org.
Chapelle, A., Crama, Y., Hübner, G., and Peters, J. (2005), Measuring and Managing Operational Risk in the Financial Sector: An Integrated Framework, Technical report, National Bank of Belgium.
Crouhy, M., Galai, D., and Mark, R. (2001), *Risk Management*, McGraw-Hill, New York.
Cruz, M. G. (2002), *Modeling, Measuring and Hedging Operational Risk*, John Wiley & Sons, New York, Chichester.
Cummins, J. D., Lewis, C. M., and Wei, R. (2004), The Market Value Impact of Operational Risk Events for U.S. Banks and Insurers, Technical report, University of Pennsylvania.
de Fontnouvelle, P., DeJesus-Rueff, V., Jordan, J., and Rosengren, E. (2003), Using Loss Data to Quantify Operational Risk, Technical report, Federal Reserve Bank of Boston.
Frost, S. M. (2004), *The Bank Analyst's Handbook: Money, Risk and Conjuring Tricks*, John Wiley & Sons, Chichester.
Geiger, H. (1999), "Die Risikopolitik der Banken, Teil 1 und Teil 2," *Der Schweizer Treuhander* 73(6/7 and 8), pp. 555–564; pp. 713–718.
Haubenstock, M. (2003), "The Operational Risk Management Framework," *in* C. Alexander, ed., *Operational Risk: Regulation, Analysis and Management*, Prentice Hall, Great Britain, pp. 241–261.

Jorion, P. (2000), *Value-at-Risk: The New Benchmark for Managing Financial Risk*, 2nd ed., McGraw-Hill, New York.

Karpoff, J. and Lott, J. R. (1993), "The Reputational Penalty Firms Bear for Committing Criminal Fraud," *Journal of Law and Economics* 36, pp. 757–802.

King, J. L. (2001), *Operational Risk: Measurement and Modelling*, John Wiley & Sons, New York.

Mori, T., and Harada, E. (2001), Internal Measurement Approach to Operational Risk Capital Charge, Technical report, Bank of Japan.

Muermann, A., and Oktem, U. (2002), "The Near-Miss Management of Operational Risk," *The Journal of Risk Finance* 4(1), pp. 25–36.

Murphy, D. L., Shrieves, R. E., and Tibbs, S. L. (2004), Determinants of the Stock Price Reaction to Allegations of Corporate Misconduct: Earnings, Risk, and Firm Size Effects, Technical report, The University of Tennessee.

Palmrose, Z., Richardson, V. J., and Scholtz, S. (2004), "Determinants of Market Reactions to Restatement Announcements," *Journal of Accounting and Economics* 37, pp. 59–89.

Perry, J., and de Fontnouvelle, P. (2005), Measuring Reputational Risk: The Market Reaction to Operational Loss Announcements, Technical report, Federal Reserve Bank of Boston.

Samad-Khan, A. (2005), "Why COSO Is Flawed," *Operational Risk*, January, pp. 1–6.

Shih, J., Samad-Khan, A. J., and Medapa, P. (2000), "Is the Size of an Operational Risk Related to Firm Size?," *Operational Risk*, January, 2000.

Tapiero, C. S. (2004), *Risk and Financial Management: Mathematical and Computational Methods*, John Wiley & Sons, Chichester.

van Greuning, H., and Bratanovic, S. B. (2003), *Analyzing and Managing Banking Risk: A Framework for Assessing Corporate Governance and Financial Risk*, 2nd edn, The World Bank, Washington, D.C.

Vaughan, E. J., and Vaughan, T. (2003), *Fundamentals of Risk and Insurance*, 9 ed., John Wiley & Sons, Hoboken, New Jersey.

CHAPTER 3

Basel II Capital Accord

I n this chapter, we review the capital requirements under the recent Basel Capital Accord as set out in its final version of June 2006. We focus on the aspects relevant to operational risk.

THE BASEL COMMITTEE ON BANKING SUPERVISION

The Basel Committee on Banking Supervision (BCBS) is the key player in the financial risk regulation network, setting risk management regulations to financial institutions worldwide. BCBS is a committee of banking supervisory authorities, established in 1975 by the central bank governors of the Group of Ten (G10) countries. Consisting of representatives from 13 countries (Belgium, Canada, France, Germany, Italy, Japan, Luxembourg, the Netherlands, Spain, Sweden, Switzerland, the United Kingdom, and the United States), it holds regular meetings at the Bank for International Settlements (BIS) in Basel, Switzerland, where its permanent Secretariat is located.

BCBS plays the leading role in establishing risk assessment and management guidelines for banks. The current (2004) Basel Capital Accord targets credit, market, and operational risks. A number of subcommittees have been established to promote consistency in its implementation. Major subcommittees include the following:[1]

- The *Accord Implementation Group* (AIG) is aimed at promoting exchange of information on the practical implementation challenges of the Capital Accord and on the strategies they are using to address these issues. The Operational Risk subgroup of AIG (AIGOR) focuses on operational risk.

---

[1]These descriptions of the subcommittees are due to BCBS.

- The *Capital Task Force* (CTF) is responsible for considering substantive modifications to, and interpretations, of the Capital Accord.
- The purpose of the *Risk Management Group* (RMG) is to develop new standards of operational risk management and methodologies for regulatory capital allocation models.
- The Basel Committee formed the *Transparency Group* that develops and reviews the disclosure principles described in Pillar III of the Capital Accord (described later in this chapter).

THE BASEL CAPITAL ACCORD

In July 1988, the Basel Committee released the Capital Accord. The Capital Accord of 1988 is now commonly referred to as *Basel I*. The primary objective of the accord was to establish minimum capital standards designed to protect against credit risk.[2] In April 1993, the inclusion of market risk into the scope of risks subject to capital requirements was discussed and the capital accord was broadened in 1996.[3]

After two years, reflecting the developments in the financial industry in the preceding years, the Basel Committee decided to undertake a comprehensive amendment of the Basel I and account for the diversity of risks taken by banks. The new capital accord of 1998 is now known as *Basel II*. The document "Operational Risk Management" was released in 1998. It discussed the importance of operational risk as a substantial financial risk factor.[4] No discussion regarding the requirement of a capital charge against operational risk had been made until January 2001, when the consultative document "Operational Risk" was released.[5]

The Basel II Capital Accord underwent a number of amendments and was finalized in June 2006.[6] Under Basel II, operational risk is subject to a regulatory capital charge. This regulatory capital—estimated separately by every bank—is designed to reflect the exposure of each individual bank to operational risk. The accord defines and sets detailed instructions on the

---

[2] Although Basel I discussed the capital requirements for only credit risk, it used a "broad-brush" approach, as it was constructed in such a way as to also implicitly cover other risks. See BIS (1988) for description.

[3] See BIS (1996) and also BIS (1998).

[4] See BIS (1998).

[5] See BIS (2001) for the full document.

[6] A number of amendments to the 2001 proposal have been released by the Basel Committee since 2001. The finalized accord is presented in BIS (2006b). See the BIS official web site www.BIS.org for a full list of downloadable publications.

capital assessment of operational risk and proposes several approaches that banks may consider to estimate the operational capital charge, as well as outlines necessary managerial and disclosure requirements.

The deadline for implementation of the Capital Accord has been provisionally set to January 2007, with some transitional adjustments that depend on a country. U.S. banks will be granted an extension to the January 2007 deadline and, as of end 2006, they have until January 2008 to comply with Basel II. Additionally, they have a three-year transition period to allow for a smooth adoption of the Capital Accord.

The scope of application is mainly holding companies that are the parent entities within a banking group, internationally active banks, and their subsidiaries including securities companies. For U.S. banks, the Basel II guidelines are mandatory for financial institutions with either $250 billion or more in assets or $10 billion or more in foreign exposure.[7]

The organization of the Basel II Capital Accord uses a three-pillar mutually reinforcing structure and addresses three types of risk: credit risk, market risk, and operational risk (see the upper half of Figure 3.1):

Pillar I: Minimum risk-based capital requirements

Pillar II: Supervisory review of an institution's capital adequacy and internal assessment process

Pillar III: Market discipline through public disclosure of various financial and risk indicators

PILLAR I: MINIMUM CAPITAL REQUIREMENTS FOR OPERATIONAL RISK

In Pillar I, the regulatory capital charge for operational risk is computed separately by every bank.

Decomposition of Capital

A bank is required to provide capital *above* the minimum required amount, the so-called *floor* capital. The regulatory capital is composed of three types: Tier I, Tier II, and Tier III. Tier I includes the following:

1. Paid-up share capital/common stock
2. Disclosed reserves

---

[7]See Silverman (2006) for a discussion of additional regulatory requirements for U.S. financial institutions.

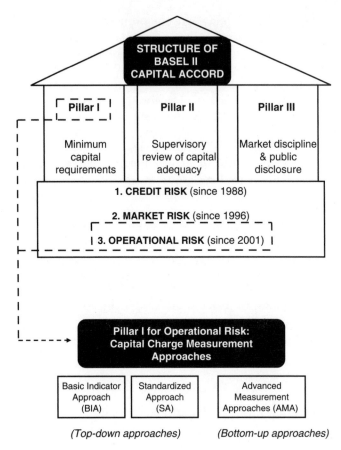

FIGURE 3.1   Structure of the Basel II Capital Accord and Pillar I for operational risk.

Tier II is composed of the following:

1. Undisclosed reserves
2. Asset revaluation reserves
3. General provisions/general loan-loss reserves
4. Hybrid (debt/equity) capital instruments
5. Long-term subordinated debt

and Tier III, if applicable, which includes short-term subordinated debt. The total of Tier II capital is limited to a maximum of 100% of the total of Tier I. Tier III capital is only eligible for market risk capitalization purposes.

Capital for Expected and Unexpected Losses

In 2001, BIS suggested that the capital charge for operational risk should cover *unexpected losses* (UL) due to operational risk, and that provisions should cover *expected losses* (EL). This is due to the fact that for many banking activities with a highly likely incidence of expected regular operational risk losses (such as fraud losses in credit card books), EL are deducted from reported income in the particular year. Therefore, in 2001 BIS proposed to calibrate the capital charge for operational risk based on both EL and UL, but to deduct the amount due to provisioning and loss deduction (rather than EL) from the minimum capital requirement.[8]

However, accounting rules in many countries do not provide a robust and clear approach to setting provisions, for example allowing for provisions set only for future obligations related to events that have already occurred. In this sense, they may not accurately reflect the true scope of EL. Therefore, in the 2004 version of the accord, it was proposed to estimate the capital charge as a sum of EL and UL first and then subtract the EL portion in those cases when the bank is able to demonstrate its ability to capture the EL by its internal business practices.[9] BIS (2006c) further clarifies the idea:

> For operational risk EL to be "measured" to the satisfaction of national supervisors, the bank's measure of EL must be consistent with the EL-plus-UL capital charge calculated using the AMA model approved by supervisors. ... Allowable offsets for operational risk EL must be clear capital substitutes or otherwise available to cover EL with a high degree of certainty over a one-year time horizon. Where the offset is something other than provisions, its availability should be limited to those business lines and event types with highly predictable, routine losses. Because exceptional operational risk losses do not fall within EL, specific reserves for any such events that have already occurred will not qualify as allowable EL offsets.

Figure 3.2 illustrates the dimensions of operational risk. *Catastrophic loss* is the loss in excess of the upper boundary of the estimated UL such as 99.9% value-at-risk.[10] It requires no capital coverage; however, insurance coverage may be considered. Catastrophic loss is often called *stress loss*.

---

[8]See the discussion in BIS (2001a).
[9]See BIS (2004), BIS (2006b), and BIS (2006c).
[10]The notion of value-at-risk will be discussed in Chapter 11.

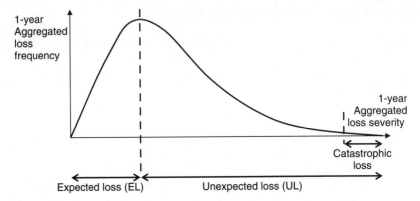

FIGURE 3.2   Aggregated loss distribution: unexpected and expected losses.

Three Approaches to Assess the Operational Risk Capital Charge

Three approaches have been finalized for assessing the operational risk capital charge:

1. Basic indicator approach
2. Standardized approach
3. Advanced measurement approaches

The basic indicator approach and the standardized approach are often referred to as the *top-down approaches* in the sense that the capital charge is allocated according to a fixed proportion of income. The Advanced Measurement Approaches are called the *bottom-up approaches* in the sense that the capital charge is estimated from actual internal loss data.[11] The lower half of Figure 3.1 shows the approaches: moving from left to right the degree of sophistication increases. A bank is allowed to adopt one of the approaches depending on its operational risk exposure and its management practices, subject to the bank meeting specific requirements. Internationally active banks with diverse business activities are to adopt the advanced measurement approaches, while smaller capital size domestic banks are generally expected to follow the basic indicator approach or the standardized approach, at least at the primary stage of the implementation. Once a bank adopts a more advanced approach, it is not allowed to switch back to a simpler approach.

---

[11]See Chapter 4 for the discussion of top-down and bottom-up models.

We now describe each of the three main approaches.

The Basic Indicator Approach The *basic indicator approach* (BIA) is the simplest approach. Under this approach, gross income is viewed as a proxy for the scale of operational risk exposure of the bank.[12] Gross income is defined by the Basel Committee as net interest income plus net noninterest income. According to the June 2006 guidelines, the operational risk capital charge under the BIA is calculated as a fixed percentage of the average over the previous three years of positive annual gross income. The fixed percentage is denoted by α.[13] The total capital charge (K_{BIA}) can be expressed as

$$K_{BIA} = \alpha \times \frac{\sum_{j=1}^{n} GI_j}{n},$$

where
GI = gross income
 n = the number of the previous three years for which GI is positive
 α = the fixed percentage of positive GI

α is currently set by the committee at 15% and is purposed to reflect the industrywide level of *minimum required regulatory capital* (MRC) to the industry-wide level of the indicator.

There are four advantages of the BIA:

1. It is easy to implement.
2. No time and resources are needed for the development of alternative sophisticated models.
3. It is useful at the primary stage of Basel II implementation, especially when loss data are insufficient to build more complex models.
4. It is particularly applicable to small and medium-size banks.

Three drawbacks of the BIA are as follows:

1. No account is given to the specifics of the bank's operational risk exposure and control, business activities structure, credit rating and other indicators, so the BIA is not risk-sensitive.

---

[12] BIS (2006b) clarifies (on p. 217) that gross income may be a suboptimal measure of operational risk exposure and may underestimate the need for operational risk capital. Banks should compare their true exposure to operational risk with that of other banks of similar size and similar business structure.
[13] See BIS (2001) on the empirical analysis of α under the BIA using banks' internal loss data.

2. It often results in overestimation of the true amount of capital required to capitalize operational risk.
3. It is not applicable for large and internationally active banks.

No quantitative and qualitative requirements are specified by Basel II regarding the use of the BIA. However, banks are encouraged to comply with the guidelines as described in BIS (2003b) and BIS (2006b). The approach is particularly convenient for small and medium-size banks in the early stage of their implementation of the capital requirements.

The Standardized Approach In the general *standardized approach* (TSA), banks' activities are divided into eight business lines. Within each business line, *gross income* (GI) is a broad indicator that serves as a proxy for the scale of business operations and operational risk exposure. The capital charge for each business line is calculated by multiplying GI by a factor, denoted by β,[14] assigned to that business line. β serves as a proxy for the industrywide relationship between the operational risk loss experience for a given business line and the aggregate level of GI for that business line. The total capital charge is calculated as the three-year average of the maximum of (a) the simple summation of the regulatory capital charges across each of the business lines and (b) zero. The total capital charge (K_{TSA}) can be expressed as

$$K_{\text{TSA}} = \frac{\sum_{j=1}^{3} \max\left\{\sum_{k=1}^{8} \text{GI}_{jk} \times \beta_k, \, 0\right\}}{3},$$

where β is a fixed percentage set by the committee, relating the level of required capital to the level of the GI for each of the eight business lines. The values of β are presented in Table 3.1

The June 2004 Basel II guidelines suggested an option to adopt an alternative version of the Standardized Approach.[15] Once a bank has been allowed to use this alternative, it will not be allowed to revert to use of the TSA without the permission of its supervisor. Under the *alternative standardized approach* (ASA), the capital charge for the Retail Banking (RB) and the Commercial Banking (CB) business lines is calculated by taking total loans and advances (LA) as the operational risk exposure indicator, instead of gross income. The β factor is further multiplied by a scaling factor denoted by m and set equal to 0.035. For the two business lines, the capital

---

[14]See BIS (2001) on the empirical analysis of beta under the TSA using banks' internal loss data.

[15]This option remains valid under the recent June 2006 guidelines.

TABLE 3.1   Beta Factors (β) Under the
Standardized Approach

Business Line	β
1. Corporate finance	18%
2. Trading and sales	18%
3. Retail banking	12%
4. Commercial banking	15%
5. Payment and settlement	18%
6. Agency services	15%
7. Asset management	12%
8. Retail brokerage	12%

Source: BIS (2006b, p. 147). Permission to use this
table was obtained from the Basel Committee on
Banking Supervision. The original table is available
free of charge from the BIS website (www.BIS.org).

charge amounts (K_{RB} and K_{CB}) are thus calculated as follows:

$$K_{RB} = \beta_{RB} \times m \times \frac{\sum_{j=1}^{3} LA_j, RB}{3},$$

$$K_{CB} = \beta_{CB} \times m \times \frac{\sum_{j=1}^{3} LA_j, CB}{3}.$$

The advantages of the TSA and ASA are the same as for the BIA with
the added advantage that they are more accurate than the BIA because
differences in the degrees of operational risk exposure by different business
lines are taken into account.

There are four drawbacks of the TSA and ASA:

1. They are not sufficiently risk sensitive: taking a fixed fraction of business
   line's gross income does not take into account specific characteristics of
   this business line for a particular bank.
2. A perfect correlation is implied between different business lines.
3. They may result in overestimation of the true amount of capital required
   to capitalize operational risk.
4. They are not applicable for large and internationally active banks.

To qualify for the TSA or ASA, banks must be able to map their
business activities into the business lines. Banks adopting the approach must
be actively involved in monitoring and controlling the bank's operational
risk profile and its changes. This includes, for example, regular reporting

of operational risk exposures, internal and/or external auditing, and valid operational risk self-assessment routines and supervision.[16]

The Advanced Measurement Approaches In the *advanced measurement approaches* (AMA), banks may use their own method for assessing their exposure to operational risk, as long as it is sufficiently comprehensive and systematic. A bank must demonstrate that its operational risk measure is evaluated for a one-year holding period and a high confidence level (such as 99.9%).[17] The AMA are the most complex and advanced, as the resulting capital charge is the risk measure directly derived from the bank's internal loss data history and employs quantitative and qualitative aspects of the bank's risk measurement system for the assessment of the regulatory capital charge. To ensure reliability of the assessment methodology, apart from the internal data, banks may supplement their databases with external data (appropriately rescaled), as well as may utilize techniques such as factor analysis, stress tests, Bayesian methods, among others. It is expected that the AMA will be uniformly adopted by all banks in the near future.[18]

In 2001, three approaches were proposed under AMA: the internal measurement approach, the loss distribution approach, and the scorecard approach. The latest regulatory capital guidelines (June 2006) no longer give the names of the possible approaches grouped under AMA, but allow banks to work out their own alternative or even more sophisticated, but robust, AMA models that would be sufficiently supported with backtesting and that would reflect their required operational risk capital. We nevertheless briefly discuss these three approaches but review in more detail the loss distribution approach.

The Internal Measurement Approach Under the Internal Measurement Approach (IMA), for each of the 56 cells, the capital charge is determined by the product of three parameters:

1. The exposure indicator (EI) (such as gross income)
2. Probability of event (PE)
3. Loss given the event (LGE)

The product $EI \times PE \times LGE$ is used to calculate the expected loss (EL) for each business line/loss type combination. The EL is then rescaled to

---

[16] Additional qualifying criteria are set out in BIS (2003b) and BIS (2006b).
[17] See BIS (2006b).
[18] See BIS (2006c) for detailed discussion of various aspects of the AMA implementation.

account for the unexpected losses (UL) using a parameter γ, different for each business line/loss type combination, but predetermined by the supervisor. The total one-year regulatory capital charge (K_{IMA}) is calculated as

$$K_{\text{IMA}} = \sum_{j=1}^{8}\sum_{k=1}^{7} \gamma_{jk} \times \text{EI}_{jk} \times \text{PE}_{jk} \times \text{LGE}_{jk}.$$

The drawbacks of this approach are the assumptions of (1) perfect correlation between the business line/loss type combinations and (2) a linear relationship between the expected and unexpected losses.[19]

The Scorecard Approach The scorecard approach (ScA) is a highly qualitative approach, under which banks determine an initial level of operational risk capital (such as based on the BIA or TSA) at the firm or business line level, and then modify these amounts over time on the basis of *scorecards*. The approach is forward-looking, as it is designed to reflect improvements in the risk-control environment that would reduce both the frequency and severity of future operational risk losses. The scorecards generally rely on a number of indicators as proxies for particular risk types within business units. The scorecards are completed by line personnel at regular intervals, for example annually, and subject to review by a central risk function. The one-year capital charge (K_{ScA}) can be computed as

$$K_{\text{ScA}} = \sum_{j=1}^{8} \text{initial } K_j \times \mathcal{R}_j,$$

where $\mathcal{R}$ is some risk score that rescales the initial capital charge K into the new one for a given business line.[20]

The Loss Distribution Approach The loss distribution approach (LDA) is an advanced measurement approach that makes use of the exact operational loss frequency and severity distributions. It was suggested by the Basel Committee in 2001 and uses an actuarial type of model for the assessment of operational risk.

---

[19]For more discussion of the IMA see BIS (2001a), Alexander (2002), Alexander and Pezier (2001a), Alexander and Pezier (2001b), Alexander (2003a), and Mori and Harada (2001).
[20]See discussions of the ScA in BIS (2001a) and also Blunden (2003).

Under the LDA, it is suggested that bank's activities are classified into a matrix of business lines/event type combinations with the actual number of business lines and event types depending on the complexity of the bank structure. For a general case of eight business lines and seven event types, a bank would have to deal with a 56-cell matrix of possible pairs. For each pair, the key task is to estimate the loss severity and loss frequency distributions. Based on these two estimated distributions, the bank then computes the probability distribution function of the cumulative operational loss.

The operational capital charge is computed as the simple sum of the one-year value-at-risk (VaR) measure[21] (with confidence level such as 99.9%) for each business line/risk type pair. The 99.9th percentile means that the capital charge is sufficient to cover losses in all but the worst 0.1% of adverse operational risk events. That is, there is a 0.1% chance that banks will not be able to cover adverse operational losses.

For the general case (eight business lines and seven loss-event types), the capital charge (K_{LDA}) can be expressed as

$$K_{\text{LDA}} = \sum_{j=1}^{8} \sum_{k=1}^{7} \text{VaR}_{jk}.$$

Note that the LDA differs from the IMA in two important respects. First, it aims to assess unexpected losses directly and not via an assumption about the linear relationship between expected loss and unexpected loss. Second, there is no need for the bank supervisor to determine a multiplication factor γ.

There are four advantages of the LDA:

1. It is highly risk sensitive, making direct use of bank's internal loss data.
2. No assumptions are made about relationship between expected and unexpected losses.
3. The approach is applicable to banks with solid databases.
4. Provided that an estimation methodology is correct, LDA provides an accurate capital charge.

A common criticism of LDA is that estimating the capital charge by a simple sum of the VaR measures implies a perfect correlation among the "business line/event type" combinations. A modified version of the LDA approach would take into consideration such correlation effects. Recent

---

[21] See Chapter 11 that reviews the notion of VaR.

guidelines point out this issue and suggest incorporating the correlation effects and other factors that may influence the accuracy of the computation of the capital charge. Four drawbacks of the LDA approach include the following:

1. Loss distributions may be complicated to estimate. Therefore, the approach can create *model risk* (i.e., wrong estimates due to the misspecification of the model).
2. VaR confidence level is not agreed upon, and whether 99.9% or higher/lower percentile is considered makes a significant difference on the capital charge.
3. Extensive internal data sets (at least five years) are required.
4. The approach lacks a forward-looking component because the risk assessment is based only on the past loss history.

Qualifying for AMA Use   To qualify for the AMA, banks must satisfy certain requirements. A crucial requirement is the availability of a minimum of five years of internal data (in the early stage of adoption of the AMA, three years of data are acceptable). Internal data may be complemented by external data (such as publicly available data and/or pooled industry data) whenever there is reason to believe that the bank is exposed to infrequent, yet potentially severe, losses, for which there is lack of data. This is related to another important quantitative prerequisite—the ability of the bank's model to capture potentially severe tail events at the 99.9th confidence level, and validate the model via backtesting (such as forecasting, scenario analysis, and stress tests).

Additionally, the quantitative standards must be sufficiently balanced with the qualitative standards that are composed of establishing a risk management group that would be in charge of design and implementation of the operational risk measurement methodology, ensuring regular reporting and documentation of loss events and management routines, internal and/or external auditing, and so on. In order to establish a forward-looking risk assessment structure, banks must also capture key business environment and internal control factors that can change its operational risk profile.

Banks are allowed to use a combination of AMA and other approaches (BIA and TSA) for various parts of its operations in some exceptional circumstances, subject to approval of the banks' supervisors.

PILLAR II: CAPITAL ADEQUACY AND REGULATORY PRINCIPLES

The role of Pillar II is to establish adequate regulatory policies to overview the capital adequacy in the banks. Supervisory review under Pillar II consists of four core principles.

1. *Establishment of (a) a process for assessing bank's overall capital adequacy in relation to risk profile, and (b) a strategy for maintaining the capital levels.* This includes board and senior management oversight, sound capital assessment, comprehensive assessment of risks, monitoring and reporting, and internal control review.

2. *Internal control review: supervisory review and evaluation of bank's internal capital adequacy assessments and strategies, and ability to monitor and ensure bank's compliance with regulatory capital ratios.* This includes onsite examinations or inspections, offsite review, discussions with bank management, review of work done by external auditors (provided it is adequately focused on the necessary capital issues), and periodic reporting. Supervisors should take appropriate supervisory actions if they are not satisfied with the result of this process.

3. *Supervisory response: requirement from banks to operate above the minimum regulatory capital ratios (i.e., the "floor"), conducted by the supervisors.* The purpose of compliance to the last principle is to create a buffer against possible losses that may not have been adequately covered by the regulatory capital charge (under Pillar I), and possible fluctuations in the risk exposure. Such buffer is expected to provide a reasonable assurance that the bank's activities are well protected.

4. *Supervisory timely intervention to prevent capital from falling below the minimum levels, and ensuring a rapid remedial action if capital is not maintained or restored.* Banks must work out actions to be undertaken if it is realized that the amount of capital is insufficient. Possible actions include tightening bank monitoring, restricting dividend payments, and reviewing the capital charge assessment model.[22]

PILLAR III: MARKET DISCIPLINE AND PUBLIC DISCLOSURE

The purpose of Pillar III is to complement Pillar I (i.e., capital requirements) and Pillar II (i.e., review of capital adequacy) with market discipline through public disclosure mechanisms. This consists of market disclosure requirements that would allow the market participants to take part in the assessment of the financial institution's key aspects: capital, risk exposures, capital adequacy, risk assessment and management practices. The disclosure

---

[22]For a detailed description of Pillar II, see BIS (2006b).

requirements for operational risk consist of two parts: qualitative disclosures and quantitative disclosures.[23]

With respect to qualitative disclosures, banks are required to provide description of bank's capital structure, risk management strategies, policies for risk mitigation and hedging, and description of the capital charge assessment approach used by the bank (with possible detailed descriptions in cases when AMA are used).

For quantitative disclosures, banks are required to disclose the information on the amount of capital charge per business line for the top consolidated group and major subsidiaries. This includes the indication of whether the "floor" is exceeded, the description of Tier I and II capital, and the description of the deductions from capital.

OVERVIEW OF LOSS DATA COLLECTION EXERCISES

Since 2001, the Risk Management Group of BIS carried out several Operational Loss Data Collection Exercises (OLDC), also called the Quantitative Impact Studies. The aim of these studies was to investigate various aspects of banks' internal operational loss data.

In 2001, 30 banks participated in the Quantitative Impact Study 2 (QIS2) study. They were asked to provide their internal quarterly aggregated data over the 1998–2000 period.[24] In May 2001, BIS launched the second study, Quantitative Impact Study 3 (QIS3), results of which were obtained in 2002. There were 89 participating banks. They were asked to provide their internal data over the 2001 fiscal year. The second study resulted in more comprehensive and accurate findings than those obtained from the earlier study.[25] The third study, Quantitative Impact Study 4 (QIS4), was performed by several countries (such as Japan, Germany, and the United States) separately.[26] Results of the study varied depending on a country. The fourth study, Quantitative Impact Study 5 (QIS5), was conducted by BIS between October and December 2005. A total of 31 countries—with the exception of the United States, all G10 countries (a total of 146 banks), and 19 other countries (a total of 155 banks)—participated in this exercise.

---

[23]For detailed description of Pillar III, see BIS (2006b), Part 4.
[24]Details of the 2001 study are described in BIS (2001b) and BIS (2002a).
[25]Details of the 2002 study are described in BIS (2002b) and BIS (2003c).
[26]See Dutta and Perry (2006) for a detailed description of the data collected in the study that took place in the United States.

The primary objective of the study was to detect potential changes in minimum required capital levels under the Basel II framework as the industry progressed toward implementation in the previous several years.[27]

Figure 3.3 demonstrates severity of losses (i.e., loss amount) and frequency of losses (i.e., number of losses) by business lines and event types, as a percentage of total operational loss amount and number of losses, respectively, obtained as a result of QIS3. The figures demonstrate the nonuniform nature of the distribution of loss amounts and frequency across various business lines and event types (the numbers were taken from BIS (2003c)).

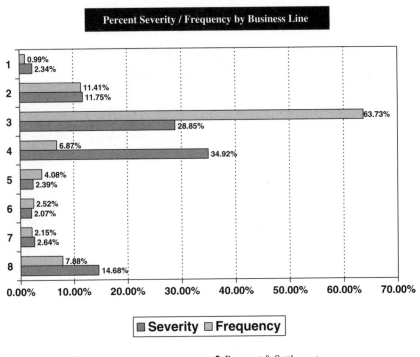

1. Corporate Finance
2. Trading & Sales
3. Retail Banking
4. Commerical Banking

5. Payment & Settlement
6. Agency Services
7. Asset Management
8. Retail Brokerage

FIGURE 3.3 Illustration of percent severity/frequency of operational losses by business line (top) and by event type (bottom), obtained as result of 2002 Loss Data Collection Exercise.

---

[27]Results of QIS5 are described in BIS (2006a).

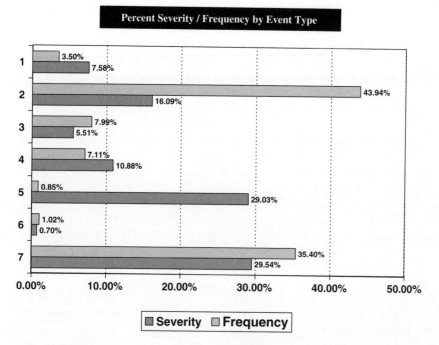

Percent Severity / Frequency by Event Type

1 — 3.50% / 7.58%
2 — 43.94% / 16.09%
3 — 7.99% / 5.51%
4 — 7.11% / 10.88%
5 — 0.85% / 29.03%
6 — 1.02% / 0.70%
7 — 35.40% / 29.54%

■ Severity □ Frequency

1. Internal Fraud
2. External Fraud
3. Employment Practices & Workplace Safety
4. Clients, Products & Business Practices
5. Damage to Physical Assets
6. Business Disruption & System Failures
7. Execution, Delivery & Process Management

FIGURE 3.3 *(continued)*

For example, the Commercial Banking business line includes losses of a relatively low frequency but the highest severity. As for the losses classified by event type, the losses in the "Damage to Physical Assets" category (such as natural disasters) account for less than 1% of the total number of losses, but almost 30% of the aggregate amount.[28]

THE ROLE OF INSURANCE

Under the Capital Accord, banks qualify for deductions from the operational risk capital charge provided that they participate in risk transfer activities,

---

[28] See BIS (2003c) for further description of the survey results.

such as insurance. This provision is limited to banks using the AMA. This is designed to encourage banks to implement, and get rewarded for, better risk management practices. Currently, the recognition of insurance mitigation is limited to 20% of the total operational risk regulatory capital charge calculated under the AMA. The Risk Management Group of the Basel Committee is still in the process of developing a uniform framework that would recognize the risk mitigating impact of insurance on the operational risk capital charge. The policies may be reviewed or changed in the near future.

A bank must have a well-reasoned and documented framework for recognizing insurance and, to comply with the Pillar III, the bank must disclose a description of its use of insurance for the purpose of mitigating operational risk. In addition,

> *The risk mitigation calculations must reflect the bank's insurance coverage in a manner that is transparent in its relationship to, and consistent with, the actual likelihood and impact of loss used in the bank's overall determination of its operational risk capital. (BIS (2006b), p. 155)*

BIS (2003d) defines three characteristics for a property and casualty risk to be insurable:

1. The risk must satisfy the requirements of the law of large numbers.
2. The occurrence of the specified event should cause an unanticipated loss.
3. The occurrence of the event and the loss should be objectively determinable.

Where an actual risk does not exhibit all three characteristics, insurers make use of deductibles, exclusions, and other techniques to compensate for that.

They are requirements for a bank to be eligible for the capital deductions via insurance:

- The insurance company must have at least an A rating or its equivalent.
- The insurance coverage must be consistent with the actual likelihood and impact of loss used in the bank's overall determination of its operational risk capital.

Other requirements are concerned with disclosure procedures and specifics of the insurance contract.[29]

---

[29]For more details, see BIS (2006b).

Unfortunately, most operational losses are not insurable. There are a limited number of traditional insurance products for operational risk:[30]

- *Fidelity bond coverage.* This product can cover a bank against losses from dishonest or fraudulent acts committed by employees, burglary or unexplained disappearances of property, counterfeiting, and forgery. It is also known as *financial institution blanket bond* or *bankers blanket bond* coverage.[31]
- *Directors' and officers' liability coverage.* This insurance policy can protect against losses incurred by directors and officers for wrongful acts and losses by the financial institution for money it paid to directors and officers to indemnify them for damages.
- *Property insurance.* This policy can protect firms against losses from fire, theft, inclement weather, and so on.
- *Electronic and computer crimes insurance.* This insurance covers intentional and unintentional incidents involving computer operations, communications, and transmissions.
- Other coverage.

Which Operational Losses Should Be Transferred?

Many banks are especially interested in using risk transfer mechanisms to address tail risk (i.e., low-frequency/high-severity losses). Low frequency/high severity losses that exceed the VaR amount—which is determined by a high confidence level such as 99%—are often called *catastrophic losses*. This means that there is a probability of 1% that losses will exceed this maximum probable total loss. Although a bank is expected to hold sufficient amount of reserves to cover the losses up to the VaR amount, it may be unable to absorb the catastrophic loss. However, if the bank obtains an insurance policy against operational risk, then it may be able to absorb at least some of the catastrophic losses. Quoting BIS (2001a):

> *Specifically, insurance could be used to externalise the risk of potentially "low frequency, high severity" losses, such as errors and omissions (including processing losses), physical loss of securities, and fraud. The Committee agrees that, in principle, such mitigation should be reflected in the capital requirement for operational risk.*

---

[30]See BIS (2003d), p. 12.

[31]Insurance against legal risks and fraud are discussed in Lewis and Lantsman (2005).

FIORI Insurance Policy by Swiss Re

Financial Institutions Operational Risk Insurance (or simply FIORI) was introduced by Swiss Re and London-based insurance broker Aon in 1999. Swiss Re offers comprehensive basket-type policies under which several sources of operational risk are aggregated in a single contract. The policy covers physical asset risks, technology risk, relationship risk, people risk, and regulatory risk. We review the details of the insurance coverage as described by van den Brink (2002).

FIORI's coverage includes a number of operational risk causes:

- Liability:
  - Losses result from neglecting legal obligations by the financial institution or one of its subsidiaries, its management or staff members, its representatives, or companies to which the financial institution has outsourced.
  - Fines are included in the coverage.
- Fidelity and unauthorized activities:
  - Dishonesty is defined in the insurance policy.
  - All trading business is covered.
  - Potential income has not been excluded from the coverage.
  - Repair costs are covered.
- Technology risks:
  - Sudden and irregular failure of own-built applications is covered.
  - Normal processing errors are not covered.
- Asset protection:
  - All risks concerning buildings and property are covered.
  - The coverage includes both own and trust assets.
- External fraud:
  - Coverage for external fraud is broadly defined.
  - The coverage includes more than existing customers.
  - Potential income is not excluded in this case.

The insurance policy has a very high deductible of $50 to $100 million per claim. The premium ranges between 3% and 8% of the covered amount, which means that if risk volume in the amount of $100 million is insured, the premium would be up to $3 to $8 million. Such requirements may not be easily affordable for small financial institutions.

Insurance Recoveries Data from the 2002 Loss Data Collection Exercise

As part of QIS3, banks were asked to provide information regarding insurance recoveries on their operational losses.

Banks filed insurance claims for 2.1% of all loss occurrences, but only 1.7% resulted in nonzero insurance payouts. This means that about 20% of all filed claims resulted in no payments by the insurer. Of all losses within a particular business line, between 0.7% and 2.7% resulted in insurance claims. Of all losses belonging to a particular event type, almost 34% of losses attributed to the Damage to Physical Assets event type resulted in insurance claims, while for the rest of the event types the percentages varied from 0.6% to 6.0%.

Regarding the recoveries (insurance recoveries and noninsurance recoveries) by business lines and event types, most recoveries were reported for the Commercial Banking business line (67%) and for the Damage to Physical Assets (58%) and the Execution, Delivery and Process Management (23%) event types. Table 3.2 summarizes the distribution of total recovery amounts by "business line/event type" combination. Of all recoveries, only 11.8% were obtained via insurance, and 88.7% were due to other recoveries.

Limitations of Insurance

There are some concerns related to the role of operational risk insurance as a risk management tool. We discuss these below.

Policy Limit   After the insurance policy deductible is met, further operational losses are covered by the policy up until the policy limit. Losses in excess of the policy limit are borne by the bank and may jeopardize the solvency of the bank. Deductibles and policy limits are illustrated in Figure 3.4. According to Allen, Boudoukh, and Saunders (2004), relatively high deductibles (that can go as high as $100 million) and relatively low policy limits result in only 10% to 13% of operational losses being coverable by an insurance policy.

High Costs of Insurance   Insurance coverage is costly. According to Marshall (2001), less than 65% of all bank insurance policy premiums have been paid out in the form of settlements. It is therefore important for a bank to identify the key areas in which it is exposed to operational risk and make an effort to mitigate the specific risks identified, and minimize the insurance premium payments.[32]

Moral Hazard   Although insurance provides a means of pooling and diversifying operational risks across the industry, the problem of moral hazard remains and may give rise to high premiums and negotiation costs. Moral hazard is the possibility that the existence of insurance protection may make the insured less diligent in taking steps to prevent the occurrence of a

---

[32]See Allen, Boudoukh, and Saunders (2004) for a discussion of this issue.

TABLE 3.2 Distribution (in %) of Total Recovery Amounts Across Various "Business Line/Event Type" Combinations

	Internal Fraud	External Fraud	Employment Practices & Workplace Safety	Clients, Products & Business Practices	Damage to Physical Assets	Business Disruptions & System Failures	Execution, Delivery, & Process Management	All Event Types
Corporate finance	0.0	0.0	0.0	1.7	0.0	0.0	0.1	1.8%
Trading & sales	0.2	0.4	0.4	0.7	2.1	0.1	0.7	1.7%
Retail banking	1.9	5.0	0.2	1.1	0.7	0.5	1.0	10.3%
Commercial banking	0.0	1.2	0.0	0.2	45.7	0.2	19.7	67.0%
Payment & settlement	0.2	0.2	0.0	0.0	0.6	2.5	0.6	4.1%
Agency services	0.0	0.0	0.0	0.0	3.3	1.3	0.4	5.0%
Asset management	0.0	0.1	0.0	0.4	0.1	0.0	0.4	1.0%
Retail brokerage	0.4	0.0	0.0	0.1	5.2	0.0	0.5	6.2%
All business lines	2.7%	6.9%	0.6%	4.0%	57.7%	4.6%	23.4%	97.1%

Source: BIS (2003c, p. 24), with modifications. Permission to use this table was obtained from the Basel Committee on Banking Supervision. The original table is available free of charge from the BIS website (www.BIS.org).

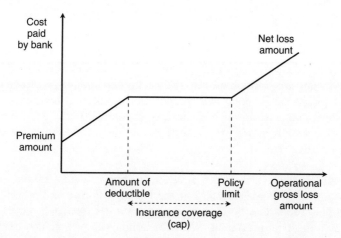

FIGURE 3.4 Illustration of deductible and its effect on the cost paid by the bank.

loss event. *Exante moral hazard* can occur in form of increased negligence by the management toward operational risk. *Expost moral hazard* is concerned with biased reporting due to the difficulty in measuring actual losses.[33]

The 20% limit on the reduction of the capital charge due to insurance has been receiving some criticism. Kuritzkes and Scott (2005) argue that this limit may have the effect of reducing the incentives of banks to obtain insurance potentially leading to an increase in bank losses. Protection sellers may use various mechanisms to mitigate the effect of moral hazard. They may increase the cost of insurance protection when the banks incurs high losses. They may also impose high deductibles, forcing the insurance buyer to share the costs.

Other questions related to insurance and its effectiveness include liquidity (i.e., the speed of insurance payouts), loss adjustment and voidability, limits in the product range, and the inclusion of insurance payouts in internal loss data.[34]

Alternatives to Insurance

Hedging catastrophic losses can be done also using the derivatives instruments such as catastrophe options and catastrophe bonds.[35]

---

[33] See Muermann and Oktem (2002).
[34] See BIS (2001a).
[35] The literature on operational risk insurance includes BIS (2003d), Chapter 14 in Cruz (2002), Mori and Harada (2001), Hadjiemmanuil (2003), Leddy (2003),

Catastrophe Options *Catastrophe options* (or simply *cat options*) were introduced in 1994 on the Chicago Board of Trade. Cat options are linked to the Property and Claims Services (PCS) Office national index of catastrophic loss claims. They can be written on outcomes due to catastrophic loss of a firm's reputation, outcome of a lawsuit, an earthquake, weather, and so on. Cat options trade like a call spread: they combine a long call position with a short call position at a higher exercise price. If the PCS index falls between the two exercise prices, then the holder of the option receives a positive payoff.

Catastrophe Bonds In the United States, trading of catastrophe bonds (or simply *cat bonds*) began in 1995 at the Chicago Board of Trade (CBOT). Catastrophe bonds can be used to hedge against catastrophic operational risk by issuing structured debt. With cat bonds, the principal is exchanged for periodic coupon payments, where the payment of the coupon and the return of the principal of the bond are linked to the occurrence of a prespecified catastrophic event.

One advantage of cat bonds over cat options is its flexible structure. There are three types of cat bonds: indemnified notes, indexed notes, and parametric notes. *Indemnified notes* are linked to a specific event that occurs as a result of a bank's internal activities. *Indexed notes* are linked to industrywide losses and can be measured by a specific index such as the PCS. When *parametric notes* are issued, the compensation payments are determined by the magnitude of a particular event and follow a prespecified formula.

Another advantage is that cat bonds provide the issuing company with access to a broader set of investors than cat options. Some investors, such as pension funds and mutual funds, are restricted from transacting in derivatives such as PCS options, but are allowed to invest in securities such as bonds or notes.[36]

Banks may also use cat options and cat bonds in order to diversify the risk of their portfolios. With a few exceptions,[37] the correlation between market risk and catastrophic risk (captured by the PCS index) is close to zero. Canter, Cole, and Sander (1996) showed that the correlation between the yearly percentage change in the PCS index and the yearly percentage change in the S&P 500 index is negative but insignificantly different from

---

Allen, Boudoukh, and Saunders (2004), Brandts (2005), and Lewis and Lantsman (2005).

[36] See Canter, Cole, and Sander (1996) for a discussion of this issue.

[37] Exceptions may include manmade catastrophic events such as the *9/11* terrorist attack.

zero. In another similar study, Hoyt and McCullough (1999) showed that there appears to be no statistically significant relationship between quarterly catastrophe losses and the S&P index, U.S. Treasury bills, and corporate bonds.

COMPLIANCE WITH BASEL II IN PRACTICE

We present two examples to illustrate how banks design and implement their operational risk management framework in their business structure to comply with Basel II.

JPMorgan Chase

JPMorgan Chase is one of the leaders in the global financial services industry, with assets over $1.3 trillion and operations in more than 50 countries. The building and implementation of the operational risk framework in JPMorgan Chase began in 1999.

JPMorgan Chase uses the Advanced Measurement Approach to quantify operational risk, which is consistent with the Basel II framework. The risk capital is estimated for each business lines using a bottom-up approach. The operational risk capital model is based on actual losses and also potential scenario-based stress losses. Further adjustments to the capital calculation are made to reflect changes in the quality of the control environment and the use of risk-transfer products.[38] Risk capital amount is disclosed in the annual reports in order to fulfill the requirements of the Pillar III of the Basel II. Table 3.3 provides an example of such risk capital disclosures for operational risk, credit risk, market risk, and other risks for the years 2004 and 2005.

Operational loss data collection process began around the year 2000. Internal data are further supplemented by the external data obtained from the Operational Riskdata eXchange database.[39]

Key risk indicators (KRI) are incorporated into JPMorgan Chase's operational risk monitoring framework and are used to detect and prevent risks before the accidents take place. JPMorgan Chase conducts over 2,700

---

[38] JPMorgan Chase 2005 Annual Report, p. 57.

[39] Operational Riskdata eXchange (ORX) is a Zurich-based association whose purpose is to assist its members with the exchange of operational risk related information. As of 2006, its membership includes 25 financial institutions, including the major banks such as JPMorgan Chase, ABN Amro, Deutsche Bank, and Bank of America.

TABLE 3.3   JPMorgan Chase's Economic Capital Allocation in 2005 and 2004

Economic Risk Capital	Yearly Average	
(in USD billions)	2005	2004
Credit risk	22.6	16.5
Market risk	9.8	7.5
Operational risk	5.5	4.5
Business risk	2.1	1.9
Private equity risk	3.8	4.5
Economic risk capital	43.8	34.9
Goodwill	43.5	25.9
Other[a]	18.2	14.8
Total common stockholders' equity	105.5	75.6

[a]Includes additional capital required to meet internal debt and regulatory rating objectives.
Source: Extracted from JPMorgan Chase Annual Report (2005), p. 56.

control self-assessments on a semiannual basis that are used to evaluate and rate over 80,000 controls and are aimed at identifying the actions required to mitigate operational risks.

Certain parties are responsible for managing operational risk:[40]

- Business practitioners who are involved in day-to-day business
- CFOs and financial analysts whose role is to analyze profits and losses, risk capital, and reconciliation process
- Business Control Committees at the review level
- Operational Risk Committee at the strategic level

In 2000, the Corporate Operational Risk Committee (ORC) was formed to supervise the operational risk management process. This committee comprises senior operational risk managers, CFOs, auditors, and legal representatives, among others. Its role is to discuss firmwide operational risk issues and implementation topics. ORC meets quarterly. In addition, JPMorgan Chase has over 130 Business Control Committees (BCC) that comprise senior management from each business unit. BCC participate in monitoring, reporting, and discussing operational risk issues.

According to JPMorgan Chase, a comprehensive and forward-looking approach to operational risk management should include the following components:[41]

---

[40]See JPMorgan Chase (2004).
[41]See JPMorgan Chase (2004).

- Reducing the probability of large loss events
- Lowering the level of expected losses
- Improving productivity of operational risk processes
- Enhancing the efficiency of economic capital

HBOS

Halifax and Bank of Scotland (HBOS) is one of the leading mortgage and savings providers in the United Kingdom, with assets of more than £540 billion. There are four Executive Risk Committees that are chaired by the group risk director:[42]

- Group Credit Risk Committee
- Group Market Risk Committee
- Group Insurance Risk Committee
- Group Operational Risk Committee

The Operational Risk Committee meets at least six times a year to discuss the operational risk exposure, operational risk capital requirements, and approval of policy and standards. The main components of the operational risk management framework include risk and control assessment, internal loss reporting and capturing of risk event information, the monitoring of key risk indicators, and evaluation of external events.[43]

HBOS uses two core operational risk systems: AspectsOR and Algo OpData. AspectsOR is a self-assessment package developed by HBOS, that allows for a bottom-up aggregation of risks from various business units to divisional level. Algo OpData is marketed by Algorithmics and is a public operational loss data provider that stores information on worldwide operational loss events and key risk indicators.

IMPLEMENTING BASEL II: SOME GENERAL CONCERNS

Many unresolved issues regarding the implementation of the Basel II Accord still remain. Some of these issues will be discussed in later chapters.

A common critique deals with the lack of a clear definition for operational risk. The definition of operational risk is argued to be subjective, ambiguous, and controversial. According to Paletta (2005), we are still "in the infancy of understanding everything about operational risk."

---

[42]HBOS 2005 Annual Report, p. 55.
[43]HBOS 2005 Annual Report, p. 60.

Moreover, *model risk* remains in that no clear-cut systematized model currently exists, according to Financial Guardian Group (2005) and S&P (2003). For example, under the loss distribution approach, the regulatory capital charge is estimated by the 99.9th percentile of the aggregate loss distribution. In light of unavailability of large datasets, the use of 99.9th (or even higher) percentile is seen as too high (i.e., too conservative) and unrealistic. As pointed out by Lawrence (2003), 99.9% of the loss distribution requires knowledge of 99.9999% of the loss severity distribution—a lack of data in such higher percentile would make the estimates highly inaccurate. Relying on an assumed model, insufficiently supported by available data, can have serious implications on the magnitude of the estimated capital charge.

Model risk may also occur in the presence of outliers (i.e., unusually high or low observations). As we already discussed, the catastrophic losses (e.g., the losses in excess of VaR under the loss distribution approach) are not covered by the capital charge. There are two ways in which banks can deal with them:

1. *Risk transfer:* A bank can cover these losses with insurance or coinsurance.
2. *Robust methods:* If the bank can demonstrate that a catastrophic loss is an outlier, then it may be allowed to exclude the loss from the database and model analysis.[44]

Another debate is related to the discrepancy between the regulatory capital amount under the accord and the true economic capital. Regulatory capital is considerably higher than economic capital,[45] particularly under the basic indicator approach and the standardized approach. Hence, as suggested by Currie (2005), adopting Basel II means regulating the models rather than the reality of operational risk. Financial Guardian Group (2005) claims that increased capital requirements mean decreased availability of funds required for financial needs and investments, and can divert finite

---

[44]This in an ongoing discussion within the Risk Management Group. Banks must present valid evidence to justify treating a data point as an outlier and removing it from the model. For example, a loss may be considered an outlier if the bank is able to provide proof (based on the event's background check) that a loss of this kind would not repeat, or if banks of similar capital size and/or operational risk exposure have no losses of similar nature in their internal databases. Robust methods and outlier detection will be examined in Chapter 12.

[45]See the definitions of regulatory capital and economic capital in the previous chapter.

resources away from needed investment in risk management systems, leaving the financial system less, rather than more, secure.[46] However, we disagree with this view: Recent banking failures indicate that the economic capital allocated to operational risk has been far less than sufficient. Furthermore, historical loss data are a reliable indicator of banks' true exposure to operational risk, provided that they are sufficiently comprehensive.

Finally, adopting Basel II entails permanent changes. Market distortions resulting from the new capital accord cannot be easily undone. An example is entering or exiting a new business line, or M&A—once implemented under the tightened capital policy, these changes are permanent. The bank can suffer a permanent damage if the policies prove wrong.

Despite the criticism, we strongly believe that adopting Basel II is in a bank's own benefit. Banks should continue collecting the data and develop operational risk models that would reflect their internal operational risk patterns. As Roger W. Ferguson, Vice Chairman of the Board of Governors of the Federal Reserve System, put it,

> *We now face three choices: we can reject Basel II, we can delay Basel II as an indirect way of sidetracking it, or we can continue the domestic and international process using the public comment and implementation process to make whatever changes are necessary to make Basel II work effectively and efficiently. The first two options require staying with Basel I, which is not a viable option for our largest banks. The third option recognizes that an international capital framework is in our self-interest since our institutions are the major beneficiary of a sound international financial system. The Fed strongly supports that third option.*[47]

SUMMARY OF KEY CONCEPTS

- The Basel Capital Accord sets out guidelines for capital requirements for credit, market, and operational risks.
- *Basel I* refers to the Capital Accord of 1988. It determines capital requirements for credit risk. *Basel II* refers to the Capital Accord of 1996, in which an amendment for market risk was made. In 2001, operational risk was included into the category of financial risks for which the regulatory capital charge is required. Basel II was finalized in June 2006.

---

[46]This concern is shared by others; see, for example, Silverman (2006).
[47]From the Hearing before the Committee on Banking, Housing and Urban Affairs, United States Senate, June 18, 2003.

- Basel II follows a three-pillar structure: minimum capital requirements (Pillar I), supervisory review of the capital adequacy (Pillar II), and market discipline and public disclosure (Pillar III).
- Under Pillar I, three approaches have been finalized for operational risk. Top-down approaches include the basic indicator approach and the standardized approach. Bottom-up approaches include the advanced measurement approaches. The first two are simplified approaches and are relevant for small and medium-size banks with limited internal operational loss databases. The advanced measurement approaches are most sophisticated and accurate and require extensive databases. Specific requirements must be met in order for a bank to qualify for either of these approaches.
- Since 2001, the Basel Committee conducted four Quantitative Impact Studies with the purpose of examining various specifics of banks' internal loss data. In particular, the results of the exercises revealed a non-uniform nature of loss frequency and severity across different banks, as well as across different business lines and loss event types.
- Banks may use several mechanisms to transfer operational risk: insurance, self-insurance, and derivatives. The Basel II Capital Accord currently allows for a reduction of the operational capital charge by up to 20% due to insurance for banks that adopted the Advanced Measurement Approach. A comprehensive operational risk insurance product FIORI is offered by Swiss Re.
- Management of operational risk is the task for every individual involved in a bank's activity: risk officers, directors, and individual employees. Because the nature of operational risk is highly bank-specific, every bank must develop its unique operational risk management structure.
- Some concerns regarding the implementation of the Basel II currently remain. They deal with the operational risk definition, data collection, and modeling issues.

REFERENCES

Alexander, C. (2002), "Understanding the Internal Measurement Approach to Assessing Operational Risk Capital Charges," *Risk* January, 2002.

Alexander, C. (2003a), "Statistical Models of Operational Loss," in Alexander, pp. 129–170.

Alexander, C., ed. (2003b), *Operational Risk: Regulation, Analysis and Management*, Prentice Hall, Upper Saddle River, NJ.

Alexander, C., and Pezier, J. (2001a) "Binomial gammas," *Operational Risk* 2 (April).

Alexander, C., and Pezier, J. (2001b), "Taking Control of Operational Risk," *Futures and Options World* 366.

Allen, L., Boudoukh, J., and Saunders, A. (2004), *Understanding Market, Credit, and Operational Risk: The Value-at-Risk Approach*, Blackwell Publishing, Oxford.

BIS (1988), "International Covergence of Capital Measurement and Capital Standard," www.BIS.org.

BIS (1996), "Amendment to the Capital Accord to Incorporate Market Risks," www.BIS.org.

BIS (1998), "Overview to the Amendment to the Capital Accord to Incorporate Market Risks," www.BIS.org.

BIS (2001a), "Consultative Document: Operational Risk," www.BIS.org.

BIS (2001b), "Working Paper on the Regulatory Treatment of Operational Risk," www.BIS.org.

BIS (2002a), "The Quantitative Impact Study for Operational Risk: Overview of Individual Loss Data and Lessons Learned," www.BIS.org.

BIS (2002b), "Operational Risk Data Collection Exercise—2002," www.BIS.org.

BIS (2003a), "Operational Risk Transfer Across Financial Sectors," www.BIS.org.

BIS (2003b), "Sound Practices for the Management and Supervision of Operational Risk," www.BIS.org.

BIS (2003c), "The 2002 Loss Data Collection Exercise for Operational Risk: Summary of the Data Collected," www.BIS.org.

BIS (2003d), "Operational Risk Transfer Across Financial Sectors," www.BIS.org.

BIS (2004), "International Convergence of Capital Measurement and Capital Standards," www.BIS.org.

BIS (2006a), "Results of the Fifth Quantitative Impact Study (QIS5)," www.BIS.org.

BIS (2006b), "International Convergence of Capital Measurement and Capital Standards," www.BIS.org.

BIS (2006c), "Observed Range of Practice in Key Elements of Advanced Measurement Approaches (AMA)," www.BIS.org.

Blunden, T. (2003), Scorecard Approaches, in Alexander (2003b), pp. 229–240.

Brandts, S. (2005), "Reducing Risk Through Insurance," in Davis (2005), pp. 305–314.

Canter, M. S., Cole, J. B., and Sander, R. L. (1996), "Insurance Derivatives: A New Asset Class for the Capital Markets and a New Hedging Tool for the Insurance Industry," *Journal of Derivatives* 4, pp. 89–104.

Cruz, M. G. (2002), *Modeling, Measuring and Hedging Operational Risk*, John Wiley & Sons, New York, Chichester.

Currie, C. (2005), A Test of the Strategic Effect of Basel II Operational Risk Requirements for Banks, Technical Report 141, University of Technology, Sydney.

Davis, E., ed. (2005), *Operational Risk: Practical Approaches to Implementation*, RISK Books, London.

Dutta, K., and Perry, J. (2006), A Tale of Tails: An Empirical Analysis of Loss Distribution Models for Estimating Operational Risk Capital, Technical Report 06-13, Federal Reserve Bank of Boston.

Financial Guardian Group (2005), The Risk of Operational Risk-Based Capital: Why Cost and Competitive Implications Make Basel II's Requirement Ill-Advised in the United States, Technical report, Financial Guardian Group.

Hadjiemmanuil, C. (2003), "Legal Risks and Fraud: Capital Charges, Control and Insurance," in Alexander (2003b), pp. 74–100.

Hoyt, R. E., and McCullough, K. A. (1999), "Catastrophe Insurance Options: Are They Zero-Beta Assets?," *Journal of Insurance Issues* 22(2).

JPMorgan Chase (2004), "The JPMorgan Chase Operational Risk Environment," in M. G. Cruz, ed., *"Operational Risk Modeling and Analysis. Theory and Practice,"* RISK Books, London, pp. 295–328.

Kuritzkes, A. P., and Scott, H. S. (2005), "Sizing Operational Risk and the Effect of Insurance: Implications for the Basel II Capital Accord," in H. S. Scott, ed., *Capital Adequacy Beyond Basel: Banking, Securities, and Insurance,* Oxford University Press, New York, pp. 258–283.

Lawrence, D. (2003), "Operational Risk Implications of Basel II," *Risk.*

Leddy, T. M. (2003), "Operational Risk and Insurance," in Alexander (2003b), pp. 101–126.

Lewis, C. M., and Lantsman, Y. (2005), "What Is a Fair Price to Transfer the Risk of Unauthorised Trading? A Case Study on Operational Risk," in Davis (2005), pp. 315–355.

Marshall, C. L. (2001), *Measuring and Managing Operational Risk in Financial Institutions: Tools, Techniques, and Other Resources,* John Wiley & Sons, Chichester.

Mori, T., and Harada, E. (2001), Internal Measurement Approach to Operational Risk Capital Charge, Technical report, Bank of Japan.

Muermann, A., and Oktem, U. (2002), "The Near-Miss Management of Operational Risk," *Journal of Risk Finance* 4(1), pp. 25–36.

Paletta, D. (2005), "For Basel Opt-Ins, Its Time to Gather Data," *American Banker,* January 21.

Silverman, E. J. (2006), "September 29: Operational Risk—Basel II, U.S. Banks Have Until January 2008 to Comply Plus 3 Year Transition Period," http://www.riskcenter.com.

S&P (2003), "Basel II: No Turning Back for the Banking Industry," Standard & Poors, Commentary and News.

Van den Brink, J. (2002), *Operational Risk: The New Challenge for Banks,* Palgrave, London.

CHAPTER 4

Key Challenges in Modeling Operational Risk

Identifying the core principles that underlie the operational risk process is the fundamental building block in deciding on the optimal model to be used. We begin the chapter with an overview of models that have been put forward for the assessment of operational risk. They are broadly classified into top-down models and bottom-up models.

Operational risk is distinct from credit risk and market risk, posing difficulties of implementation of the Basel II guidelines and strategic planning. We discuss some key aspects that distinguish operational risk from credit risk and market risk. They are related to the arrival process of loss events, the loss severity, and the dependence structure of operational losses across a bank's business units.

Finally, in this chapter we reconsider the normality assumption—an assumption often made in modeling financial data—and question its applicability for the purpose of operational risk modeling.

OPERATIONAL RISK MODELS

Broadly speaking, operational risk models stem from two fundamentally different approaches: (1) the top-down approach, and (2) the bottom-up approach. Figure 4.1 illustrates a possible categorization of quantitative models.

Top-down approaches quantify operational risk without attempting to identify the events or causes of losses.[1] That is, the losses are simply

---

[1] An exception is the scenario analysis models in which specific events are identified and included into internal databases for stress testing. These events are, however, imaginable and do not appear in the banks' original databases.

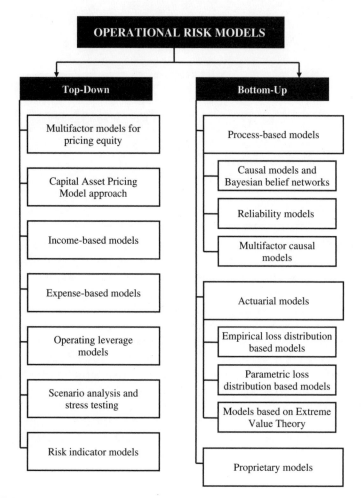

FIGURE 4.1 Topology of operational risk models.

measured on a macrobasis. The principal advantage of this approach is that little effort is required with collecting data and evaluating operational risk. Bottom-up approaches quantify operational risk on a microlevel being based on identified internal events, and this information is then incorporated into the overall capital charge calculation. The advantage of bottom-up approaches over top-down approaches lies in their ability to explain the mechanism of *how* and *why* operational risk is formed within an institution. Banks can either start with top-down models and use them as a temporary tool to estimate the capital charge and then slowly shift to the more advanced bottom-up models, or they can adopt bottom-up models from the start, provided that they have robust databases.

Models Based on Top-Down Approaches

In this section we provide a brief look at the seven top-down approaches shown in Figure 4.1.[2]

Multifactor Equity Pricing Models *Multifactor equity pricing models*, also referred to as *multifactor models*, can be utilized to perform a global analysis of banking risks and may be used for the purpose of integrated risk management, in particular for publicly traded firms. The stock return process R_t can be estimated by regressing stock return on a large number of external risk factor indices I_t related to market risk, credit risks, and other nonoperational risks (such as interest rate fluctuations, stock price movements, and macroeconomic effects). Operational risk is then measured as the volatility of the residual term. Such models rely on the assumption that operational risk is the residual banking risk, after credit and market risks are accounted for.[3]

$$R_t = a_t + b_1 I_{1t} + \cdots + b_n I_{nt} + \varepsilon_t,$$

in which ε_t is the residual term, a proxy for operational risk.

This approach relies on the widely known Efficient Market Hypothesis that was introduced by Fama (1970), which states that in efficient capital markets all relevant past, publicly and privately available information is reflected in current asset prices.

Capital Asset Pricing Model Under the *Capital Asset Pricing Model* (CAPM) approach, all risks are assumed to be measurable by the CAPM and represented by beta (β). CAPM, developed by Sharpe (1964), is an equilibrium model that describes the pricing of assets. It concludes that the expected security risk premium (i.e., expected return on security minus the risk-free rate of return) equals beta times the expected market risk premium (i.e., expected return on the market minus the risk-free rate of return).

Under the CAPM approach, operational risk is obtained by measuring market, credit, and other risks' betas and deducting them from the total

---

[2]Some of these models are described in Allen, Boudoukh, and Saunders (2004).
[3]In Chapter 2 we provided an example of an empirical study that utilized such model in order to to evaluate the sensitivity of operational risk to macroeconomic factors.

beta. With respect to applications to operational risk, the CAPM approach was discussed by Hiwatashi and Ashida (2002) and van den Brink (2002). According to van den Brink (2002), the CAPM approach has some limitations and so has not received a wide recognition for operational risk, but was in the past considered by Chase Manhattan Bank.

Income-Based Models   *Income-based models* resemble the multifactor equity price models: Operational risk is estimated as the residual variance by extracting market, credit, and other risks from the historical income (or earnings) volatility. Income-based models are described by Allen, Boudoukh, and Saunders (2004), who refer to them as *earnings at risk models*, and by Hiwatashi and Ashida (2002), who refer to them as the *volatility approach*. According to Cruz (2002), the profit and loss (P&L) volatility in a financial institution is attributed 50%, 15%, and 35% to credit risk, market risk, and operational and other risks, respectively.

Expense-Based Models   *Expense-based models* measure operational risk as fluctuations in historical expenses rather than income. The unexpected operational losses are captured by the volatility of direct expenses (as opposed to indirect expenses, such as opportunity costs, reputational risk, and strategic risk, that are outside the agreed scope of operational risk),[4] adjusted for any structural changes within the bank.

Operating Leverage Models   *Operating leverage models* measure the relationship between operating expenses and total assets. Operating leverage is measured as a weighted combination of a fraction of fixed assets and a portion of operating expenses. Examples of calculating operating leverage amount per business line include taking 10% of fixed assets plus 25% times three months' operating expenses for a particular business, or taking 2.5 times the monthly fixed expenses.[5]

Scenario Analysis and Stress Testing Models   *Scenario analysis* and *stress testing models* can be used for testing the robustness properties of loss models, in monetary terms, in the presence of potential events that are not part of banks' actual internal databases. These models, also called *expert judgment models* (van den Brink, 2002), are estimated based on the what-if scenarios generated with reference to expert opinion, external data, catastrophic events occurred in other banks, or imaginary high-magnitude

---

[4]See the discussion of varous risk types in Chapter 2.
[5]See Marshall (2001).

events. Experts estimate the expected risk amounts and their associated probabilities of occurrence. For any particular bank, examples of scenarios include the following:[6]

- The bank's inability to reconcile a new settlement system with the original system
- A class action suit alleging incomplete disclosure
- Massive technology failure
- High-scale unauthorized trading (e.g., adding the total loss borne by the Barings Bank preceeding its collapse[7] into the database, and reevaluating the model)
- Doubling the bank's maximum historical loss amount

Additionally, stress tests can be used to see the likely increase in risk exposure due to removing a control or reducing risk exposure due to tightening of controls.

Risk Indicator Models *Risk indicator models* rely on a number (one or more) of operational risk exposure indicators[8] to track operational risk. In the operational risk literature, risk indicator models are also called *indicator approach models*,[9] *risk profiling models*,[10] and *peer-group comparison*.[11] A necessary aspect of such models is testing for possible correlations between risk factors. These models assume that there is a direct and significant relationship between the indicators and target variables. For example, Taylor and Hoffman (1999) illustrate how training expenditure has a reverse effect on the number of employee errors and customer complaints, and Shih, Samad-Khan, and Medapa (2000) illustrate how a bank's size relates to the operational loss amount.[12]

Risk indicator models may rely on a single indicator or multiple indicators. The former model is called the *single-indicator approach*;[13] an example of such model is the Basic Indicator Approach for quantification of the operational risk regulatory capital, proposed by the Basel II. The latter model is called the *multiindicator approach*; an example of such model is the Standardized Approach.

---

[6]The first four examples are due to Marshall (2001).
[7]See Chapter 1 for a description of this incident.
[8]See Chapter 2 on a list of possible operational risk exposure indicators.
[9]See Hiwatashi and Ashida (2002).
[10]See Allen, Boudoukh and Saunders (2004).
[11]See van den Brink (2002).
[12]We gave a description of this study in Chapter 2.
[13]See van den Brink (2002).

Models Based on Bottom-Up Approaches

An ideal internal operational risk assessment procedure would be to use a balanced approach, and include both top-down and bottom-up elements into the analysis.[14] For example, scenario analysis can prove effective for the backtesting purposes, and multifactor causal models are useful in performing operational value-at-risk (VaR)[15] sensitivity analysis. Bottom-up approach models can be categorized into three groups:[16] process-based models, actuarial-type models (or statistical models), and proprietary models.

Process-Based Models   There are three types of process-based models: (1) causal models and Bayesian belief networks, (2) reliability models, and (3) multifactor causal models.

The first group of process-based models is the *causal models and Bayesian belief networks*. Also called *causal network models, causal models* are *subjective self-assessment models*. Causal models form the basis of the *scorecard models.*[17] These models split banking activities into simple steps; for each step, bank management evaluates the number of days needed to complete the step, the number of failures and errors, and so on, and then records the results in a *process map* (or scorecards) in order to identify potential weak points in the operational cycle. Constructing associated event trees that detect a sequence of actions or events that may lead to an operational loss is part of the analysis.[18] For each step, bank management estimates a probability of its occurrence, called the *subjective* (or prior) probability. The ultimate event's probability is measured by the posterior probability. Prior and posterior probabilities can be estimated using the *Bayesian belief networks.*[19] A variation of the causal models, *connectivity models*, focuses on the *ex ante* cause of operational loss event, rather than the *ex post* effect.

---

[14]The Internal Measurement Approach (see description in Chapter 3 and BIS (2001)) combines some elements of top-down approach and bottom-up approach: the gamma parameter in the formula for the capital charge is set externally by regulators, while the expected loss is determined based on internal data.

[15]Refer to Chapter 11 on the discussion of value-at-risk.

[16]See Allen, Boudoukh, and Saunders (2004).

[17]In February 2001 the Basel Committee suggested the Scorecard Approach as one possible Advanced Measurement Approach to measure the operational risk capital charge. See Chapter 3 for a description of the Scorecard Approach.

[18]See, for example, Marshall (2001) on the "fishbone analysis."

[19]Relevant Bayesian belief models with applications to operational risk are discussed in Alexander and Pezier (2001), Neil and Tranham (2002), and Giudici (2004), among others.

The second group of process-based models encompasses *reliability models*. These models are based on the frequency distribution of the operational loss events and their interarrival times. Reliability models focus on measuring the likelihood that a particular event will occur at some point or interval of time.

If $f(t)$ is the density of a loss amount occurring at time t, then the reliability of the system is the *probability of survival* up to at least time t, denoted by $R(t)$ and calculated as

$$R(t) = 1 - \int_0^t f(s)ds.$$

The *hazard rate* (or the *failure rate*), $h(t)$, is the rate at which losses occur per unit of time t, defined as

$$h(t) = \frac{f(t)}{R(t)}.$$

In practical applications, it is often convenient to use the Poisson-type arrival model to describe the occurrence of operational loss events.[20] Under the simple Poisson model with the intensity rate λ (which represents the average number of events in any point of time), the interarrival times between the events (i.e., the time intervals between any two consecutive points of time in which an event takes place) follow an exponential distribution having density of form $f(t) = \lambda e^{-\lambda t}$ with mean interarrival time equal to $1/\lambda$. The parameter λ is then the hazard rate for the simple Poisson process.

Finally, the third group of process-based models is the *multifactor causal models*. These models can be used for performing the factor analysis of operational risk. These are regression-type models that examine the sensitivity of aggregate operational losses (or, alternatively, VaR) to various internal risk factors (or risk drivers). Multifactor causal models have been discussed in the VaR and operational risk literature.[21] Examples of control factors include system downtime in minutes per day, number of employees in the back office, data quality (such as the ratio of the number of transactions with no input errors to the total number of transactions), total number of transactions, skill levels, product complexity, level of automation, customer satisfaction, and so on. Cruz (2002) suggests using manageable explanatory

---

[20] See Chapter 5 for the discussion of various frequency distributions.
[21] See also Haubenstock (2003) and Cruz (2002). Note that in Chapter 2 we described the Allen-Bali empirical study in which they examined the sensitivity of operational value-at-risk to macroeconomic rather than a bank's internal risk factors.

factors.[22] In multifactor causal models, operational losses OR, or VaR, in a particular business unit at a point t, are regressed on a number of control factors:

$$OR_t = a_t + b_1 X_{1t} + \cdots + b_n X_{nt} + \varepsilon_t,$$

where X_k, $k = 1, 2, \ldots, n$ are the explanatory variables, and b's are the estimated coefficients. The model is forward-looking (or *ex ante*) as operational risk drivers are predictive of future losses. Extensions to the simple regression model may include auto-regressive models, regime-switching models, ARMA/GARCH models, and others.

Actuarial Models *Actuarial models* (or *statistical models*) are generally parametric statistical models. They have two key components: (1) the loss frequency and (2) the loss severity distributions of the historic operational loss data. Operational risk capital is measured by VaR of the aggregated one-year losses. A major focus of this book will be to develop and examine such models.[23]

For the frequency of the loss data it is common to assume a Poisson process, with possible generalizations, such as a Cox process.[24]

Actuarial models can differ by the type of the loss distribution.[25] *Empirical loss distribution models* do not specify a particular class of loss distributions, but directly utilize the empirical distribution derived from the historic data. *Parametric loss distribution models* make use of a particular parametric distribution for the losses (or part of them), such as lognormal, Weibull, Pareto, and so on. Models based on *extreme value theory* (EVT)[26] restrict attention to the tail events (i.e., the losses in the upper quantiles of the severity distribution), and VaR or other analyses are carried out upon fitting the generalized Pareto distribution to the data beyond a fixed high threshold. Van den Brink (2002) suggests using all three models simultaneously; Figure 4.2, inspired by his discussions, illustrates possible approaches. Yet another possibility is to fit ARMA/GARCH model to the losses below a high threshold and the generalized Pareto distribution to the data exceeding it.

---

[22] See also Chapter 2 on a description of possible risk indicators.

[23] Actuarial models form the basis of the Loss Distribution Approach, an Advanced Measurement Approach for operational risk. See BIS (2001) and Chapter 3.

[24] Frequency models are presented in Chapter 5.

[25] Operational loss distributions are reviewed in Chapter 6.

[26] Chapter 8 provides a review of extreme value theory.

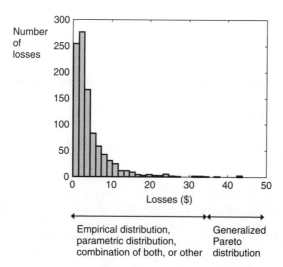

FIGURE 4.2 An example of a histogram of the operational loss severity distribution.

Proprietary Models *Proprietary models* for operational risk have been developed by major financial service companies and use a variety of bottom-up and top-down quantitative methodologies, as well as qualitative analysis, to evaluate operational risk. Banks can input their loss data into ready and systematized spreadsheets, which would be further categorized. The system then performs a qualitative and quantitative analysis of the data, and can carry out multiple tasks such as calculating regulatory capital, pooling internal data with external, performing Bayesian network analysis, and so on.

Examples of currently available proprietary software include:

- *Algo OpVantage*, marketed by Algorithmics, Inc. The product provides a framework for operational risk self-assessment, data mapping, modeling and mixing of internal data and external data, and capital modeling.
- *Six Sigma*, developed by General Electric and modified for operational risk by Citigroup and GE Capital.
- *Horizon*, offered by JPMorgan Chase and Ernst & Young.

SPECIFICS OF OPERATIONAL LOSS DATA

The nature of operational risk is very different from that of market risk and credit risk. In fact, operational losses share many similarities with insurance claims, suggesting that most actuarial models can be a natural choice of the model for operational risk, and models well developed by the insurance industry can be almost exactly applied to operational risk. In this section we discuss some key issues characterizing operational risk that must be taken into consideration before quantitative analysis is undertaken.

Scarcity of Available Historical Data

The major obstacle banks face in developing comprehensive models for operational risk is the scarcity of available historical operational loss data. As of 2006, generally, even the largest banks have no more than five to six years of loss data. Shortage of relevant data means that the models and conclusions drawn from the available limited samples would lack sufficient explanatory power. This, in turn, means that the estimates of the expected loss and VaR may be highly volatile and unreliable. In addition, complex statistical or econometric models cannot be tested on small samples.

The problem becomes amplified when dealing with modeling extremely high operational losses. One cannot model tail events when only a few such data are present in the internal loss database. Three solutions have been proposed: (1) pooling internal and external data, (2) supplementing actual losses with near-miss losses,[27] and (3) using scenario analysis and stress tests (discussed earlier in this chapter).

The idea behind pooling internal and external data is to populate a bank's existing internal database with data from outside the bank. The rationale is twofold: (1) to expand the database and hence increase the accuracy of statistical estimations; and (2) to account for losses that have not occurred within the bank but that are not completely improbable based on the histories of other banks. According to BIS,

> a bank's internal measurement system must reasonably estimate unexpected losses based on the combined use of internal and relevant external loss data ... (BIS (2006, p. 150))

Baud, Frachot, and Roncalli (2002) propose a statistical methodology to pool internal and external data. Their methodology accounts for the fact that external data are truncated from below (banks commonly report their loss data to external parties in excess of $1 million) and that bank size may be correlated with the magnitudes of losses. They showed that pooling internal and external data may help avoid underestimation of the capital charge. We discuss the methodology in Chapter 9.

---

[27]We provided discussion on near-misses in Chapter 2.

Data Arrival Process

One difficulty that arises with modeling operational losses has to do with the irregular nature of the event arrival process. In market risk models, market positions are recorded on a frequent basis, many times daily depending on the entity, by *marking to market*. Price quotes are available daily or, for those securities that are infrequently traded, model-based prices are available for marking a position to market. As for credit risk, rating agencies provide credit ratings. In addition, rating agencies provide credit watches to identify credits that are candidates for downgrades. In contrast, operational losses occur at irregular time intervals suggesting a process of a discrete nature. This makes it similar to the reduced-form models for credit risk, in which the frequency of default (i.e., failure to meet a credit agreement) is of nontrivial concern. Hence, while in market risk it is needed to model only the return distribution in order to obtain VaR, in operational risk both loss severity and frequency distributions are important.

Another problem is related to timing and data recording issue. In market and credit risk models, the impact of a relevant event is almost immediately reflected in the market and credit returns. In an ideal scenario, banks would know how much of operational loss would be borne by the bank from an event at the very moment the event takes place, and would record the loss at this moment. However, from the practical point of view, this appears nearly impossible to implement, because it takes time for the losses to accumulate after an event takes place.[28] Therefore, it may take days, months, or even years for the full impact of a particular loss event to be evaluated. Hence, there is the problem of discrepancy (i.e., a time lag) between the occurrence of an event and the time at which the incurred loss is being recorded.

This problem directly affects the method in which banks choose to record their operational loss data. When banks record their operational loss data, they record (1) the amount of loss, and (2) the corresponding date. We can identify three potential scenarios for the types of date banks might use:[29]

1. *Date of occurrence.* The bank chooses the date on which the event that has led to operational losses actually took place.
2. *Date on which the existence of event has been identified.* The date is when bank authorities realize that an event that has led to operational

---

[28]Recall the discussion in Chapter 2 on the distinction between the hazard, event, and loss due to operational risk.

[29]Identification of the three types of dates are based on discussions with Marco Moscadelli (Banking Supervision Department, Bank of Italy).

losses has taken or is continuing to take place. Recording a loss at this date may be relevant in cases when the true date of occurrence is impossible or hard to track.

3. *Accounting date.* The bank uses the date on which the total amount of operational losses due to a past event are realized and fully measured, and the state of affairs of the event is closed or assumed closed.

Depending on which of the three date types is used, the models for operational risk and conclusions drawn from them may be considerably different. For example, in the third case of accounting dates, we are likely to observe cyclicality/seasonal effects in the time series of the loss data (e.g., many loss events would be recorded around the end of December), while in the first and second cases such effects are much less likely to be present in the data. Fortunately, however, selection of the frequency distribution does not have a serious impact on the resulting capital charge.[30]

Loss Severity Process

There are three main problems that operational risk analysts must be aware of with respect to the severity of operational loss data: (1) the nonnegative sign of the data, (2) the high degree of dispersion of the data, and (3) the shape of the data.

The first problem related to the loss severity data deals with the sign of the data. Depending on the movements in the interest or exchange rates, the oscillations in the market returns and indicators can take either positive or negative sign. This is different in the credit and operational risk models—usually, only losses (i.e., negative cashflows) are assumed to take place.[31] Hence, in modeling operational loss magnitudes, one should either consider fitting the loss distributions that are defined only on positive values, or should use distributions that are defined on negative and positive values, truncated at zero.

The second problem deals with the high degree of dispersion of loss data. Historical observations suggest that the movements in the market indicators are generally of relatively low magnitude. Bigger losses are usually attributed to credit risk. Finally, although most of the operational losses occur on a daily basis and hence are small in magnitude, the excessive losses of financial institutions are in general due to the operational losses, rather

---

[30] See Carillo Menéndez (2005).

[31] Certainly, it is possible that an event due to operational risk can incur unexpected profits for a bank, but usually this possibility is not considered. See also the relevant discussion in Chapter 2.

than credit or market risk-related losses. We provided in Chapter 1 examples of high-magnitude operational losses from the financial industry. Empirical evidence indicates that there is an extremely high degree of dispersion of the operational loss magnitudes, ranging from near-zero to billions of dollars. In general, this dispersion is measured by variance or standard deviation.[32]

The third problem concerns the shape of the loss distribution. The shape of the data for operational risk is very different from that of market or credit risk. In market risk models, for example, the distribution of the market returns is often assumed to be nearly symmetric around zero. Asymmetric cases refer to the data whose distribution is either *left-skewed* (i.e., the left tail of the distribution is very long) or *right-skewed* (i.e., the right tail of the distribution is very long) and/or whose distribution has two or more peaks of different height. Operational losses are highly asymmetric, and empirical evidence on operational risk indicates that the losses are highly skewed to the right. This is in part explained by the presence of "low frequency/high severity" events.[33] See Figure 4.2 for an exemplary histogram of operational losses.

As previously discussed, empirical evidence on operational losses indicates a majority of observations being located close to zero, and a small number of observations being of a very high magnitude. The first phenomenon refers to a high kurtosis (i.e., peak) of the data, and the second one indicates heavy tails (or fat tails). Distributions of such data are often described as *leptokurtic*.

The Gaussian (or normal) distribution is often used to model market risk and credit risk. It is characterized by two parameters, μ and σ, that are its mean and standard deviation. Figure 4.3 provides an example of a normal density. Despite being easy to work with and having attractive features (such as symmetry and stability under linear transformations), the Gaussian distribution makes several critical assumptions about the loss data:

- The Gaussian assumption is useful for modeling the distribution of events that are symmetric around their mean. It has been empirically demonstrated that operational losses are not symmetric and severely *right-skewed*, meaning that the right tail of the loss distribution is very long.

- In most cases (except for the cases when the mean is very high), the use of Gaussian distribution allows for the occurrence of negative values.

---

[32] Some very heavy-tailed distributions, such as the heavy-tailed Weibull, Pareto, or alpha-stable, can have an infinite variance. In these situations, robust measures of spread must be used.

[33] The notion of "low frequency/high severity" losses was described in Chapter 2.

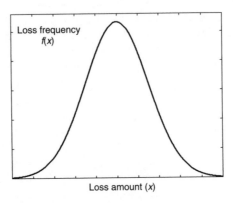

FIGURE 4.3   An example of a Gaussian density.

This is not a desirable property for modeling loss severity because negative losses are usually not possible.[34]

- More importantly, the Gaussian distribution has an exponential decay in its tails (this property puts the Gaussian distribution into the class of *light-tailed* distributions), which means that the tail events (i.e., the events of an unusually high or low magnitude) have a near-zero probability of occurrence. However, we have already seen in Chapter 1 how very-high-magnitude operational losses can seriously jeopardize a financial institution. Thus, it would be inappropriate to model operational losses with a distribution that essentially excludes the possibility of high-impact individual losses. Empirical evidence strongly supports the conjecture that the distribution of operational losses is in fact very *leptokurtic*—that is, it has a high peak and very heavy tails (i.e., very rare events are assigned a positive probability). The supporting evidence will be provided later in this book.

For the reasons already presented, it is unlikely that the Gaussian distribution would find much application for the assessment of operational risk.[35] Heavier-tailed distributions such as lognormal, Weibull, and even Pareto and alpha-stable, ought to be considered.[36]

---

[34]Certainly, it is possible to use a truncated (at zero) version of the Gaussian distribution to fit operational losses. Truncated distributions will be presented in Chapter 9.

[35]Of course, a special case is fitting the Gaussian distribution to the natural logarithm of the loss data. This is equivalent (in terms of obtaining the maximum likelihood parameter estimates) to fitting the lognormal distribution to the original loss data.

[36]The large class of alpha-stable distributions is discussed in Chapter 7.

Dependence between Business Units

In order to increase the accuracy of operational risk assessment, banks are advised to classify their operational loss data into groups of different degrees and nature of exposure to operational risk. Following this principle, the Advanced Measurement Approaches (AMA) for the quantification of the operational risk capital charge, proposed by Basel II,[37] suggest estimating operational risk capital separately for each "business line/event type" combination. Such procedure is not common in market risk and credit risk models.

The most intuitive approach to combine risk measures collected from each of these business line/event type combinations is to add them up.[38] However, such an approach may result in overestimation of the total capital charge because it implies a perfect positive correlation between groups. To prevent this from happening, it is essential to account for dependence between these combinations. *Covariance* and *correlation* are the simplest measures of dependency, but they assume a linear type of dependence, and therefore can produce misleading results if the linearity assumption is not true. An alternative approach would involve using *copulas* that are more flexible with respect to the form of the dependence structure that may exist between different groups. Another attractive property of copulas is their ability to capture the tail dependence between the distributions of random variables. Both properties are preserved under linear transformations of the variables.[39]

SUMMARY OF KEY CONCEPTS

- Operational risk measurement models are divided into top-down and bottom-up models.
- *Top-down models* use a macrolevel regulatory approach to assess operational risk and determine the capital charge. They include multifactor equity price models, income and expense based models, operating leverage models, scenario analysis and stress testing models, and risk indicator models.
- *Bottom-up models* originate from a microlevel analysis of a bank's loss data and consideration for the process and causes of loss events in determination of the capital charge. They include process-based

---

[37]The AMA were described in Chapter 3.
[38]This is the approach that was proposed in BIS (2001).
[39]Copulas and their application to the operational risk modeling will be examined in Chapter 13.

models (such as causal network and Bayesian belief models, connectivity models, multifactor causal models, and reliability models), actuarial models, and proprietary models.

- Scarcity and reliability of available internal operational loss data remains a barrier preventing banks from developing comprehensive statistical models. Sufficiently large datasets are especially important for modeling low-frequency, high-severity events. Three solutions have been put forward to help expand internal databases: pooling together internal and external data, accounting for near-misses, and stress tests.
- The nature of operational risk is fundamentally different from that of credit and market risks. Specifics of operational loss process include discrete data arrival process, delays between time of event and loss detection/accumulation, loss data taking only positive sign, high dispersion in magnitudes of loss data, distribution of loss data being severely right-skewed and heavy-tailed, and dependence between business units and event types.
- While many market and credit risk models make the convenient Gaussian assumption on the market returns or stock returns, this distribution is unlikely to be useful for the operational risk modeling because it is unable to capture the nonsymmetric and heavy-tailed nature of the loss data.

REFERENCES

Alexander, C., and Pezier, J. (2001), "Taking Control of Operational Risk," *Futures and Options World* 366.

Allen, L., Boudoukh, J. and Saunders, A. (2004), *Understanding Market, Credit, and Operational Risk: The Value-at-Risk Approach*, Blackwell Publishing, Oxford.

Baud, N., Frachot, A., and Roncalli, T. (2002), Internal Data, External Data, and Consortium Data for Operational Risk Measurement: How to Pool Data Properly?, Technical report, Groupe de Recherche Opérationnelle, Crédit Lyonnais, France.

BIS (2001), "Consultative Document: Operational Risk," www.BIS.org.

BIS (2006), "International Convergence of Capital Measurement and Capital Standards," www.BIS.org.

Carillo Menéndez, S. (2005), Operational Risk, Presentation at International Summer School on Risk Measurement and Control, Rome, June 2005.

Cruz, M. G. (2002), *Modeling, Measuring and Hedging Operational Risk*, John Wiley & Sons, New York, Chichester.

Fama, E. F. (1970), "Efficient Capital Markets: A Review of Theory and Empirical Work", *Journal of Finance* 25, pp. 383–417.

Giudici, P. (2004), "Integration of Qualitative and Quantitative Operational Risk Data: A Bayesian Approach," in M. G. Cruz, ed., *Operational Risk Modelling and Analysis. Theory and Practice,* RISK Books, London, pp. 131–138.

Haubenstock, M. (2003), "The Operational Risk Management Framework," in C. Alexander, ed., *Operational Risk: Regulation, Analysis and Management,* Prentice Hall, Upper Saddle River, NJ, pp. 241–261.

Hiwatashi, J., and Ashida, H. (2002), Advancing Operational Risk Management Using Japanese Banking Experiences, Technical report, Federal Reserve Bank of Chicago.

Marshall, C. L. (2001), *Measuring and Managing Operational Risk in Financial Institutions: Tools, Techniques, and Other Resources,* John Wiley & Sons, Chichester.

Neil, M., and Tranham, E. (2002), "Using Bayesian Networks to Predict Op Risk," *Operational Risk,* August, pp. 8–9.

Sharpe, W. F. (1964), "Capital Asset Prices: A Theory of Market Equilibrium Under Conditions of Risk," *Journal of Finance* 19, pp. 425–442.

Shih, J., Samad-Khan, A. J., and Medapa, P. (2000), "Is the Size of an Operational Risk Related to Firm Size?," *Operational Risk,* January.

Taylor, D. and Hoffman, D. (1999), "How to Avoid Signal Failure," *Risk,* November, pp. 13–15.

van den Brink, J. (2002), *Operational Risk: The New Challenge for Banks,* Palgrave, London.

CHAPTER 5

Frequency Distributions

Most operational losses occur and are detected nearly on a daily basis. Frequent operational losses are associated with minor errors committed by inexperienced employees or with product defects, credit card frauds, process slowdowns, delays attributed to computer problems, and so on. However, some losses may occur once in 5, 10, or 50 years, such as substantial property damage due to natural disasters or terrorist attacks. Moreover, some losses take place over an extended period of time, but may remain undetected for months or years, such as long-lasting unauthorized trading activities. In either scenario, observed losses arrive on an irregular fashion, with the interarrival times (i.e., the time intervals between the occurrences of events) ranging from several hours to several years or even decades. In this light, it appears appropriate to incorporate the specifics of the arrival process into the model for operational losses, and to model losses of every type as a process that is characterized by a random frequency of events and a random monetary magnitudes of their effect.

An essential prerequisite for developing a solid operational risk model is a systematized mechanism for data recording. In particular, a bank should be consistent in the way it records the *date* associated with every loss event. Currently, there does not seem to exist a standardized policy on this. In Chapter 4 we described three possible ways in which the date might be recorded.

In this chapter we review distributions that can be used to model the frequency of operational losses. We refer the reader to the appendix to this chapter for a brief review of useful properties of discrete random variables. The key model that is the focus of our attention in this chapter is the Poisson counting process and its variants.[1] Goodness-of-fit tests for discrete distributions will be described in Chapter 10.

---

[1]Useful literature on statistics and probability includes Casella and Berger (2001), Ross (2002), Klugman, Panjer, and Willmot (2004), Bickel and Doksum (2001), and

BINOMIAL DISTRIBUTION

The binomial distribution is one of the simplest distributions that can be used to model the frequency of loss events in a fixed time interval. It relies on four main assumptions:

1. Each trial can result in only two possible outcomes, *success* and *failure*.
2. The total number of identical trials n is fixed, $n > 0$.
3. The probability of success p is constant for each trial ($0 \leq p \leq 1$).
4. All trials are independent from each other.

In the context of operational losses, success could be, for example, the event that at least one operational loss has occurred in one day. The number of trials can be the total number of days in question; for example, 250 working days (i.e., one year), so that in each of these days at least one loss occurs or it does not, and in any single day a loss is equally likely to take place. In this example, we define the random variable as the number of days in which at least one operational loss takes place.

The probability that a binomial random variable X takes a value k out of n maximum possible (for example, the probability that one will observe operational losses on k days in one year) is then

$$P(X = k) = \binom{n}{k}p^k(1 - p)^{n-k}, \quad k = 0, 1, \ldots, n.$$

The mean and the variance of X can be calculated as follows:

$$\text{mean}(X) = np, \quad \text{var}(X) = np(1 - p).$$

For example, if, on average, 7 out of every 10 days a risk manager observes a particular loss (i.e., $p = 0.7$), then he should expect to see

$$250 \times 0.7 = 175$$

total number of days in one year on which this loss takes place, with standard deviation

$$\sqrt{250 \times 0.7 \times 0.3} = 7.25.$$

Cizek, Härdle, and Weron (2005). References on simulation of random variables include Ross (2001), Ross (2002), and Devroye (1986). Advanced references on the Poisson and Cox processes include Bening and Korolev (2002), Grandell (1976), Grandell (1991), Grandell (1997), Haight (1967), and Kingman (1993).

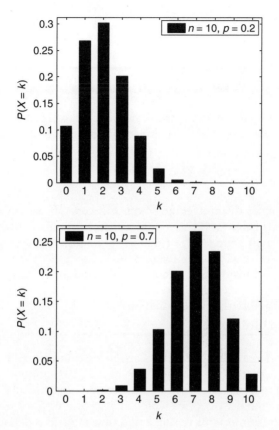

FIGURE 5.1 Illustration of the histogram of a binomial random variable.

Exemplary histograms of binomial random variables are depicted in Figure 5.1. Note that when p is small and n is large, as explained shortly, the binomial distribution can be approximated by the Poisson distribution with parameter $\lambda = np$. In addition, when n is sufficiently large, then one can use a normal approximation with the parameters $\mu = np$ and $\sigma = \sqrt{np(1-p)}$.

GEOMETRIC DISTRIBUTION

The geometric distribution is useful to model the probability that an event occurs for the first time, given that it has not occurred before. It assumes independence between events and a constant probability of its happening.

If the probability of an incidence of a success event is p, $0 \leq p \leq 1$, in a particular period of time, then the probability that an event will be observed on the kth interval of time for the first time is[2]

$$P(X = k) = (1 - p)^{k-1}p, \quad k = 1, 2, \ldots$$

which means that the first $k - 1$ trials must be failures, and the kth trial must be a success. The mean and the variance of a geometric random variable are

$$\text{mean}(X) = \frac{1}{p}, \quad \text{var}(X) = \frac{1-p}{p^2}.$$

For example, if, on average, 7 out of every 10 days a risk manager observes a particular loss (i.e., $p = 0.7$), then he should expect to see a loss event immediately after $1/0.7 = 1.42$ days of no loss. The standard deviation in this case is $(1 - 0.7)/0.7^2 = 0.61$ days.

Examples of histograms of a geometric random variable are presented in Figure 5.2.

POISSON DISTRIBUTION

The main difference between the Poisson distribution and the binomial distribution is that the former does not make an assumption regarding the total number of trials. The Poisson distribution is used to find the probability that a certain number of events would arrive within a fixed time interval. If the mean number of events during a unit time interval is denoted by λ, then the probability that there will be k events during this interval of time can be estimated by the following expression:

$$P(X = k) = \frac{e^{-\lambda}\lambda^k}{k!}, \quad k = 0, 1, \ldots$$

The mean and the variance of a Poisson random variable are

$$\text{mean}(X) = \lambda, \quad \text{var}(X) = \lambda.$$

A Poisson process assumes a constant mean (which is also referred to as the *intensity rate* or the *intensity factor*) and is therefore often called a

---

[2]Another parameterization is sometimes used, with the probability mass function defined by $P(X = k) = (1 - p)^k p$, $k = 0, 1, \ldots$ The mean and the variance are then $\text{mean}(X) = \frac{1-p}{p}$ and $\text{var}(X) = \frac{1-p}{p^2}$.

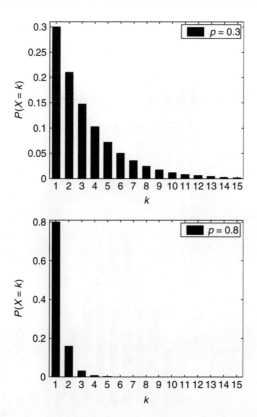

FIGURE 5.2 Illustration of the histogram of a geometric random variable.

homogeneous Poisson process. To fit the Poisson distribution to data, one needs to estimate the mean number of events in a prespecified time interval. Examples of the histograms of Poisson random variables are portrayed in Figure 5.3.

Note that the mean number of events is going to be different, depending on the length of the time interval considered. To rescale the distribution to adjust for a longer time horizon, simply multiply the parameter λ by the length of time. For example, suppose an average number of operational loss events that occur in a one-day period is 5. The mean (and the variance) of the corresponding Poisson process are 5 also. Then we expect the number of loss events that arrive during a one-week (i.e., five business days) period to equal $5 \times 5 = 25$.

As a simple way to check whether a counting process can be characterized as a Poisson distribution, one can plot equal time intervals on a

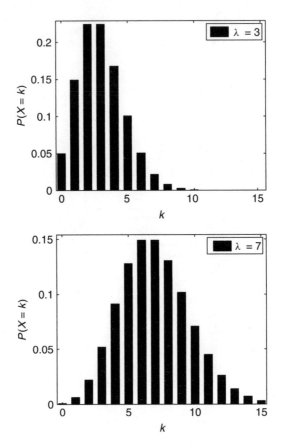

FIGURE 5.3   Illustration of the histogram of a Poisson random variable.

horizontal axis, and total number of events that occurred in each interval on the vertical axis. The plot should roughly look like a straight horizontal line, centered around the mean. If the plot is steadily increasing, decreasing, or significantly oscillating, this may indicate that the assumption of a constant intensity rate is not valid, and alternative models should be sought. Another method is to compare the mean and the variance of the numbers of events and see if they are fairly equal.

The Poisson distribution has a convenient property: if X and Y are two independent Poisson random variables with parameters λ_X and λ_Y, respectively, then the distribution of $X + Y$ is a Poisson distribution with parameter $\lambda_X + \lambda_Y$. This property can be useful if one wishes to consider the frequency distribution of losses from, for example, two independent

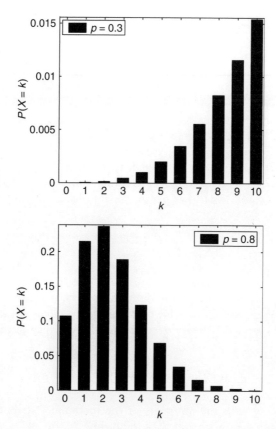

FIGURE 5.4   Illustration of the histogram of a negative binomial random variable.

business units or even all units of a bank. The analysis will not change structurally.

Another important property of the Poisson distribution is related to the distribution of the associated interarrival times between events. The interval length between two consecutive events follows an exponential distribution[3] with parameter λ, which is the same as the parameter of the corresponding Poisson distribution defined for this time interval. The mean of the Poisson distribution is inversely related to the mean interarrival time. For example, if in a 10-day interval we expect to see 7 loss events, then we expect the mean interarrival time to be 10/7 = 1.4 days between events.

---

[3] We review properties of the exponential distribution in Chapter 6.

NEGATIVE BINOMIAL DISTRIBUTION

The negative binomial distribution is a special generalized case of the Poisson distribution, in which the intensity rate λ is no longer taken to be constant but is assumed to follow a gamma distribution.[4] This Poisson-gamma mixture relaxes the assumption of a constant mean (and hence the assumption regarding the independence of events) and allows for a greater flexibility in the number of loss events within a period of time.

Given a particular value of λ, X is distributed Poisson with the parameter λ. The random variable λ is gamma distributed with parameters n and β ($n > 0$ and $\beta > 0$). The probability mass function of such random variable X is expressed as follows (other parameterizations are possible):

$$P(X = k) = \binom{n + k - 1}{k} p^k (1 - p)^n, \quad k = 0, 1, \ldots$$

where $p = \frac{\beta}{1+\beta}$.

To fit a negative binomial distribution to data, one can fit the gamma distribution to the random variable representing the intensity rate and obtain the values for n and β.[5] Then the mean and the variance of the number of events are

$$\text{mean}(X) = n\beta, \quad \text{var}(X) = n\beta(1 + \beta).$$

Comparing these with the moments of the binomial distribution suggests that the variance is now greater than the mean.

NONHOMOGENEOUS POISSON PROCESS (COX PROCESS)

In practice, it is plausible to expect that the mean number of events in a given time interval does not remain constant, but behaves in a more random fashion or even evolves and changes with time. Later in this chapter we provide empirical evidence to support such conjecture. The Cox process is a generalization of a simple Poisson process that, as we discussed earlier, has a constant intensity rate. A Cox process is a *nonhomogenous* process that,

---

[4] The gamma distribution will be described in Chapter 6.
[5] See Chapter 6 on the estimation of the gamma distribution parameters using the maximum likelihood estimation procedure.

given a particular instance of time (and hence a particular realization of the intensity rate λ), follows a Poisson distribution with parameter λ.

We stress that a necessary requirement for applying such advanced models is the availability of extensive data sets. We distinguish between a variety of frequency models that can fall into the category of Cox processes.

Mixture Distributions

In mixture distributions, the intensity rate λ is taken to follow a particular distribution, defined only on the positive support (i.e., the positive part of the real line because the interval of time between any two events takes only positive values). Such models allow for an extra variability of the underlying Poisson random variable through the variability of the parameter value. The negative binomial distribution that we discussed earlier is an example of a Poisson-gamma mixture distribution in which λ is assumed to follow a gamma distribution. Certainly, other generalizations are possible. The class of mixture distributions is often included into the class of nonhomogeneous Poisson processes.

Nonhomogeneous Poisson Process with Stochastic Intensity

Unlike mixture distributions in which λ follows a particular distribution of its own, in nonhomogeneous Poisson processes, the stochastic intensity λ is believed to evolve with time in a fashion that can be expressed by some mathematical function $\lambda(t)$. For example, a possible cyclical component in the time series of the number of loss events may be captured by a sinusoidal rate function, an upward-sloping tendency may be captured by a quadratic function, and so on. Moreover, a chaotic behavior of the intensity rate may be captured by a random stochastic process, such as Brownian motion.

We propose the following algorithms that allow one to determine an optimal stochastic model for operational loss frequency distribution. We take a unit of time equal to one year. Later in this chapter we present two examples with loss data that demonstrate the success of such algorithms.

Algorithm 1

1. Split the total time frame [0, t], into m small time intervals of equal length, such as days, months, or quarters;[6] express the intervals in terms of years.

---

[6]Note that the frequency distribution will change depending on the chosen intervals.

2. Calculate the total number of loss events that have occurred within each interval.
3. Construct the following plot:
   (a) On the horizontal axis that represents time, locate the numbers 1:m.
   (b) On the vertical axis that represents number of events, locate the *cumulative* number of loss events.
4. The resulting plot represents an approximation to the cumulative intensity function $\Lambda(t) = \int_0^t \lambda(s)ds$.
5. Choose a function that fits best the plot, using the mean square error (MSE) or the mean absolute error (MAE) minimization technique.

Algorithm 2

1. Sort the data so that the dates of the loss events are in increasing order.
2. Calculate the interarrival times between the dates in days (or other units) and then divide by 365 in order to express the interarrival times in terms of years.[7]
3. Suppose we have a total of n events. Construct the following plot:
   (a) Split the horizontal axis that represents total time frame $[0, t]$, t being one year, into $n - 1$ small time intervals that represent the *cumulative* interarrival times between n total number of loss events.
   (b) On the vertical axis that represents number of events, locate the numbers 1:n.
4. The resulting plot represents an approximation to the cumulative intensity function $\Lambda(t) = \int_0^t \lambda(s)ds$.
5. Choose a function that fits best the plot, using the mean square error (MSE) or the mean absolute error (MAE) minimization technique.

ALTERNATIVE APPROACH: INTERARRIVAL TIMES DISTRIBUTION

An alternative methodology for examining the frequency of losses is to investigate the properties of the interarrival times instead. This approach appears most relevant for a homogeneous Poisson process or mixture distributions. For example, we already pointed out that the interarrival

---

[7]In this example, we use 365 because we are interested in the actual number of days between the occurrences of the events. If one is interested in the number of working days instead, then 250 should be used.

times of a homogeneous Poisson process follow an exponential distribution. However, if the goodness-of-fit tests for an exponential distribution fail to support it, then alternative models should be sought.[8]

It is reasonable to model the interarrival times distribution with a continuous distribution defined on a positive support. This is discussed further in the next chapter, where we cover continuous distributions.

EMPIRICAL ANALYSIS WITH OPERATIONAL LOSS DATA

We now review some empirical studies with frequency distributions. A simple Poisson assumption is prevalent in these studies. According to Chapelle, Crama, Hübner, and Peters (2005), a simple Poisson assumption for annually aggregated losses provides a good approximation for the true frequency distribution. Such assumption has been made in numerous studies.[9] More advanced models have been considered. We classify empirical studies into two groups: those in which real data were used to estimate the parameters of frequency distribution and those in which simulated data were used.

Studies with Real Data

We review some recent empirical studies that use real data to estimate the frequency distribution.

Cruz Study of Fraud Loss Data   Cruz (2002, Chapter 5) examines the frequency distribution of 3,338 operational losses obtained from the fraud database of a major British retail bank (name undisclosed). The data were collected between 1992 and 1996.[10] He considers the Poisson and the negative binomial distributions. On average, three frauds were observed daily. The upper panel of Table 5.1 depicts the observed frequency distribution of the number of losses per day and the parameter estimates for the Poisson and negative binomial distributions.[11] Figure 5.5 shows the actual and fitted frequency distributions. Although the negative binomial distribution better captures the peak of the empirical distribution, the Poisson model

---

[8] We discuss various goodness-of-fit tests in Chapter 10.
[9] See, for example, Ebnöther, Vanini, McNeil, and Antolinez-Fehr (2001), Cruz (2002), Baud, Frachot, and Roncalli (2002b), Chernobai, Menn, Rachev, and Trück (2005a), Lewis and Lantsman (2005), and Rosenberg and Schuermann (2004).
[10] The loss data, aggregated monthly, are tabulated in Cruz (2004), Chapter 4, p. 69.
[11] The parameter value $p = 0.4038$ is based on $\beta = 0.67737$.

TABLE 5.1 Frequency distribution of fraud loss data in the Cruz study

1. Daily Frequency																
Number of Losses	0	1	2	3	4	5	6	7	8	9	10	11	12	13	14	15	16+
Frequency	221	188	525	112	73	72	44	40	14	7	2	2	4	3	2	1	0

Parameter Estimates

Poisson	$\lambda = 2.379$
Negative Binomial	$n = 3.51, p = 0.4038$

2. Annual Frequency						
			Year			Parameter Estimates
	1992	1993	1994	1995	1996	
Total Number of Frauds	586	454	485	658	798	$\lambda = 596.2$
Number of Frauds $> £100,000$	21	17	17	19	21	$\lambda = 19$

Source: Cruz (2002, pp. 82 and 94), with modifications.

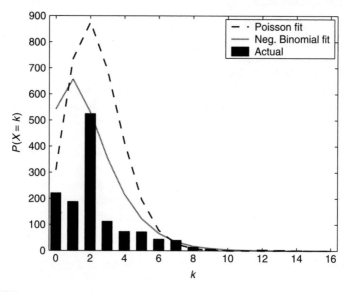

FIGURE 5.5 Poisson and Negative Binomial distributions fitted to the frequency of fraud loss data in the Cruz study.
Source: Cruz (2002, p. 95), with modifications.

seems to better capture the data overall. Cruz therefore concludes that using the simpler of the two—the Poisson distribution—would be a reasonable solution.

For the same data set, Cruz aggregated losses on a yearly basis, and also separately examined the frequency of high-magnitude events that exceed £100,000. Note the change of the Poisson parameter. The bottom panel of Table 5.1 reports the annual number of frauds for each year and the Poisson intensity rate.[12]

Moscadelli Study of 2002 LDCE Operational Loss Data Moscadelli (2004) examines the data collected by the Risk Management Group (RMG) of the Basel Committee in its June 2002 Operational Risk Loss Data Collection Exercise (LDCE).[13] There were 89 participating banks from 19 countries worldwide that provided their internal loss data for the year 2001. The data were classified into eight business lines and pooled together across all banks:

BL1: Corporate finance

BL2: Trading and sales

BL3: Retail banking

BL4: Commercial banking

BL5: Payment and settlement

BL6: Agency services

BL7: Asset management

BL8: Retail brokerage

The Poisson and the negative binomial distributions were fitted to the annual number of loss events for each business line. Moscadelli (2004) concludes that the negative binomial distribution provides a better fit than the Poisson and reports only the estimates of the negative binomial distribution and the resulting expected frequency value. We show them in Table 5.2.

---

[12]Note that the number of events per year tends to increase over time. This suggests that a homogeneous Poisson process may not be the right model for the data: the frequency rate tends to increase with time. However, the short time span of the data set does not allow us to make any formal conclusions.

[13]See Chapter 3 for a review of the Basel II Capital Accord. See also BIS (2003) on the description of the data used in the QIS2 study.

TABLE 5.2 Parameters of frequency distributions fitted to LDCE operational loss frequency data in the Moscadelli study

	\multicolumn{8}{c}{Negative Binomial Parameters (n, p) and the Mean Value (μ)}
	BL1	BL2	BL3	BL4	BL5	BL6	BL7	BL8
n	0.59	0.45	N/A	0.52	0.61	0.47	0.60	0.34
p	0.04	0.01	N/A	0.01	0.02	0.01	0.03	0.00
μ	12.67	74.45	347.45	43.90	32.00	35.03	20.02	75.55

Source: Moscadelli (2004, p. 65).

De Fontnouvelle, Rosengren, and Jordan Study of 2002 LDCE Operational Loss Data De Fontnouvelle, Rosengren, and Jordan (2005) examined the same data set analyzed by Moscadelli (2004). They limited their analysis to the data collected from six banks, and performed the analysis on a bank-by-bank basis, rather than pooling the data, as was done by Moscadelli.

They consider the Poisson and the negative binomial models for the annual number of events. For confidentiality reasons, they do not report the parameter estimates. Instead, they use a cross-sectional regression model. The number of losses n_i of an individual bank i is regressed on X_i under the Poisson distribution function in which the mean is expressed as bX_i, and also regressed on X_i under the negative binomial distribution with mean $b_1 X_i$ and variance b_2. X_i represents individual bank's size of assets (in billions of dollars) and b, b_1, and b_2 are the coefficients. The coefficients were estimated to be $b = 8.2$, $b_1 = 7.4$, and $b_2 = 0.43$.

They conclude that, based on the Poisson model, on average every billion dollars in assets is associated with 8.2 loss events per year. This result is consistent with their earlier study; see de Fontnouvelle, DeJesus-Rueff, Jordan, and Rosengren (2003). They report that a typical large internationally active bank experiences an average of 50 to 80 losses above $1 million per year, while smaller banks may encounter significantly fewer such losses and extremely large banks weighted toward more risky business lines may experience larger losses. In their study, they consider a wide range of values for the Poisson parameter λ between 30 and 100 losses in excess of $1 million per year.[14] Furthermore, this result was used by Rosenberg and Schuermann (2004), who used the midpoint average of 50 and 80 and take $\lambda = 65/365$ for the Poisson intensity of the daily loss occurrence.

---

[14]See de Fontnouvelle, DeJesus-Rueff, Jordan, and Rosengren (2003). They also mention that the Poisson assumption may not be the most appropriate, as the occurrence of large losses may be time-variant.

Lewis and Lantsman Study of Unauthorized Trading Data   Lewis and Lantsman (2005) examine industrywide losses due to *unauthorized trading* (UAT) for financial service companies over the period 1980 to 2001. The data were obtained from the OpVaR operational risk database marketed by OpVantage. To examine only the "material" UAT losses, they excluded losses under $100,000 for small and medium-size firms and losses under $1 million for large firms.[15] The remaining data set consisted of 91 events. Due to the scarcity of data, the analysis did not permit using advanced frequency models, so the homogeneous Poisson model was considered. The mean frequency per year was estimated to be $\lambda = 2.4$.

Chernobai, Burneçki, Rachev, Trück, and Weron Study of U.S. Natural Catastrophe Insurance Claims Data   Chernobai, Burneçki, Rachev, Trück, and Weron (2006) examine the U.S. natural catastrophe insurance loss data for the period 1990 to 1999. The data were obtained from the Insurance Services Office Inc. (ISO) Property Claims Services (PCS). Such data can be used as a proxy for external type operational loss data due to natural catastrophes.

The time series of the quarterly number of losses do not exhibit any trends (see the first graph in Figure 5.6) but an annual seasonality can be very well observed using the periodogram (see the second graph in Figure 5.6) with a distinct peak at frequency 0.25 implying a period of $1/0.25 = 4$ quarters (i.e., one year).[16] This suggests that calibrating a nonhomogeneous Poisson process with a time-varying sinusoidal rate function would provide a good model. The least squares estimation was used to calibrate the intensity function of quarterly aggregated losses. Table 5.3 shows the intensity rate function of the nonhomogeneous Poisson process (NHPP), and compares the mean square error (MSE) and mean absolute error (MAE) estimates with those obtained by fitting a homogeneous Poisson process.[17] Significantly higher error estimates under the constant intensity rate indicate an inferior fit.

Chernobai, Menn, Rachev, and Trück Study of 1980−2002 Public Operational Loss Data   Chernobai, Menn, Rachev, and Trück (2005b) examine operational

---

[15]The original loss amounts were converted into dollars and adjusted for inflation using base year 2001.

[16]See also Burneçki and Weron (2005) for the description and analysis of the data set.

[17]The Poisson parameter was estimated by fitting the exponential distribution to the respective interarrival times in years. Alternatively, λ can be obtained by multiplying the quarterly number of points by four and averaging, yielding $\lambda = 31.7143$, and resulting in MSE = 38.2479 and MAE = 5.3878.

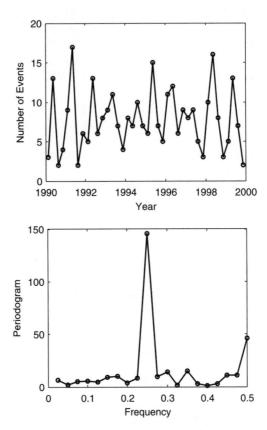

FIGURE 5.6 Time series (top) and periodogram (bottom) of quarterly number of insurance claims data in the Chernobai, Burneçki, Rachev and Trück, and Weron study.
Source: Reprinted with permission of Springer Science and Business Media: Figure 1 in *Computational Statistics*, Vol. 21, 2006, "Modelling Catastrophe Claims with Left-Truncated Severity Distributions," A. Chernobai, K. Burneçki, S.T. Rachev, S. Trück, and R. Weron, p. 545.

TABLE 5.3 Nonhomogeneous and homogeneous Poisson processes fitted to natural catastrophe insurance claims data in the Chernobai, Burneçki, Rachev, Trück, and Weron study

NHPP	$\lambda(t) = a + b \cdot 2\pi \cdot \sin 2\pi(t - c)$	MSE = 18.9100	MAE = 3.8385
Poisson	$\lambda = 33.0509$	MSE = 115.5730	MAE = 10.1308

Source: Chernobai, Burneçki, Rachev, Trück, and Weron (2006).

loss data for the period 1980 to 2002 for five loss types obtained from a major European data provider:

1. *Relationship:* These events are related to legal issues, negligence, and sales-related fraud.
2. *Human:* Events are related to employee errors, physical injury, and internal fraud.
3. *Processes:* Events are related to business errors, supervision, security, and transactions.
4. *Technology:* Events are related to technology and computer failure and telecommunications.
5. *External:* Events are related to natural and man-made disasters and external fraud.

Following Algorithm 1 described earlier in this chapter, they aggregate loss events on the annual basis. Visual inspection of the plot suggests that the accumulation resembles a continuous cumulative distribution-like (cdf) process.[18] As a result, they fit two nonhomogeneous Poisson process models with a deterministic intensity function to each of the five data sets:

Type I: a lognormal cdf-like process of form

$$\Lambda(t) = a + b \exp\left\{-\frac{(\log t - d)^2}{2c^2}\right\} (2\pi)^{-1/2} c^{-1}$$

Type II: a log-Weibull cdf-like process of form

$$\Lambda(t) = a - b \exp\left\{-c \log^d t\right\}$$

Table 5.4 shows the parameter and error estimates for the external type losses, and compares the fit to the homogeneous Poisson process.

Figure 5.7 plots actual annual frequency of loss events with the fitted Poisson and Types I and II nonhomogeneous processes for the external type loss data. Clearly, the nonhomogeneous processes provide with a superior fit.

Chernobai and Rachev Study of 1950–2002 Public Operational Loss Data   Chernobai and Rachev (2004) examine similar data sets as in Chernobai, Menn, Rachev, and Trück (2005b), but for the 1950 to 2002 period. They consider instead a homogeneous intensity process and investigate the distribution of the interarrival times. Table 5.5 demonstrates the Kolmogorov-Smirnov (KS) and the Anderson-Darling (AD) statistics for the fitted continuous

---

[18]Such model appears plausible for this particular data set and time frame.

TABLE 5.4 Nonhomogeneous and homogeneous Poisson processes fitted to external operational loss data in the Chernobai, Menn, Rachev, and Trück study

Process	Parameter Estimates				MSE	MAE
Type I	a	b	c	d		
	2.02	305.91	0.53	3.21	16.02	2.708
Type II	a	b	c	d		
	237.88	236.30	0.00026	8.27	14.56	2.713
Poisson				λ		
				10.13	947.32	24.67

Source: Chernobai, Menn, Rachev, and Trück (2005b).

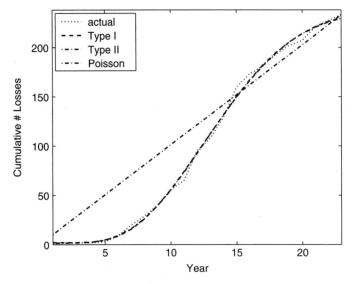

FIGURE 5.7 Empirical annual frequency and fitted Poisson and nonhomogeneous Poisson processes for the *External* type loss data in the Chernobai, Menn, Rachev, and Trück study.

distributions.[19] Cauchy and symmetric stable distributions were fitted to the data symmetrized around zero.

It is clear from Table 5.5 that the α-stable and symmetric α-stable appear reasonable models for the distribution of the inter-arrival times, based on their lowest statistic values.

---

[19]α-Stable distributions are discussed in Chapter 7.

TABLE 5.5 Interarrival time distributions fitted to the operational loss frequency data in the Chernobai and Rachev study

Distribution		Rel.	Hum.	Proc.	Tech.	Ext.
Exponential	KS	0.3447	0.2726	0.2914	0.2821	0.3409
	AD	1.6763	13.592	2.3713	3.4130	2.0864
Lognormal	KS	0.3090	0.2550	0.2575	0.2821	0.3409
	AD	1.1354	0.9823	1.2383	2.8887	1.5302
Pareto	KS	0.3090	0.2222	0.2649	0.2821	0.3409
	AD	1.1127	0.4614	1.3883	2.3497	1.9164
α-Stable	KS	0.1020	0.0944	0.1090	0.1153	0.1013
	AD	0.2256	0.2149	0.2740	0.3318	0.2302
Cauchy	KS	0.2643	0.2630	0.3252	0.3924	0.3157
	AD	1.8138	1.4750	2.5744	4.7790	2.5338
Symm. α-Stable	KS	0.1234	0.1068	0.0899	0.0931	0.1084
	AD	0.2469	0.2144	0.1798	0.1882	0.2169

Source: Chernobai and Rachev (2004, p. 162), with modifications.

Studies with Simulated Data

We now review some studies that use simulated rather than real operational frequency data.

Laycock Study of Mishandling Losses and Processing Errors Data   Laycock (1998) analyzes mishandling losses and processing errors that occur as a result of late settlement of cash or securities in financial transactions, using hypothetical data. He fitted the Poisson distribution that resulted in a reasonable fit. However, a closer inspection of the fitted and actual frequency distributions suggests that there is a degree of correlation between the occurrences of the events: "bad" days on which many losses take place occur more often than suggested by the Poisson distribution; the same is true for "good" days in which no losses take place.

Cruz Study with Internal Fraud Data   Cruz (2002, Chapter 5) simulates internal fraud data of a hypothetical commercial bank. On average, 4.88 loss events occurred daily, resulting in the Poisson parameter of $\lambda = 4.88$, with one day taken as a unit of time. Table 5.6 shows the actual daily count and fitted Poisson count.[20] The chi-squared test performed on the data suggested

---

[20]The Poisson count was obtained by multiplying the Poisson frequency by 33, the total number of observations.

TABLE 5.6 Poisson distribution fitted to the internal fraud frequency data

Number of Losses	0	1	2	3	4	5	6	7	8	9	10	11	12	13–
Actual Count	2	3	3	5	7	2	1	1	2	3	2	1	1	0
Poisson Count	0.25	1.23	2.99	4.86	5.93	5.78	4.70	3.28	2.00	1.08	0.53	0.23	0.10	0.04

Chi-Squared Test

$\chi^2 = 0.000112521$ p-value $= 1$

Adopted from Cruz (2004, p. 93) with modifications.

a good fit of the model, as indicated by the low chi-statistic value and a high *p*-value.

Similar simulation studies were performed in Lewis (2004, Chapter 8), and King (2001, Chapter 7). For example, King (2001) uses simulated data for a fictitious firm named Genoa Bank.[21] There are a total of 25 losses over the one-year period. The average number of losses per month is two, corresponding to the Poisson parameter $\lambda = 2$.

SUMMARY OF KEY CONCEPTS

- Arrival of operational loss events is of a rather chaotic nature, and events occur at irregular instances of time. It is therefore important to examine the frequency distribution in order to understand the underlying loss arrival process.
- Common frequency distributions include binomial, geometric, Poisson, and negative binomial. The most common among these, the Poisson distribution, assumes a constant intensity rate.
- More advanced models admit the possibility of a random or time-dependent intensity rate. These models form the basis of Cox processes, or nonhomogeneous Poisson processes.
- The intensity rate of a Cox process can have a distribution (mixture models), or can be modeled with a deterministic function or a function that allows for randomness.
- An alternative approach is to examine the distribution of the intervals between successive events. Common distributions that can be used are discussed in the next chapter.
- Empirical studies with operational loss data mainly emphasize the use of a simple Poisson process or the negative binomial distribution. However, a few studies have succeeded in fitting more complex models to the data.

APPENDIX: BASIC DESCRIPTIVE TECHNIQUES FOR DISCRETE RANDOM VARIABLES

Suppose we observe a sample of *n* realizations of a random variable *X* that are independent and identically distributed (*iid*). These constitute a random sample. Based on the sample $x = \{x_1, x_2, \ldots, x_n\}$ we are able to make inferences about the entire population of *X*. A discrete random variable *X* is assumed to take discrete values: 0, 1, 2, and so on.

---

[21] The data sample for one year is presented in King (1991), Chapter 7, p. 133.

Sample

- *Histograms* are useful to visualize the distribution of the data sample. For discrete distributions, they are usually obtained by constructing a bar plot for the number of observations corresponding to each value of X. *Relative histograms* plot proportions of data instead of the number of data points.

The center of the sample can be measured by mean, median, or mode.

- *Sample mean* is calculated as the average sample value:

$$\bar{x} = \frac{\sum_{j=1}^{n} x_j}{n}.$$

- *Sample median* indicates the value of the ordered sample so that exactly half of the data have values below and half have values above: median is exactly the midpoint of the ordered data if n is odd, and is the average of the two midpoints if n is even.
- *Sample mode* denotes the most frequent value of the data, i.e., is the value of x that corresponds to the peak of the histogram. *Note:* there can be more than one mode.

There are several possible measures of the spread of discrete data. These include range, interquartile range, variance, standard deviation, and mean absolute deviation. Among these, the variance and standard deviation are the ones most commonly used in practice.

- *Sample variance* is calculated by

$$s^2 = \frac{\sum_{j=1}^{n} (x_j - \bar{x})^2}{n - 1}.$$

- *Sample standard deviation* (denoted s) is the square root of the sample variance:

$$s = \sqrt{\frac{\sum_{j=1}^{n} (x_j - \bar{x})^2}{n - 1}}.$$

Population

- The *probability mass function* of a discrete random variable X is denoted by $p(x) = P(X = x)$. The *cumulative distribution* $F(x)$ is related to the probability mass function by the following expression:

$$F(x) = \sum_{k=0}^{x} p(k).$$

- The right *tail* of a distribution is denoted $\overline{F}$ so that

$$\overline{F}(x) = 1 - F(x).$$

Graphically, the cumulative distribution function looks like a step plot. Figure 5.8 illustrates the notions of cumulative distribution and right tail for a discrete random variable.

- *Quantiles* (or *percentiles*) indicate a value a of a random variable X under which lies a fraction p of the data, so that $F(a) = p$. For example, the 95th quantile denotes the value of X under which lie 95% of the data; median is the 50th percentile. *1st quartile (Q1)* is the 25th percentile (and is the mode of the first half of the ordered data), and *3rd quartile (Q3)* is the 75th percentile (and is the mode of the second half of the ordered data).

The three common measures of the population center are the mean, median, and mode. In practice, the one most commonly used is the mean.

- *Population mean* (often denoted by μ) of a random variable X is measured by the expectation of X:

$$\text{mean}(X) = \mathbb{E}(X) = \sum_{k=0}^{\infty} kp(k).$$

- *Population median* of a random variable X is the 50th percentile.
- *Population mode* is the most frequent value of X.

The most common measures of population spread are the variance and the standard deviation.

- *Population variance* (often denoted by σ^2) is measured as

$$\text{var}(X) = \mathbb{E}\left[(X - \text{mean}(X))^2\right] = \sum_{k=0}^{\infty} (k - \text{mean}(X))^2 p(k).$$

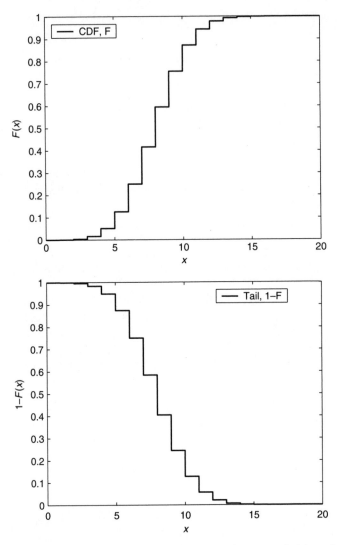

FIGURE 5.8 Illustration of empirical cumulative distribution and right tail of empirical distribution.

- *Population standard deviation* (often denoted by σ) is the square root of the population variance:

$$\text{stdev}(X) = \sqrt{\mathbb{E}\left[(X - \text{mean}(X))^2\right]} = \sqrt{\sum_{k=0}^{\infty} (k - \text{mean}(X))^2 p(k)}.$$

REFERENCES

Baud, N., Frachot, A., and Roncalli, T. (2002b), How to Avoid Over-Estimating Capital Charge for Operational Risk, Technical report, Groupe de Recherche Opérationnelle, Crédit Lyonnais, France.

Bening, V. E. and Korolev, V. Y. (2002), *Generalized Poisson Models and Their Applications in Insurance and Finance*, VSP International Science Publishers, Utrecht, Boston.

Bickel, P. J., and Doksum, K. A. (2001), *Mathematical Statistics: Basic Ideas and Selected Topics*, Vol. 1, 2nd ed., Prentice Hall, Upper Saddle River, New Jersey.

BIS (2003), "The 2002 Loss Data Collection Exercise for Operational Risk: Summary of the Data Collected," www.BIS.org.

Burneçki, K. and Weron, R. (2005), Modeling of the Risk Process, *in* Cizek et al. (2005).

Casella, G., and Berger, R. L. (2001), *Statistical Inference*, 2nd ed., Duxbury Press, Pacific Grove, CA.

Chapelle, A., Crama, Y., Hübner, G., and Peters, J. (2005), Measuring and Managing Operational Risk in the Financial Sector: An Integrated Framework, Technical report, National Bank of Belgium.

Chernobai, A., Burneçki, K., Rachev, S. T., Trück, S., and Weron, R. (2006), "Modelling Catastrophe Claims with Left-Truncated Severity Distributions," *Computational Statistics* 21(3), pp. 537–555.

Chernobai, A., Menn, C., Rachev, S. T., and Trück, S. (2005a), "A Note on the Estimation of the Frequency and Severity Distribution of Operational Losses," *Mathematical Scientist* 30(2), pp. 87–97.

Chernobai, A., Menn, C., Rachev, S. T., and Trück, S. (2005b), Estimation of Operational Value-at-Risk in the Presence of Minimum Collection Thresholds, Technical report, University of California at Santa Barbara.

Chernobai, A. and Rachev, S. T. (2004), Stable Modelling of Operational Risk, *in* M. G. Cruz, ed., "Operational Risk Modelling and Analysis. Theory and Practice," RISK Books, London, pp. 139–169.

Cizek, P., Härdle, W., and Weron, R. eds. (2005), *Statistical Tools for Finance and Insurance*, Springer, Heidelberg.

Cruz, M. G. (2002), *Modeling, Measuring and Hedging Operational Risk*, John Wiley & Sons, New York, Chichester.

de Fontnouvelle, P., DeJesus-Rueff, V., Jordan, J., and Rosengren, E. (2003), Using Loss Data to Quantify Operational Risk, Technical report, Federal Reserve Bank of Boston.

de Fontnouvelle, P., Rosengren, E., and Jordan, J. (2005), Implications of Alternative Operational Risk Modelling Techniques, Technical report, Federal Reserve Bank of Boston and Fitch Risk.

Devroye, L. (1986), *Non-Uniform Random Variate Generation*, Springer-Verlag, New York.

Ebnöther, S., Vanini, P., McNeil, A. J., and Antolinez-Fehr, P. (2001), Modelling Operational Risk, Technical report, ETH Zürich.

Grandell, J. (1976), Doubly Stochastic Poisson Processes, in *Lecture Notes in Mathematics*, Vol. 529, Springer-Verlag, Berlin, New York.

Grandell, J. (1991), *Aspects of Risk Theory*, Springer-Verlag, New York.

Grandell, J. (1997), *Mixed Poisson Processes*, Chapman & Hall, London.

Haight, F. A. (1967), *Handbook of the Poisson Distribution*, John Wiley & Sons, New York.

King, J. L. (2001), *Operational Risk: Measurement and Modelling*, John Wiley & Sons, New York.

Kingman, J. F. C. (1993), *Poisson Processes*, Clarendon Press, Oxford.

Klugman, S. A., Panjer, H. H., and Willmot, G. E. (2004), *Loss Models: From Data to Decisions*, 2nd ed., John Wiley & Sons, Hoboken, New Jersey.

Laycock, M. (1998), Analysis of Mishandling Losses and Processing Errors, *in* "Operational Risk and Financial Institutions," pp. 131–145.

Lewis, C. M., and Lantsman, Y. (2005), What Is a Fair Price to Transfer the Risk of Unauthorised Trading? A Case Study on Operational Risk, *in* E. Davis, ed., *Operational Risk: Practical Approaches to Implementation*, RISK Books, London, pp. 315–355.

Lewis, N. (2004), *Operational Risk with Excel and VBA*, John Wiley & Sons, Hoboken, New Jersey.

Moscadelli, M. (2004), The Modeling of Operational Risk: Experience with the Analysis of the Data Collected by the Basel Committee, Technical report, Bank of Italy.

Rosenberg, J. V., and Schuermann, T. (2004), A General Approach to Integrated Risk Management with Skewed, Fat-Tailed Risks, Technical report, Federal Reserve Bank of New York.

Ross, S. M. (2001), *Simulation*, 3rd ed., Academic Press, Boston.

Ross, S. M. (2002), *Introduction to Probability Models*, 8th ed., Academic Press, Boston.

CHAPTER **6**

Loss Distributions

R epresenting a stream of uncertain operational losses with a specified model is a difficult task. Data can be wrongly recorded, fuzzy, incomplete (e.g., truncated or censored), or simply limited. Two main approaches may be undertaken:

1. *Nonparametric approach.* One approach would be to directly use the empirical density of the data or its smoothed curve version.[1] This *nonparametric approach* can be relevant in two circumstances: first, when the available data are not believed to follow any conventional distribution,[2] and second, when the data set available at hand is believed to be sufficiently comprehensive.[3]

2. *Parametric approach.* The task is considerably simplified if we can fit a curve of a simple analytical form that satisfies certain properties. The general goal of this *parametric approach* is to find a loss distribution that would most closely resemble the distribution of the loss magnitudes of the available data sample.

Figure 6.1 shows a common histogram for the operational loss data with a fitted continuous curve. A visual examination suggests that magnitudes of the majority of the losses are very close to zero, as is seen from the high peak around zero of the histogram. An insignificant fraction of data account for the long right tail of the histogram. Clearly, if we choose the parametric approach and if the fitted curve represents a density of some chosen parametric distribution, the loss distributions that would be adequate for modeling operational losses are those that are right-skewed, possibly leptokurtic, and have support on the positive values.

---

[1] An example is cubic spline approximation as is done in Rosenberg and Schuermann (2004). Useful references on this approach include Silverman (1986) and Scott (1992).
[2] See Rosenberg and Schuermann (2004).
[3] See Cizek, Härdle, and Weron (2005).

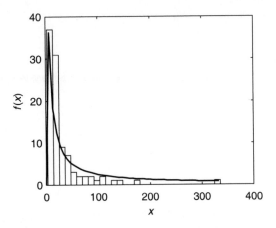

FIGURE 6.1   Illustration of a histogram of loss data and fitted continuous density.

Figure 6.2 summarizes possible approaches to modeling operational loss severity. This chapter focuses on the nonparametric approach, common loss distributions, and mixture distributions. We begin by reviewing the nonparametric approach to modeling operational losses and then proceed to the parametric approach and review some common continuous distributions

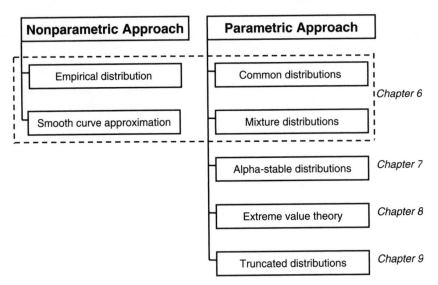

FIGURE 6.2   Approaches to modeling loss severity.

that can be relevant for modeling operational losses. For each of the distributions, we focus on its major characteristics that are important when using them to model the operational loss data: density, distribution, tail behavior, mean, variance, mode, skewness, and kurtosis. We also discuss how they can be simulated. Readers familiar with these distributions and their properties may proceed to the review of the recent empirical studies that use real operational loss data.

In later chapters we present other nonstandard approaches: the class of heavy-tailed, alpha-stable distributions (Chapter 7), the extreme value theory (Chapter 8), and truncated distributions (Chapter 9). We assume that the reader is familiar with basic probability and statistics concepts. A brief review of necessary terminology is supplemented in the appendix to this chapter.[4]

NONPARAMETRIC APPROACH: EMPIRICAL DISTRIBUTION FUNCTION

Modeling operational losses with their empirical distribution function is a *nonparametric* approach, as it does not involve estimation of the parameters of a loss distribution. In this sense, it is the simplest approach. On the other hand, it makes the following two critical assumptions regarding future loss data:

1. Historic loss data are sufficiently comprehensive.
2. All past losses are equally likely to reappear in the future, and losses of other magnitudes (such as potential extreme events that are not a part of existent database) cannot occur.

Suppose we want to find the empirical distribution function of a random variable X. It is found by

$$P(X \leq x) = \frac{\text{number of losses} \leq x}{\text{total number of losses}}.$$

Empirical distribution function looks like a step function, with a step-up occurring at each observed value of X. Figure 6.3 provides an illustration.

---

[4]Useful literature on statistics and probability includes Casella and Berger (2001), Ross (2002), Klugman, Panjer, and Willmot (2004), and Cizek, Härdle, and Weron (2005). References on simulation of random variables include Ross (2001), Ross (2002), and Devroye (1986).

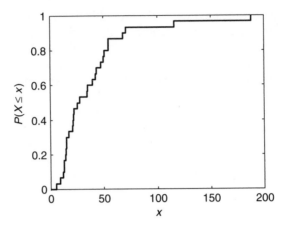

FIGURE 6.3   Illustration of empirical distribution function.

The density function[5] is simply a relative frequency histogram with a bar at each observed data value, and the height of each bar shows the proportion of losses of this magnitude out of total.

Note that the empirical distribution is often used in goodness-of-fit tests. One can compare it with a fitted loss distribution. If the fitted loss distribution closely follows the empirical distribution, then this indicates a good fit; if it does not follow closely the empirical distribution function, then the loss distribution is not optimal.

PARAMETRIC APPROACH: CONTINUOUS LOSS DISTRIBUTIONS

In this section, we review several popular loss distributions. Certainly, a variety of additional distributions may be created by using some transformation of the original data and then fitting a distribution to the transformed data. A popular transformation involves taking the natural logarithm of the data. It is notable that if the original data are severely right-skewed, then the distribution of the log-data often becomes *bell-shaped* and nearly symmetric. For example, fitting the normal distribution to the log-data is equivalent to fitting the lognormal distribution to the original data.

---

[5]To be more precise, for a discrete random variable it is called *probability mass function*.

Exponential Distribution

The exponential distribution for a random variable X of length n is described by its density f and distribution F of the following form:

$$f(x) = \lambda e^{-\lambda x}, \quad F(x) = 1 - e^{-\lambda x}, \quad x > 0.$$

The distribution is characterized by only one parameter λ ($\lambda > 0$), which is the scale parameter.

Examples of exponential densities are illustrated in Figure 6.4. The *maximum likelihood estimate* (MLE) for λ is

$$\widehat{\lambda} = \frac{1}{n} \sum_{j=1}^{n} x_j.$$

Raw moments are calculated as

$$\mathbb{E}(X^k) = \frac{k!}{\lambda^k},$$

and so the population mean and variance are

$$\text{mean}(X) = 1/\lambda, \quad \text{var}(X) = 1/\lambda^2.$$

The mode of an exponential distribution is located at zero. The skewness and kurtosis coefficients are $\gamma_1 = 2$ and $\gamma_2 = 6$, respectively.

The inverse of the distribution has a simple form $F^{-1}(p) = -1/\lambda \log(1 - p)$, $p \in (0, 1)$, and so an exponential random variate can be simulated using the inverse transform method by $X = -\frac{1}{\lambda} \log U$, where U is distributed

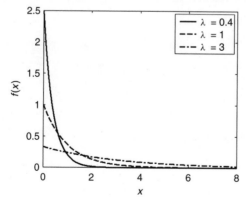

FIGURE 6.4 Illustration of exponential density.

uniformly on the (0,1) interval. Another popular simulation method uses the Von Neumann Algorithm.

The exponential density is monotonically decreasing toward the right and is characterized by exponentially decaying right tail of the form $\overline{F}(x) = e^{-\lambda x}$, which means that high-magnitude events are given a near-zero probability. For this reason, it is unlikely that it would find much use in modeling operational losses, where arguably the central concern is the losses of a very high magnitude (unless, perhaps, some generalizations of the exponential distribution or mixture models are considered).[6]

Note that another parameterization of the exponential distribution is possible, with the density specified as $f(x) = \frac{1}{\lambda}e^{-\frac{1}{\lambda}x}$.

Lognormal Distribution

A random variable X has a lognormal distribution[7] if its density and distribution are

$$f(x) = \frac{1}{\sqrt{2\pi}\sigma x}e^{-\frac{(\log x - \mu)^2}{2\sigma^2}}, \quad F(x) = \Phi\left(\frac{\log x - \mu}{\sigma}\right), \quad x > 0,$$

where $\Phi(x)$ is the distribution of a standard normal, $N(0, 1)$, random variable, and can be obtained by looking up the table of the standard normal quantiles.

Examples of the lognormal density are illustrated in Figure 6.5. The parameters $\mu(-\infty < \mu < \infty)$ and $\sigma(\sigma > 0)$ are the location and scale parameters, respectively, and can be estimated with MLE as

$$\widehat{\mu} = \frac{1}{n}\sum_{j=1}^{n}\log x_j, \quad \widehat{\sigma^2} = \frac{1}{n}\sum_{j=1}^{n}(\log x_j - \widehat{\mu})^2. \tag{6.1}$$

Raw moments are calculated as

$$\mathbb{E}(X^k) = e^{\mu k + \frac{\sigma^2 k^2}{2}},$$

and so the population mean and variance are calculated to be

$$\text{mean}(X) = e^{\mu + \frac{\sigma^2}{2}}, \quad \text{var}(X) = (e^{\sigma^2} - 1)e^{2\mu + \sigma^2}.$$

---

[6] See also Figure 6.12 and the accompanying example later in this chapter.
[7] The lognormal distribution is sometimes called Cobb-Douglas distribution. The lognormal distribution was proposed by the Basel Committee for the operational risk modeling in 2001.

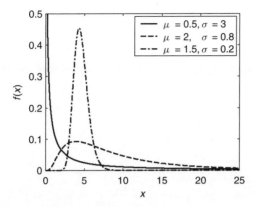

FIGURE 6.5 Illustration of lognormal density.

The mode is located at $e^{\mu-\sigma^2}$. The skewness and kurtosis coefficients are

$$\gamma_1 = \sqrt{e^{\sigma^2} - 1}(2 + e^{\sigma^2}), \quad \gamma_2 = e^{4\sigma^2} + 2e^{3\sigma^2} + 3e^{2\sigma^2} - 6.$$

The inverse of the distribution is $F^{-1}(p) = e^{\Phi^{-1}(p)\sigma+\mu}$, and so a lognormal random variate can be simulated by $X = e^{\Phi^{-1}(U)\sigma+\mu}$, where Φ is the standard normal distribution. Note that a lognormal random variable can be obtained from a normal random variable Y with parameters μ and σ (this is often written as $N(\mu, \sigma)$) via the transformation $X = e^Y$. Thus, if X has a lognormal distribution, then $\log X$ has a normal distribution with the same parameters.

The lognormal distribution is characterized by moderately heavy tails, with the right tail $\overline{F}(x) \sim x^{-1}e^{-\log^2 x}$. To fit a lognormal distribution to the data, one can take the natural logarithm of the data set, and then fit to it the normal distribution. Note that the MLE will produce the same estimates, but the method of moments will produce different parameter estimates.

Weibull Distribution

The Weibull distribution is a generalization of the exponential distribution: two parameters instead of one parameter allow for greater flexibility and heavier tails. The density and distribution are[8]

$$f(x) = \alpha\beta x^{\alpha-1}e^{-\beta x^\alpha}, \quad F(x) = 1 - e^{-\beta x^\alpha}, \quad x > 0,$$

---

[8]$\Gamma(a)$ is the complete gamma function, $\Gamma(a) = \int_0^\infty t^{a-1}e^{-t}\,dt$. When a is an integer, then $\Gamma(a) = (a-1)!$.

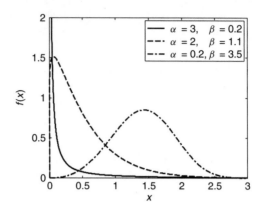

FIGURE 6.6 Illustration of Weibull density.

with β ($\beta > 0$) being the scale parameter and α ($\alpha > 0$) the shape parameter.

Examples of the density are illustrated in Figure 6.6. The MLE estimators for the parameters do not exist in closed form, and should be evaluated numerically. Raw moments are calculated as

$$\mathbb{E}(X^k) = \beta^{-k/\alpha} \Gamma\left(1 + \frac{k}{\alpha}\right),$$

and so the population mean and variance are

$$\text{mean}(X) = \beta^{-1/\alpha} \Gamma\left(1 + \frac{1}{\alpha}\right),$$

$$\text{var}(X) = \beta^{-2/\alpha} \left(\Gamma\left(1 + \frac{2}{\alpha}\right) - \Gamma^2\left(1 + \frac{1}{\alpha}\right)\right).$$

The mode is located at mode $= \beta^{-1}(1 - \alpha^{-1})^{1/\alpha}$ for $\alpha > 0$ and at zero otherwise. The formulae for the skewness and kurtosis coefficients are

$$\gamma_1 = \frac{2\Gamma^3\left(1 + \frac{1}{\alpha}\right) - 3\Gamma\left(1 + \frac{1}{\alpha}\right)\Gamma\left(1 + \frac{2}{\alpha}\right) + \Gamma\left(1 + \frac{3}{\alpha}\right)}{\left[\Gamma\left(1 + \frac{2}{\alpha}\right) - \Gamma^2\left(1 + \frac{1}{\alpha}\right)\right]^{3/2}},$$

$$\gamma_2 = \frac{-6\left[\begin{array}{c}\Gamma^4\left(1 + \frac{1}{\alpha}\right) + 12\Gamma^2\left(1 + \frac{1}{\alpha}\right)\Gamma\left(1 + \frac{2}{\alpha}\right) - 3\Gamma^2\left(1 + \frac{2}{\alpha}\right) \\ -4\Gamma\left(1 + \frac{1}{\alpha}\right)\Gamma\left(1 + \frac{3}{\alpha}\right) + \Gamma\left(1 + \frac{4}{\alpha}\right)\end{array}\right]}{\left[\Gamma\left(1 + \frac{2}{\alpha}\right) - \Gamma^2\left(1 + \frac{1}{\alpha}\right)\right]^2}.$$

The inverse of a Weibull random variable does not exist in a simple closed form. To generate a Weibull random variable, one can first generate an exponential random variable Y with parameter β and then follow the transformation $X = Y^{1/\alpha}$.

The right tail behavior of a Weibull random variable follows the form $\overline{F}(x) = e^{\beta x^{\alpha}}$, and so the distribution is heavy-tailed for $\alpha < 1$. Weibull distribution has been found to be the optimal distribution in reinsurance models as well as in asset returns models.[9]

Note the following regarding the Weibull distribution. First, if $\alpha = 1$, then the Weibull distribution reduces to the exponential distribution. Second, other parameterizations of the Weibull distribution are possible. For example, some literature uses $1/\beta$ instead of β. Sometimes $1/\beta^{\alpha}$ is used instead of β.

Gamma Distribution

The gamma distribution is another generalization of an exponential distribution and is specified by its density and distribution given by[10]

$$f(x) = \frac{\beta^{\alpha}}{\Gamma(\alpha)} x^{\alpha-1} e^{-\beta x}, \quad F(x) = \Gamma(\alpha; \beta x), \quad x > 0,$$

where the two parameters, α ($\alpha > 0$) and β ($\beta > 0$), characterize the shape and scale, respectively.

Examples of the density are illustrated in Figure 6.7 . The MLE estimates for the parameters can only be evaluated numerically. The raw moments are found by

$$\mathbb{E}(X^k) = \frac{\Gamma(\alpha + k)}{\Gamma(\alpha)\beta^k},$$

yielding the population mean and variance as

$$\text{mean}(X) = \frac{\alpha}{\beta}, \quad \text{var}(X) = \frac{\alpha}{\beta^2}.$$

The mode is $\frac{\alpha-1}{\beta}$ for $\alpha > 1$ and zero otherwise. The skewness and kurtosis coefficients are found by

$$\gamma_1 = \frac{2}{\sqrt{\alpha}}, \quad \gamma_2 = \frac{6}{\alpha}.$$

---

[9]See Madan and Unal (2004) and Kremer (1998). Also see Mittnik and Rachev (1993a,b).

[10]$\Gamma(a;b)$ is the incomplete gamma function defined as $\Gamma(a; b) = \frac{1}{\Gamma(a)} \int_0^b t^{a-1} e^{-t}\, dt$.

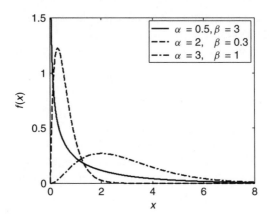

FIGURE 6.7 Illustration of gamma density.

If α is an integer,[11] then to generate a gamma random variable with parameters α and β one can generate a sum of α exponential random variables each with parameter β. Hence, if $U_1, U_2, \ldots, U_\alpha$ are independent uniform $(0, 1)$ random variables, then $X = -1/\beta \log(\prod_{j=1}^{\alpha} U_j)$ has the desired distribution. A variety of methods for generation of a gamma random variable is described in Devroye (1986) and references therein.

Beta Distribution

The beta distribution has density and distribution of the following form:[12]

$$f(x) = \frac{\Gamma(\alpha + \beta)}{\Gamma(\alpha)\Gamma(\beta)} x^{\alpha-1}(1 - x)^{\beta-1}, \quad F(x) = I(x; \alpha, \beta), \quad 0 \le x \le 1.$$

Examples of the density are illustrated on Figure 6.8. Note that X has a bounded support on $[0, 1]$. Certainly, operational loss data may be rescaled to fit this interval. In this case, the following version of the beta density and distribution is possible (the parameter θ is assumed known):

$$f(x) = \frac{\Gamma(\alpha)\Gamma(\beta)}{\Gamma(\alpha + \beta)} \left(\frac{x}{\theta}\right)^{\alpha-1} \left(1 - \frac{x}{\theta}\right)^{\beta-1} \frac{1}{x},$$

$$F(x) = I\left(\frac{x}{\theta}; \alpha, \beta\right), \quad 0 < x < \theta, \quad \theta > 0.$$

---

[11] In this case, the gamma distribution is called the Erlang distribution.
[12] $I(x;\alpha, \beta)$ is the regularized beta function equal to $\int_0^x u^{\alpha-1}(1 - u)^{\beta-1} du \cdot \frac{\Gamma(\alpha)\Gamma(\beta)}{\Gamma(\alpha+\beta)}$.

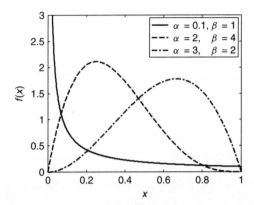

FIGURE 6.8 Illustration of Beta density.

The parameters α ($\alpha > 0$) and β ($\beta > 0$) determine the shape of the distribution. The MLE estimators can be evaluated numerically. The raw moments for the regular version of the beta density can be found by

$$\mathbb{E}(X^k) = \frac{(\alpha + \beta - 1)!(\alpha + k - 1)!}{(\alpha - 1)!(\alpha + \beta + k - 1)!},$$

yielding the mean and the variance:

$$\text{mean}(X) = \frac{\alpha}{\alpha + \beta}, \qquad \text{var}(X) = \frac{\alpha\beta}{(\alpha + \beta)^2(\alpha + \beta + 1)}.$$

The mode is equal to $(\alpha - 1)/(\alpha + \beta - 2)$. The skewness and kurtosis coefficients are estimated by

$$\gamma_1 = \frac{2(\beta - \alpha)\sqrt{1 + \alpha + \beta}}{\sqrt{\alpha + \beta}(2 + \alpha + \beta)},$$

$$\gamma_2 = \frac{6\left[\alpha^3 + \alpha^2(1 - 2\beta) + \beta^2(1 + \beta) - 2\alpha\beta(2 + \beta)\right]}{\alpha\beta(\alpha + \beta + 2)(\alpha + \beta + 3)}.$$

The beta random variate can be generated using an algorithm described in Ross (2001), Ross (2002), or Devroye (1986).

Note that the beta distribution is related to the gamma distribution. Suppose we have two gamma random variables X and Y with parameters α_1, β_1 and α_2, β_2, respectively. Then the variable $Z = X/(X + Y)$ has a beta distribution with parameters α_1, α_2. This property can be used to generate a beta random variate from two gamma random variates.

Pareto Distribution

The Pareto distribution is characterized by its density and distribution of the form:

$$f(x) = \frac{\alpha \beta^\alpha}{x^{\alpha+1}}, \quad F(x) = 1 - \left(\frac{\beta}{x}\right)^\alpha, \quad \beta < x < \infty.$$

Note that the range of permissible values of X depends on the scale parameter β ($\beta > 0$). The parameter α ($\alpha > 0$) determines the shape.

Figure 6.9 illustrates some examples of the density. No closed-form expressions for the MLE estimators exist (except for the case when $\beta = 1$, in which case $\widehat{\alpha} = n/\sum_{j=1}^{n} \log x_j$), so they have to be evaluated numerically.

The raw moments are estimated by

$$\mathbb{E}(X^k) = \frac{\alpha \beta^k}{\alpha - k},$$

from which the population mean and variance are found to be

$$\text{mean}(X) = \frac{\alpha \beta}{\alpha - 1} \quad \text{for } \alpha > 1, \qquad \text{var}(X) = \frac{\alpha \beta^2}{(\alpha - 1)^2 (\alpha - 2)} \quad \text{for } \alpha > 2.$$

The mode is equal to zero. The skewness and kurtosis coefficients are

$$\gamma_1 = \sqrt{\frac{\alpha - 2}{\alpha}} \frac{2(\alpha + 1)}{\alpha - 3}, \qquad \gamma_2 = \frac{6(\alpha^3 + \alpha^2 - 6\alpha - 2)}{\alpha(\alpha - 3)(\alpha - 4)}.$$

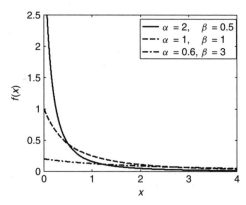

FIGURE 6.9 Illustration of Pareto density.

The inverse of the distribution is $F^{-1}(p) = \beta\big((1-p)^{-1/\alpha} - 1\big)$, which can be used to generate a Pareto random variate.

Pareto distribution is a very heavy-tailed distribution, as is seen from the tail behavior. α determines the heaviness of the right tail, which is monotonically decreasing for the Pareto distribution: The closer it is to zero, the thicker the tail, $\overline{F}(x) = \left(\frac{\beta}{\beta+x}\right)^\alpha$. Tails proportional to $x^{-\alpha}$ are called the *power tails* (as opposed to the exponentially decaying tails) because they follows a power function. The case when $\alpha \leq 1$ refers to a very heavy-tailed case, in which the mean and the variance are infinite (see the formulae for mean and variance earlier), which means that losses of an infinitely high magnitude are possible.

While on one hand the Pareto distribution appears very attractive for modeling operational risk, as it is expected to capture very high-magnitude losses, on the other hand, from the practical point of view, the possibility of infinite mean and variance could pose a problem.

Note the following:

- Different versions of the Pareto distribution are possible. Occasionally a simplified, 1-parameter, version of the Pareto distribution is used, with $\beta = 1$.
- A 1-parameter Pareto random variable may be obtained from an exponential random variable via a simple transformation. If a random variable Y follows an exponential distribution with parameter λ, then $X = e^Y$ has the 1-parameter Pareto distribution with the same shape parameter.
- A 2-parameter Pareto distribution may be reparameterized in such a way that we obtain the generalized Pareto distribution (GPD). The GPD can be used to model extreme events that exceed a high threshold. This is reviewed in Chapter 8, where we cover the extreme value theory.

Burr Distribution

The Burr distribution is a generalized three-parameter version of the Pareto distribution and allows for greater flexibility in the shape due to additional shape parameter γ ($\gamma > 0$). The density and distribution functions can be written as

$$f(x) = \gamma\alpha\beta^\alpha \frac{x^{\gamma-1}}{(\beta + x^\gamma)^{\alpha+1}}, \quad F(x) = 1 - \left(\frac{\beta}{\beta + x^\gamma}\right)^\alpha, \quad x > 0.$$

Examples of the density are depicted in Figure 6.10. The MLE estimators for the parameters can generally be evaluated only numerically. The raw

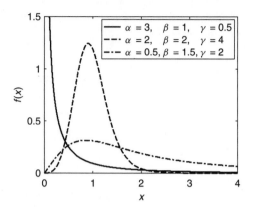

FIGURE 6.10   Illustration of Burr density.

moments are estimated as

$$\mathbb{E}(X^k) = \frac{\beta^{k/\gamma}}{\Gamma(\alpha)} \Gamma\left(1 + \frac{k}{\gamma}\right) \Gamma\left(\alpha - \frac{k}{\gamma}\right), \quad -\gamma < k < \gamma\alpha,$$

from which the population mean and variance are calculated as

$$\text{mean}(X) = \frac{\beta^{1/\gamma}}{\Gamma(\alpha)} \Gamma\left(1 + \frac{1}{\gamma}\right) \Gamma\left(\alpha - \frac{1}{\gamma}\right), \quad \gamma\alpha > 1,$$

$$\text{var}(X) = \frac{\beta^{2/\gamma}}{\Gamma(\alpha)} \Gamma\left(1 + \frac{2}{\gamma}\right) \Gamma\left(\alpha - \frac{2}{\gamma}\right)$$

$$- \frac{\beta^{2/\gamma}}{\Gamma^2(\alpha)} \Gamma^2\left(1 + \frac{1}{\gamma}\right) \Gamma^2\left(\alpha - \frac{1}{\gamma}\right), \quad \gamma\alpha > 2.$$

Mode is equal to $\frac{1}{\beta^{1/\gamma}}\left(\frac{\gamma-1}{\alpha\gamma+1}\right)^{1/\gamma}$ for $\gamma > 1$ and zero otherwise. The expressions for skewness and kurtosis are complicated and can be found by directly using the formulae given in the appendix to this chapter.

The Burr random variable can be generated by the inverse transform method, using $F^{-1}(p) = \left(\beta((1-p)^{-1/\alpha} - 1)\right)^{1/\gamma}$.

The right tail has the power law property and obeys $\overline{F}(x) = \left(\frac{\beta}{\beta+x^\gamma}\right)^\alpha$. The distribution is heavy-tailed for the case $\alpha < 2$ and is very heavy-tailed when $\alpha < 1$. The Burr distribution has been used in the insurance industry and has been found to provide an optimal distribution for natural catastrophe insurance claims.[13]

---

[13] See Cizek, Härdle, and Weron (2005).

Note the following two points. First, if $\tau = 1$, then the Burr distribution reduces to the Pareto distribution. Second, other parameterizations of the Burr distribution are possible. For example, the Burr distribution with $\beta = 1$ is known as the *loglogistic distribution*.

EXTENSION: MIXTURE LOSS DISTRIBUTIONS

Histograms of the operational loss data often reveal a very high peak close to zero and a smaller but distinct peak toward the right tail. This may suggest that the operational loss data often do not follow a pattern of a single distribution, even for data belonging to the same loss type (such as operational losses due to business disruptions) and the same business line (such as commercial banking). One approach in modeling such losses would be to consider the GPD to model the tail events and an empirical or other distribution for the remaining lower-magnitude losses. Alternatively, one may consider a single distribution composed by a mixture of two or more loss distributions.

The density and distribution of a m-point mixture distribution can be expressed as

$$f(x) = \sum_{j=1}^{m} w_j f_j(x), \quad F(x) = \sum_{j=1}^{m} w_j F_j(x),$$

where $w_j, j = 1, 2, \ldots, m$ are the positive weights attached to each member distribution, adding up to 1. It is possible to have a mixture of different types of distributions, such as exponential and Weibull, or of the same type of distribution but with different parameters.

An example of a mixture of two lognormal distributions ($\mu_1 = 0.9$, $\sigma_1 = 1, \mu_2 = 3, \sigma_2 = 0.5$) is depicted in Figure 6.11.

The MLE estimates of the parameters (including the weights) of mixture distributions can generally be evaluated only numerically. A commonly used procedure to estimate the parameters of mixture distributions is the *expectation-maximization algorithm*. The raw moments are found as the weighted sum of the kth moments evaluated individually for each of the m member distributions. The population mean and variance are found by

$$\text{mean}(X) = \sum_{j=1}^{m} w_j \mathbb{E}_j(X), \quad \text{var}(X) = \sum_{j=1}^{m} w_j^2 \sigma_j^2(X),$$

where the subscripts j refer to each member density. The right tail follows $\overline{F}(x) = \sum_{j=1}^{m} w_j \overline{F}_j(x)$.

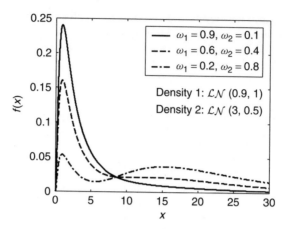

FIGURE 6.11 Illustration of two-point lognormal mixture density.

The advantage of using mixture distributions is that they can be fitted to practically all shapes of loss distributions. However, the models may lack reliability due to a large number of parameters that need to be estimated (in particular, when the available loss data set is not large enough). For example, a two-point mixture of exponential distributions requires only three parameters, but a four-point mixture of exponential distributions requires seven parameters. In some cases, this problem may be overcome when certain simplifications are applied to the model. For example, it is possible to achieve a two-point mixture of Pareto distributions with four, instead of five, unknown parameters; the following distribution has been successfully applied to liability insurance:

$$F(x) = 1 - a \left(\frac{\beta_1}{\beta_1 + x} \right)^{\alpha} - (1 - a) \left(\frac{\beta_2}{\beta_2 + x} \right)^{\alpha+2},$$

with the first distribution covering smaller magnitude events and having a higher weight a attached, and the second distribution covering infrequent large-magnitude events.[14]

An extension to mixture distributions may be to allow m to be a parameter, and "let the data decide" on how many distributions should enter the mixture. This, however, makes the model data-dependent and more complex.[15]

---

[14] See Klugman, Panjer, and Willmot (2004).
[15] See Klugman, Panjer, and Willmot (2004).

Note that the term *mixture distribution* is sometimes also used for distributions in which an unknown parameter is believed to be random and follows some distribution rather than being fixed. For example, a mixture of Poisson and gamma distributions (i.e., the parameter of the Poisson distribution follows a gamma distribution) will result in a hypergeometric distribution.

A NOTE ON THE TAIL BEHAVIOR

In Chapter 1 we described the failures of major banks due to operational loss events. Incidents of this magnitude are extremely rare, but their occurrence cannot be ruled out. Operational risk managers are concerned with finding a model that would capture the *tail events*.[16] A crucial task in operational risk modeling is to produce a model that would give a realistic account to the possibility of losses exceeding a very high amount. (This becomes critical in the estimation of the value-at-risk.)

In operational risk modeling, thin-tailed distributions should be used with caution. The following example illustrates the danger of fitting a light-tailed distribution to the data whose true distribution is heavy-tailed.[17] We generated 5,000 points from the Pareto distribution (heavy-tailed) with parameters $\alpha = 1.67$ and $\beta = 0.6$. We then fitted an exponential distribution (light-tailed) to the data. The MLE procedure resulted in the exponential parameter of $\lambda = 1.61$. Figure 6.12 demonstrates the difference in the behavior of the tails of both distributions. In the far right, the probability of exceeding any high point is significantly lower (roughly, by 5%) under the exponential fit. This indicates that the probability of high-value events (and exceeding them) will be underestimated if one commits the mistake of fitting a thin-tailed loss distribution to the loss data. Such mistakes may be costly and lead to serious consequences in the operational risk management, if the potential for high-magnitude losses is being inadequately assessed.

In Table 6.1 common distributions are classified into two categories depending on the heaviness of the right tail. Note that the Weibull distribution can be thin-tailed or heavy-tailed depending on the value of the shape parameter. Regarding the lognormal distribution, some literature refers to

---

[16] In the context of operational losses, it is understood that tail events refer to the events in the upper tail of the loss distribution.

[17] In literature, thin-tailed distributions are also called light-tailed distributions, and heavy-tailed distributions are also called fat-tailed distributions. We will use the corresponding terms interchangeably throughout the book.

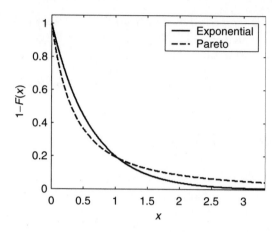

FIGURE 6.12 Tails of Pareto and exponential distributions fitted to simulated Pareto random variable.

TABLE 6.1 Tail behavior of common loss distributions

Name	Tail $\overline{F}(x)$	Parameters
Thin-Tailed Distributions		
Normal	$\overline{F}(x) = 1 - \Phi\left(\frac{x-\mu}{\sigma}\right)$	$-\infty < \mu < \infty, \sigma > 0$
Exponential	$\overline{F}(x) = e^{-\lambda x}$	$\lambda > 0$
Gamma	$\overline{F}(x) = 1 - \Gamma(\alpha; \beta x)$	$\alpha, \beta > 0$
Weibull	$\overline{F}(x) = e^{-\beta x^{\alpha}}$	$\alpha \geq 1, \beta > 0$
Beta	$\overline{F}(x) = 1 - I(x; \alpha, \beta)$	$\alpha, \beta > 0$
Medium-Tailed and Heavy-Tailed Distributions		
Lognormal	$\overline{F}(x) = 1 - \Phi\left(\frac{\log x - \mu}{\sigma}\right)$	$-\infty < \mu < \infty, \sigma > 0$
Weibull	$\overline{F}(x) = e^{-\beta x^{\alpha}}$	$0 < \alpha < 1, \beta > 0$
Pareto	$\overline{F}(x) = \left(\frac{\beta}{\beta+x}\right)^{\alpha}$	$\alpha, \beta > 0$
Burr	$\overline{F}(x) = \left(\frac{\beta}{\beta+x^{\gamma}}\right)^{\alpha}$	$\alpha, \beta, \gamma > 0$

it as a thin-tailed distribution, but we follow Embrechts, Klüppelberg, and Mikosch (1997) who put it in the class of medium-tailed distributions. The beta distribution has a bounded support, which makes it a thin-tailed distribution.

EMPIRICAL EVIDENCE WITH OPERATIONAL LOSS DATA

In this section we provide results from empirical studies based on operational loss data that apply the distributions described in this chapter. There are two types of studies: Those based on real operational loss data and those based on simulated data.

The empirical studies indicate that practitioners try a variety of possible loss distributions for the loss data and then determine an optimal one on the basis of goodness-of-fit tests. It is common to use the Kolmogorov-Smirnov (KS) and Anderson-Darling (AD) tests to examine the goodness of fit of the model to the data. The two tests use different measures of the discrepancy between the fitted continuous distribution and the empirical distribution functions. The KS test better captures the discrepancy around the median of the data, while the AD test is more optimal for the tails. A smaller value of the test statistic indicates a better fit. Other goodness-of-fit tests include Kuiper, Cramér-von Mises, Pearson's χ^2 test, among others.[18]

Studies with Real Data

We review some empirical studies based on real operational loss data from financial institutions.

Müller Study of 1950–2002 Operational Loss Data   Müller (2002) carried out empirical analysis with external operational loss data obtained from worldwide institutions in the 1950–2002 period, made available then by the IC^2 Operational Loss F1RST Database. Only data in U.S. dollars for the events whose state of affairs was "closed" or "assumed closed" on an indicated date were considered for the analysis. The data were available for five loss types, as defined in Chapter 5: relationship, human, processes, technology, and external.

Figure 6.13 shows the histograms of the five data sets. There is a clear peak in the beginning, which is captured by the excessive kurtosis; a heavy right tail is also evident and is captured by the high degree of positive skewness (see Table 6.2).

From the common distributions discussed in this chapter, exponential, lognormal, Weibull, gamma, and Pareto distributions were used. Table 6.2 demonstrates the five samples' MLE parameter estimates and KS and AD statistic values for the five distributions. The center of the data is best explained by the lognormal distribution, and is concluded from the lowest *KS* statistic values, for all except *technology* type losses for which Weibull is the best. The same conclusions are drawn regarding the tails of the data sets.

---

[18]Various goodness-of-fit tests will be described in Chapter 10.

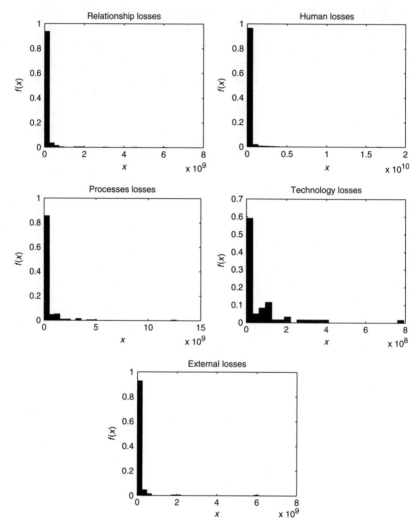

FIGURE 6.13 Relative frequency histograms of operational loss data in Müller study.

Cruz Study of Legal Loss Data Cruz (2002) applies exponential, Weibull, and Pareto distributions to a sample (in U.S. dollars) from a legal database (from an undisclosed source), consisting of 75 points.[19] The sample's descriptive

---

[19] Original data set are available from Cruz (2002), Chapter 3, p. 57.

TABLE 6.2 Sample description, parameter estimates, and goodness-of-fit tests in the Müller study

	Relationship	Human	Processes	Technology	External
1. Sample Description					
# obs.	585	647	214	61	220
Mean (\$ '000,000)	0.0899	0.1176	0.3610	0.0770	0.0930
Median (\$ '000)	12.8340	6.3000	50.1708	11.0475	8.9076
St. Dev. (\$ '000,000)	0.3813	0.7412	1.0845	0.1351	0.4596
Skewness	11.1717	18.8460	7.8118	3.0699	10.9407
Kurtosis	152.2355	418.8717	81.5218	14.7173	136.9358
2. MLE Parameter Estimates and Goodness-of-Fit Test Statistics					
Exponential distribution					
λ	$9.0 \cdot 10^7$	$0.15 \cdot 10^7$	$0.36 \cdot 10^7$	$7.7 \cdot 10^7$	$9.3 \cdot 10^7$
KS test	0.4024	0.5489	0.3864	0.3909	0.4606
AD test	$1.2 \cdot 10^5$	8460	3.9185	1.9687	430.2
Lognormal distribution					
μ	16.2693	15.9525	17.6983	16.1888	15.9696
σ	2.1450	2.4551	2.2883	2.5292	2.2665
KS test	0.0301	0.0530	0.0620	0.1414	0.0449
AD test	0.0787	0.1213	0.1600	0.3043	0.1597
Weibull distribution					
α	0.0002	0.0008	0.0001	0.0003	0.0004
β	0.4890	0.4162	0.4822	0.4692	0.4527
KS test	0.0608	0.0907	0.0656	0.1179	0.0749
AD test	0.4335	0.2231	0.2247	0.2372	0.2696
Gamma distribution					
α	—	—	0.3372	0.3425	—
β	—	—	$1.07 \cdot 10^9$	$0.2 \cdot 10^9$	—
KS test	—	—	0.1344	0.1357	—
AD test	—	—	—	—	—
Pareto distribution					
α	0.8014	0.8936	0.7642	0.6326	0.8498
β	$1.8 \cdot 10^7$	$1.6 \cdot 10^7$	$8.5 \cdot 10^7$	$2.8 \cdot 10^7$	$1.4 \cdot 10^7$
KS test	0.1296	0.1979	0.1504	0.2812	0.1783
AD test	0.4031	0.5566	0.6256	1.0918	0.4784

statistics, as well as the MLE parameters for the three distributions[20] and goodness-of-fit statistics are depicted in Table 6.3 The data are highly

---

[20]Note that the density specification for the exponential and Weibull distributions in Cruz (2002) are different. We report the parameter values based on this book's specification.

TABLE 6.3 Sample descriptive statistics, parameter estimates, and goodness-of-fit tests in the Cruz study

1. Sample Description	
Mean ($)	439,725.99
Median ($)	252,200
St. dev. ($)	538,403.93
Skewness	4.42
Kurtosis	23.59

2. MLE Parameter Estimates and Goodness-of-Fit Test Statistics			
Exponential	$\lambda = 440{,}528.63$	KS test: 0.2104	W^2 test: 1.3525
Weibull	$\alpha = 2.8312$	KS test: 0.3688	W^2 test: 4.8726
	$\beta = 0.00263$		
Pareto	$\alpha = 6.1737$	KS test: 0.1697	W^2 test: 0.8198
	$\beta = 2{,}275{,}032.12$		

Source: Cruz (2002, pp. 57, 58, and 60), with modifications.

leptokurtic and significantly right-skewed. Based on visual and formal tests for the goodness of fit,[21] Cruz concluded that the Pareto distribution fits the data best. Nevertheless, none of the considered loss distributions is able to capture well the heaviness of the upper tail.

Moscadelli Study of 2002 LDCE Operational Loss Data Moscadelli (2004) explores the data (in euros) collected by the Risk Management Group (RMG) of the Basel Committee in June 2002's Operational Risk Loss Data Collection Exercise (LDCE).[22] There were 89 participating banks from 19 countries worldwide that provided their internal loss data for the year 2001. As already expressed in Chapter 5, the data were classified into eight business lines and pooled together across all banks.

The lognormal, gamma, Gumbel, Pareto, and exponential distributions were fitted to the data. The estimation procedure used in the study was somewhat simplified, for two reasons. First, different banks used different minimum truncation levels for their internal data, roughly between euro

---

[21]The KS values reported in Table 6.3 should be further scaled by $\sqrt{n}$ (n being the sample length) if we want to compare the goodness of fit across samples of different lengths; see also the discussion in Chapter 10.

[22]See Chapter 3 for a review of the Basel II Capital Accord. See also BIS (2003) on the description of the data.

TABLE 6.4 Sample descriptive statistics, parameter estimates, and goodness-of-fit statistics in Moscadelli study

	BL1	BL2	BL3	BL4	BL5	BL6	BL7	BL8
			1. Sample Description					
# obs.	423	5,132	28,882	3,414	1,852	1,490	1,109	3,267
Mean '000	646	226	79	356	137	222	195	125
St. dev. '000	6,095	1,917	887	2,642	1,320	1,338	1,473	1,185
Skewness	16	23	55	15	24	13	25	32
Kurtosis	294	674	4,091	288	650	211	713	1,232
			2. MLE Parameter Estimates and Goodness-of-Fit Test Statistics					
Lognormal distribution								
μ	3.58	3.64	3.17	3.61	3.37	3.74	3.79	3.58
σ	1.71	1.27	0.97	1.41	1.10	1.28	1.28	1.08
KS test	0.18	0.14	0.18	0.16	0.15	0.12	0.11	0.12
AD test	22.52	181	1,653	174	73.74	46.33	25.68	87.67
Gumbel distribution								
μ	93.96	51.76	25.63	48.30	35.86	54.82	56.78	41.03
σ	602	185	58.80	204	110	181	154	93.51
KS test	0.43	0.37	0.34	0.37	0.36	0.35	0.32	0.31
AD test	125	1,224	6,037	831	436	333	204	577

Source: Moscadelli (2004, p. 19 and p. 25).

6,000 to 10,000. This issue was ignored in the estimation process.[23] Second, the data across all participating banks were pooled together without any consideration given for bank characteristics such as size.

Table 6.4 reproduces the sample descriptive statistic (based on 1,000 bootstrapped samples generated from the original data), MLE parameter estimates (based on the original data), and goodness-of-fit test statistics[24] for the lognormal and Gumbel distributions.[25] Other considered distributions showed a poor fit. Although lognormal and Gumbel fit the main body of the data rather well, they performed poorly in the upper tail, according to Moscadelli. This was confirmed by the test statistic values above the 90%

---

[23] See the discussion of a correct estimation procedure with truncated data in Chapter 9.

[24] The test statistics are unadjusted to the length of data.

[25] The Gumbel distribution is light-tailed and has density $f(x) = \frac{1}{\sigma} \exp\{-\frac{x-\mu}{\sigma} - \exp\{-\frac{x-\mu}{\sigma}\}\}$, defined on $x \in \Re$. The support allows for negative loss values, so the Gumbel distribution is unlikely to find much application in operational risk modeling.

critical values, meaning that it is unlikely that the data come from a selected distribution at the 90% confidence level.

He further performs the analysis of the data using the *extreme value theory* argument for modeling high losses with the GPD, finding that GPD outperforms other considered distributions.[26] He also confirms the findings from other empirical studies that operational losses follow a very heavy-tailed distribution.

De Fontnouvelle, Rosengren, and Jordan Study of 2002 LDCE Operational Loss Data

The data set examined in Moscadelli was also analyzed by de Fontnouvelle, Rosengren, and Jordan (2005). They limited their analysis to the data collected from six banks, and performed the analysis on the bank-by-bank basis, rather than pooling the data, as was done in Moscadelli. For confidentiality reasons, only the data belonging to the four business lines—Trading and Sales (BL1), Retail Banking (BL2), Payment and Settlement (BL3), and Asset Management (BL4)—and five loss types— Internal Fraud (LT1), External Fraud (LT2), Employment Practices and Workplace Safety (LT3), Clients, Products and Business Practices (LT4), and Execution, Delivery and Process Management (LT5)—were included in the analysis.

The following distributions were considered for the study: exponential, Weibull, lognormal, gamma, loggamma (i.e., log of data is gamma-distributed), 1-parameter Pareto, Burr, and loglogistic.[27] The distributions were fitted using the MLE method. Overall, heavy-tailed distributions—Burr, loggamma, loglogistic, and one-parameter Pareto—fit the data very well, while thin-tailed distributions' fit is poor, as expected. In particular, losses of LT3 are well fit by most of the heavy-tailed distributions and lognormal. In many cases, the estimated parameters would be unreasonable, for example resulting in a negative mean loss. For some BL and LT data sets, the models failed the χ^2 goodness-of-fit test for all considered cases. Hence, de Fontnouvelle, Rosengren, and Jordan performed additional analysis using the extreme value theory and fitting the GPD to the data exceeding a high threshold, results that we will provide in Chapter 8.[28]

---

[26]We will present the results of this and other empirical studies with operational loss data in Chapter 8 on the Extreme Value Theory.

[27]The density of the Loglogistic distribution is $f(x) = ax^{1/b-1}/[b(1 + ax^{1/b})^2]$.

[28]For the tables with the χ^2 goodness-of-fit statistic values and other details of this empirical study we refer the reader to de Fontnouvelle, Rosengren, and Jordan (2005).

TABLE 6.5 Goodness-of-fit test results in the Lewis study

Distribution	AD Test Statistic
Normal	8.090
Exponential	0.392
Weibull	0.267

Lewis Study of Legal Liability Loss Data Lewis (2004) reports his findings for a sample (in British pounds) of legal liability losses (from an undisclosed source), consisting of 140 points.[29] The data are highly leptokurtic and significantly right-skewed. He fits the normal, exponential, and Weibull distributions[30] to the data. The MLE parameter estimates resulted in $\mu = 151,944.04$ and $\sigma = 170,767.06$ for normal, $\lambda = 151,944.04$ for exponential, and $\alpha = 0.95446$ and $\beta = 0.00001$ for the Weibull distributions. Table 6.5 shows the results of the AD goodness-of-fit test. As expected, the normal distribution results in a very poor fit, and the Weibull distribution seems the most reasonable candidate, based on the lowest value of the AD test statistic.

Studies with Simulated Data

A number of studies on operational risk that have appeared in literature used simulated rather than real data. We present a few examples here.

Reynolds and Syer Study Reynolds and Syer (2003) apply a nonparametric approach to modeling operational loss severity. They use a hypothetical sample of six-year internal operational loss data of a firm, with a total of 293 observations, with the total number of annual observations ranging from 43 to 64 and the average loss amount ranging from \$75,700 to \$117,900. Using the sample of simulated data, sampling is repeated a large number of times, and 1,000 simulated years are created. For each year, the simulated losses are summed up. The distribution of yearly aggregated operational losses is assumed to follow the resulting empirical distribution.

---

[29]Original dataset is available from Lewis (2004), Chapter 7, p. 87. The mean loss was £151,944.04, the median was £103,522.90, the standard deviation was £170,767.06, and the skewness and kurtosis coefficients were 2.84 and 12.81, respectively.

[30]Lewis (2004) does not report the parameter estimates for the Gaussian and Weibull cases. We computed them directly by fitting the ditributions to the data.

Rosenberg and Schuermann Study   Rosenberg and Schuermann (2004) use a Monte Carlo approach to generate a sample of 200,000 operational losses. For the loss distribution they consider a 1-parameter Pareto distribution with parameter $1/0.65 = 1.5385$. This parameter is based on the average of the exponential parameters[31] of 1/0.64 and 1/0.66, obtained for logarithmic losses from the OpRisk Analytics database and OpVantage database, respectively, in the empirical study carried out by de Fontnouvelle, DeJesus-Rueff, Jordan, and Rosengren (2003). Recall that since the shape parameter is less than one, then such Pareto distribution has a finite mean but an infinite variance. To guarantee the existence of the first two moments, Rosenberg and Schuermann set a log-loss greater than 1,000 standard deviations equal to a loss of 1,000 standard deviations.

SUMMARY OF KEY CONCEPTS

- Broadly, one can classify the approaches to model operational loss magnitudes into two groups: nonparametric approach and parametric approach.
- Under the nonparametric approach, one can either model the losses using the empirical distribution function, or one can fit a smooth curve to the histogram of the data and analyze the properties of the curve instead.
- Under the parametric approach, one can fit one (or more) of common parametric distributions directly to the data (and compare them).
- Because of the specific nature of the operational loss data, the distributions that are most likely to find application to modeling the losses are those that are right-skewed and are defined only on the positive values of the underlying random variable. In particular, the exponential, lognormal, Weibull, gamma, beta, Pareto, Burr, and mixture distributions were reviewed.
- Special attention was given to discussing the tail behavior of various loss distributions. Common loss distributions were classified into light-tailed and heavy-tailed, according to their right-tail behavior.
- We reviewed several studies from the recent literature on the empirical findings with operational loss data. Two types of empirical studies are distinctive: studies that use real loss data and studies that use simulated

---

[31]We stated earlier that an exponential transformation of an Exponentially distributed random variable follows a one-parameter Pareto distribution.

data. Generally, most of the studies suggest that heavy-tailed loss distributions (such as lognormal or Pareto) best describe operational loss magnitudes.

APPENDIX: BASIC DESCRIPTIVE TECHNIQUES FOR CONTINUOUS RANDOM VARIABLES

Suppose we observe a sample of n realizations of a random variable X that are independent and identically distributed (*iid*). These constitute a random sample. Based on the sample $x = \{x_1, x_2, \ldots, x_n\}$, we can make inference about the entire population of X.

Sample

- *Histograms* are useful to visualize the distribution of the data sample. They are obtained by dividing the range of the data into a number of classes (e.g., 30) and constructing a bar plot for the number of observations in each class. *Relative frequency histograms* plot proportions of data instead of the number of data points.

  The center of the sample can be measured by mean, median, or mode.

- *Sample mean* is calculated as the average sample value:

$$\bar{x} = \frac{\sum_{j=1}^{n} x_j}{n}.$$

- *Sample median* indicates the value of the ordered sample so that exactly half of the data have values below and half have values above: median is exactly the midpoint of the ordered data if n is odd, and is the average of the two midpoints if n is even.
- *Sample mode* denotes the most frequent value of the data (i.e., the value of x that corresponds to the peak of the histogram). *Note:* There can be more than one mode.

  There are various possible measures of the spread of the data. These include range, inter-quartile range, variance, standard deviation, and mean absolute deviation. Among these, variance and standard deviation are the ones most commonly used in practice.

- *Sample variance* is the most common measure of spread. It is estimated by the second central moment. Its unbiased estimate is calculated by

$$s^2 = \frac{\sum_{j=1}^{n}(x_j - \bar{x})^2}{n-1}.$$

- *Sample standard deviation* (denoted s) is the square root of the sample variance:

$$s = \sqrt{\frac{\sum_{j=1}^{n}(x_j - \bar{x})^2}{n-1}}.$$

The shape of the data can be described by its kurtosis and skewness. Examples of skewness and kurtosis are illustrated in Figure 6.14.

- *Skewness* indicates asymmetry in the data. The data is *left-skewed* if the left tail of the distribution is longer than the right tail. In this case, generally, the following holds: mean < median < mode. Similarly, the data are *right-skewed* if the right tail is longer than the left tail. In this case, generally, the following holds: mode < median < mean. The degree and sign of skewness in the data can be measured by the *sample skewness coefficient*. There are several versions of the skewness coefficient. The most common version is calculated as the ratio of the third central moment to the 3/2th power of the second central moment:

$$\text{Sample skewness} = \frac{\sum_{j=1}^{n}(x_j - \bar{x})^3}{(n-1)s^3}.$$

- *Kurtosis* indicates the peakedness of the data. A higher kurtosis means that there is a high peak in the center of the data. It also means heavy tails. The data that are severely kurtotic and have also heavy tails are often called *leptokurtic*. The degree of kurtosis in a sample is measured by the *sample kurtosis coefficient*. There are several versions of it. The most common version is calculated as the ratio of the fourth central moment to the squared second central moment:

$$\text{Sample kurtosis} = \frac{\sum_{j=1}^{n}(x_j - \bar{x})^4}{(n-1)(s^2)^2} - 3.$$

The reason for subtracting 3 is to make the estimate more comparable to that of a standard normal random variable (whose kurtosis coefficient is 0, once 3 is subtracted). This version of the kurtosis coefficient is also known as *excess kurtosis*. Note that in some literature they do not subtract 3 in the formula.

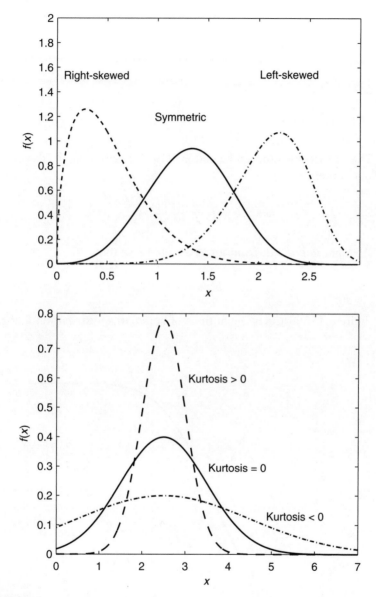

FIGURE 6.14 Illustration of a symmetric and skewed densities (top) and densities with varying kurtosis (bottom).

Population

- The *density* of a continuous random variable X is denoted by $f(x)$. The *cumulative distribution* $F(x)$ is related to the density by the following expression:

$$F(x) = \int_{-\infty}^{x} f(s)\, ds.$$

The density function can be obtained by differentiating the distribution function once:

$$f(x) = \frac{dF(x)}{dx}.$$

- The right *tail* of a distribution is denoted $\bar{F}$ so that

$$\bar{F}(x) = 1 - F(x).$$

Figure 6.15 illustrates the notions of cumulative distribution and right tail.

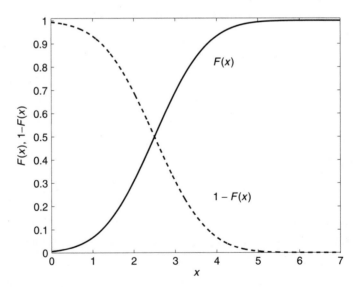

FIGURE 6.15 Illustration of cumulative distribution and right tail of a continuous distribution.

■ *Expectation* of a function $g(X)$ of a random variable X is computed by

$$\mathbb{E}[g(X)] = \int_{-\infty}^{+\infty} g(x) f(x)\, dx.$$

■ *kth raw moment* (m_k) of a random variable X is the expectation of $g(X) = X^k$:

$$m_k := \mathbb{E}(X^k) = \int_{-\infty}^{+\infty} x^k f(x)\, dx.$$

For example, population mean is the first raw moment; population variance is obtained by the difference between the second raw moment and the squared first raw moment.

■ *kth central moment* (μ_k) of a random variable X is the expectation of $g(X) = (X - \mathbb{E}(X))^k$:

$$m_k := \mathbb{E}[(X - \mathbb{E}(X))^k] = \int_{-\infty}^{+\infty} (x - \mathbb{E}(X))^k f(x)\, dx.$$

■ *Quantiles* (or *percentiles*) indicate a value a of a random variable X under which lies a fraction p of the data. It is often denoted by the inverse of the distribution function: $a = F^{-1}(p)$). For example, the 95th quantile denotes the value of X under which lie 95% of the data; median is the 50th percentile. *1st quartile (Q1)* is the 25th percentile (and is the mode of the first half of the ordered data), and *3rd quartile (Q3)* is the 75th percentile (and is the mode of the second half of the ordered data).

The three common measures of the population center are the mean, median, and mode. In practice, the one most commonly used in the mean.

■ *Population mean* (often denoted by μ) of a random variable X is measured by the expectation of $g(X) = X$, and is the first raw moment m_1:

$$\mathrm{mean}(X) = \mathbb{E}(X) = \int_{-\infty}^{+\infty} x f(x)\, dx.$$

■ *Population median* of a random variable X is the 50th percentile. It is measured by the inverse of the cumulative distribution function at point 0.5:

$$\mathrm{median} = F^{-1}(0.5).$$

- *Population mode* can be obtained by differentiating the density with respect to x, and finding the value of x that would set the quantity to zero. For those densities with a steadily decaying right tail, the mode is equal to zero.

The most common measures of population spread are the variance and the standard deviation.

- *Population variance* (often denoted by σ^2) is measured by the 2nd central moment μ_2, and is:

$$\text{var}(X) = \mathbb{E}[(X - \text{mean}(X))^2] = \int_{-\infty}^{+\infty} (x - \text{mean}(X))^2 f(x)\, dx.$$

- *Population standard deviation* (denoted by σ) is the square root of the population variance:

$$\text{stdev}(X) = \sqrt{\mathbb{E}[(X - \text{mean}(X))^2]} = \sqrt{\int_{-\infty}^{+\infty} (x - \text{mean}(X))^2 f(x)\, dx}.$$

The shape of the distribution can be measured by its skewness and kurtosis.

- *Population skewness coefficient* is measured by

$$\gamma_1 = \frac{\mu_3}{\sigma^3}.$$

- *Population kurtosis coefficient* is measured by

$$\gamma_2 = \frac{\mu_4}{(\sigma^2)^2} - 3.$$

Transformations of Random Variables

Suppose that a random variable X has a density $f_X(x)$. A random variable Y is a transformation of X via $Y = g(X)$. Using the fact that $x = g^{-1}(y)$, the density $f_Y(y)$ of Y can be generally found by the Jacobian transformation method:

$$f_Y(y) = \left| \frac{dx}{dy} \right| \cdot f_X(g^{-1}(y)).$$

For example, if X is exponentially distributed with parameter a, and $Y = e^X$, then using the methodology, the density of Y is $f_Y(y) = d \log(y)/dy \cdot ae^{-a \log(y)} = ay^{-a-1}$, which we recognize as the density of a 1-parameter Pareto random variable. Note that since the support of X is $(0, +\infty)$, the support of Y is $(1, +\infty)$.

Parameter Estimation Methods

There are several methods for estimating the unknown parameters of the density function. They include the method of *maximum likelihood estimation* (MLE), the *method of moments* (MOM), and the *method of probability weighted moments*. MLE is the most popular method because of its attractive properties: (1) Maximum likelihood estimators are consistent and (2) maximum likelihood estimators are asymptotically normally distributed, which makes them easy to analyze. We describe the MLE method here.

We assume that a sample of length n consists of *iid* observations. Then their joint density function is simply a product of their densities. This joint density is called the *likelihood function*:

$$\mathcal{L}(x) = \prod_{j=1}^{n} f(x_j)$$

It is easier to work with its logarithmic form, called the *log-likelihood function*:

$$l(x) = \sum_{j=1}^{n} \log f(x_j)$$

The optimal values of the unknown parameters are those that maximize the likelihood of the sample, that is, those that maximize the log-likelihood function. Hence, the MLE parameter can be found by: (step 1) differentiating $l(x)$ with respect to the parameter; (step 2) setting the quantity to zero, and (step 3) finding the parameter value that satisfies this equation.

For example, if X has a lognormal distribution, then the log-likelihood is expressed as

$$l(x) = -(n/2) \log(2\pi) - n \log(\sigma) - \sum_{j=1}^{n} \log(x_j) - \frac{1}{2\sigma^2} \sum_{j=1}^{n} (\log(x_j) - \mu)^2.$$

Differentiating it with respect to μ and setting to zero, we get

$$0 = \frac{1}{\sigma^2} \sum_{j=1}^{n} \log(x_j) - \frac{n\mu}{\sigma^2},$$

from which the estimate for μ is found to be $\hat{\mu} = \sum_{j=1}^{n} \log(x_j)/n$. Similarly, differentiating $l(x)$ with respect to σ^2 and using the previously obtained MLE estimate for μ, we get $\widehat{\sigma^2} = \sum_{j=1}^{n} (\log(x_j) - \hat{\mu})^2/n$.

REFERENCES

BIS (2003), "The 2002 Loss Data Collection Exercise for Operational Risk: Summary of the Data Collected," www.BIS.org.

Casella, G., and Berger, R. L. (2001), *Statistical Inference*, 2nd ed., Duxbury Press, Pacific Grive, CA.

Cizek, P., Härdle, W., and Weron, R., eds. (2005), *Statistical Tools for Finance and Insurance*, Springer, Heidelberg.

Cruz, M. G. (2002), *Modeling, Measuring and Hedging Operational Risk*, John Wiley & Sons, New York, Chichester.

de Fontnouvelle, P., DeJesus-Rueff, V., Jordan, J., and Rosengren, E. (2003), Using Loss Data to Quantify Operational Risk, Technical report, Federal Reserve Bank of Boston.

de Fontnouvelle, P., Rosengren, E., and Jordan, J. (2005), Implications of Alternative Operational Risk Modeling Techniques, Technical report, Federal Reserve Bank of Boston and Fitch Risk.

Devroye, L. (1986), *Non-Uniform Random Variate Generation*, Springer-Verlag, New York.

Embrechts, P., Klüppelberg, C., and Mikosch, T. (1997), *Modeling Extremal Events for Insurance and Finance*, Springer-Verlag, Berlin.

Klugman, S. A., Panjer, H. H., and Willmot, G. E. (2004), *Loss Models: From Data to Decisions*, 2nd ed., John Wiley & Sons, Hoboken, New Jersey.

Kremer, E. (1998), "Largest Claims Reinsurance Premiums for the Weibull Model," in *Blätter der Deutschen Gesellschaft für Versicherungsmathematik*, pp. 279–284.

Lewis, N. (2004), *Operational Risk with Excel and VBA*, John Wiley & Sons, Hoboken, New Jersey.

Madan, D. B., and Unal, H. (2004), Risk-Neutralizing Statistical Distributions: With an Application to Pricing Reinsurance Contracts on FDIC Losses, Technical Report 2004-01, FDIC, Center for Financial Research.

Mittnik, S., and Rachev, S. T. (1993a), Modelling Asset Returns with Alternative Stable Distributions, *Econometric Reviews* 12, pp. 261–330.

Mittnik, S. and Rachev, S. T. (1993b), Reply to Comments on Modelling Asset Returns with Alternative Stable Distributions and Some Extensions, *Econometric Reviews* 12, pp. 347–389.

Moscadelli, M. (2004), The Modelling of Operational Risk: Experience with the Analysis of the Data Collected by the Basel Committee, Technical report, Bank of Italy.

Müller, H. (2002), Quantifying Operational Risk in a Financial Institution, Master's thesis, Institut für Statistik und Wirtschaftstheorie, Universität Karlsruhe.

Reynolds, D., and Syer, D. (2003), A General Simulation Framework for Operational Loss Distributions, in C. Alexander, ed., *Operational Risk: Regulation, Analysis and Management*, Prentice Hall, Upper Saddle River, NJ, pp. 193–214.

Rosenberg, J. V., and Schuermann, T. (2004), A General Approach to Integrated Risk Management with Skewed, Fat-Tailed Risks, Technical report, Federal Reserve Bank of New York.

Ross, S. M. (2001), *Simulation*, 3rd ed., Academic Press, Boston.

Ross, S. M. (2002), *Introduction to Probability Models*, 8th ed., Academic Press, Boston.

Scott, D. W. (1992), *Multivariate Density Estimation: Theory, Practice, and Visualization*, John Wiley & Sons, New York.

Silverman, B. W. (1986), *Density Estimation for Statistics and Data Analysis*, Chapman & Hall, London.

CHAPTER 7

Alpha-Stable Distributions

O perational losses due to errors and omissions, physical loss of securities, natural disasters, and internal fraud are infrequent in nature but can have serious financial consequences for an institution. Such low frequency/high severity operational losses can be extreme in magnitude when compared to the rest of the data. If one constructs a histogram of the loss distribution, these events would be located in the far right end. Because of this, they are often classified as *tail events*. We say that the data are *heavy-tailed* when such tail events are present.

In Chapter 6 we discussed common loss distributions that can be used to describe the operational loss distribution. According to BIS (2001 Annex 1, p. 18):[1]

> *The internal risk measurement system must capture the impact of infrequent, but potentially severe, operational risk events. That is, the internally generated risk measure must accurately capture the "tail" of the operational risk loss distribution.*

Loss distributions, such as lognormal, gamma, and Weibull, are classified as moderately heavy-tailed and thus may not be sufficient to capture the infrequent but potentially severe operational loss events. In Chapter 6 we also emphasized the importance of the tail behavior of loss distributions to modeling heavy-tailed operational losses.

In this chapter we continue the discussion of modeling operational loss severity with heavy-tailed distributions. In particular, we discuss a wide class of alpha-stable or α-stable distributions.[2] Nonexistence of a closed

---

[1]BIS (2006, p. 151) confirmed this by stating that "a bank must be able to demonstrate that its [advanced measurement] approach captures potentially severe 'tail' loss events."
[2]Alpha-stable distributions are often referred to as stable Paretian distributions.

form for the density function (in the general case) poses an obstacle from the standpoint of their practical applications. However, their attractive features make them worth investigating in applications to operational risk data where these properties become crucial. Alpha-stable distributions have been receiving increasing recognition in the financial markets research.[3]

In this chapter we review the definition and the basic properties of the alpha-stable distribution. We further illustrate some empirical studies with operational risk data.

DEFINITION OF AN ALPHA-STABLE RANDOM VARIABLE

We begin with a definition of an alpha-stable random variable.[4] Suppose that $X_1, X_2, \ldots, X_n$ are independent and identically distributed (*iid*) random variables, independent copies of X. Then a random variable X is said to follow an alpha-stable distribution if there exist a positive constant C_n and a real number D_n such that the following relation holds:

$$X_1 + X_2 + \cdots + X_n \stackrel{d}{=} C_n X + D_n.$$

The notation $\stackrel{d}{=}$ denotes equality in distribution. The constant $C_n = n^{1/\alpha}$ dictates the stability property, which we discuss later. When $\alpha = 2$, we have the Gaussian (normal) case. In subsequent discussions of the alpha-stable distributions in this chapter, we restrict ourselves to the *non-Gaussian case* in which $0 < \alpha < 2$.

---

[3]Early applications of the alpha-stable distribution to financial data include Fama (1963, 1965a,b), in which the distribution was applied to stock market prices and portfolio analysis. Many applications to financial time series can be found in Rachev and Mittnik (2000), Rachev (2003), and Rachev, Menn, and Fabozzi (2005). Applications to nonlife insurance are described in Cizek, Härdle, and Weron (2005). Recently, the distributions have been applied to real estate market analysis by Brown (2005).

Alpha-stable distribution has been built into some risk and portfolio management software. For example, *cognity* is a risk and portfolio management software product of the U.S.-based FinAnalytica Inc. It is the only commercial system that offers the alpha-stable Paretian distributions framework. More information regarding the software and products can be obtained from the company's permanent home page: www.finanalytica.com.

[4]Extensive analysis of alpha-stable distributions and their properties can be found in Samorodnitsky and Taqqu (1994), and Rachev and Mittnik (2000), and Stoyanov and Racheva-Iotova (2004a,b).

For the general case, the density does not have a closed form. The distribution is expressed by its characteristic function:[5]

$$
\mathbb{E}[e^{itX}] =
\begin{cases}
\exp\left(-|\sigma t|^\alpha (1 - i\beta(\text{sign } t)\tan\dfrac{\pi\alpha}{2}) + i\mu t\right), & \alpha \neq 1 \\
\exp\left(-\sigma|t|(1 + i\beta\dfrac{2}{\pi}(\text{sign } t)\ln|t|) + i\mu t\right), & \alpha = 1,
\end{cases}
$$

where sign t equals 1 when $t \geq 0$, 0 when $t = 0$, and -1 when $t \leq 0$.

The distribution is characterized by four parameters:[6]

1. α: the index of stability or the shape parameter, $\alpha \in (0, 2)$
2. β: the skewness parameter, $\beta \in [-1, +1]$
3. σ: the scale parameter, $\sigma \in (0, +\infty)$
4. μ: the location parameter, $\mu \in (-\infty, +\infty)$

The exceptions of closed-form densities are three special cases: the Gaussian case ($\alpha = 2$), Cauchy case ($\alpha = 1, \beta = 0$), and Lévy case ($\alpha = 1/2$, $\beta = \pm 1$) with the following densities:

- Gaussian: $f(x) = \dfrac{1}{2\sigma\sqrt{\pi}}e^{-\frac{(x-\mu)^2}{4\sigma^2}}$, $\quad -\infty < x < \infty$
- Cauchy: $f(x) = \dfrac{\sigma}{\pi((x-\mu)^2 + \sigma^2)}$, $\quad -\infty < x < \infty$
- Lévy: $f(x) = \dfrac{\sqrt{\sigma}}{\sqrt{2\pi}(x-\mu)^{3/2}}e^{-\frac{\sigma}{2(x-\mu)}}$, $\quad \mu < x < \infty$

Because of the four parameters, the distribution is highly flexible and suitable for modeling nonsymmetric, highly kurtotic, and heavy-tailed data. Figure 7.1 illustrates the effects of the shape (top) and skewness (bottom) parameters on the shape of the distribution, other parameters kept constant. As is evident from part a of Figure 7.1, a lower value for α is attributed to heavier tails and higher kurtosis.

---

[5]There is a one-to-one correspondence between the distribution function and the characteristic function. Therefore, expressing the distribution by its characteristic function is equivalent to expressing it by the density function. The appendix to this chapter provides a technical discussion of the notion of characteristic functions.

[6]The parameterization of alpha-stable distribution is not unique. The one presented here is due to Samorodnitsky and Taqqu (1994). An overview of the different approaches can be found in Zolotarev (1986).

Alpha-Stable Densities for Varying α's, with $\beta = 0$, $\sigma = 1$, and $\mu = 0$

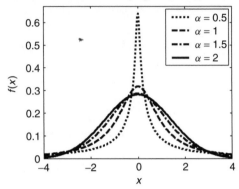

Alpha-Stable Densities for Varying β's, with $\alpha = 1$, $\sigma = 1$, and $\mu = 0$

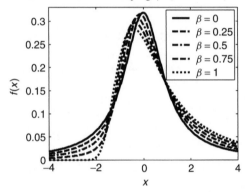

FIGURE 7.1 Illustration of alpha-stable densities.

USEFUL PROPERTIES OF AN ALPHA-STABLE RANDOM VARIABLE

We briefly present four basic properties of the alpha-stable distribution.[7]

  Property 1. The *power tail decay* property means that the tail of
  the density function decays like a power function (slower than the

---

[7]The properties of alpha-stable distribution are treated in depth in Samorodnitsky and Taqqu (1994) and Rachev and Mittnik (2000).

exponential decay), which is what allows the distribution to capture extreme events in the tails:

$$P(|X| > x) \propto \text{const} \cdot x^{-\alpha}, \quad x \to \infty$$

Property 2. Raw moments satisfy the property:

$$\mathbb{E}|X|^p < \infty \quad \text{for any} \quad 0 < p < \alpha,$$

$$\mathbb{E}|X|^p = \infty \quad \text{for any} \quad p \geq \alpha.$$

Property 3. Because of Property 2, the mean is finite only for $\alpha > 1$:

$$\text{mean}(X) = \mu \quad \text{for} \quad \alpha > 1,$$

$$\text{mean}(X) = \infty \quad \text{for} \quad 0 < \alpha \leq 1.$$

Furthermore, the second and higher moments are infinite, leading to infinite variance together with the skewness and kurtosis coefficients.

Property 4. The stability property is a useful and convenient property and dictates that the distributional form of the variable is preserved under linear transformations. The stability property is governed by the stability parameter α in the constant C_n (which appeared earlier in the definition of an alpha-stable random variable): $C_n = n^{1/\alpha}$. As was stated earlier, smaller values of α refer to a heavier-tailed distribution. The standard central limit theorem does not apply to the non-Gaussian case: Appropriately standardized large sum of *iid* random variables converges to an alpha-stable random variable instead of normal random variable.

The following examples illustrate the stability property. Suppose that $X_1, X_2, \ldots, X_n$ are independent alpha-stable random variables with the same index of stability α and respective parameters $\{\beta_i, \sigma_i, \mu_i\}, i = 1, 2, \ldots, n$. Then:

- The distribution of $Y = \sum_i^n X_i$ is alpha-stable with the index of stability α and parameters

$$\beta = \frac{\sum_i^n \beta_i \sigma_i^\alpha}{\sum_i^n \sigma_i^\alpha}, \quad \sigma = \left(\sum_i^n \sigma_i^\alpha\right)^{1/\alpha}, \quad \mu = \sum_i^n \mu_i.$$

- The distribution of $Y = X_1 + a$ for some real constant a is alpha-stable with the index of stability α and parameters

$$\beta = \beta_1, \quad \sigma = \sigma_1, \quad \mu = \mu_1 + a.$$

- The distribution of $Y = aX_1$ for some real constant a ($a \neq 0$) is alpha-stable with the index of stability α and parameters

$$\beta = (\text{sign } a)\beta_1, \quad \sigma = |a|\sigma_1, \quad \mu = a\mu_1 \qquad \text{for } \alpha \neq 1,$$
$$\beta = (\text{sign } a)\beta_1, \quad \sigma = |a|\sigma_1, \quad \mu = a\mu_1 - \frac{2}{\pi}a(\ln a)\sigma_1\beta_1 \quad \text{for } \alpha = 1.$$

- The distribution of $Y = -X_1$ is alpha-stable with the index of stability α and parameters

$$\beta = -\beta_1, \quad \sigma = \sigma_1, \quad \mu = -\mu_1.$$

ESTIMATING PARAMETERS OF THE ALPHA-STABLE DISTRIBUTION

Since the density of the alpha-stable distribution does not exist in closed form, the traditional *maximum likelihood estimation* (MLE) procedure (under which the likelihood function is maximized subject to the unknown parameters) cannot be applied.[8] There are two methodologies commonly used to estimate the four parameters:

1. *Sample characteristic function approach:* Use the observed data to evaluate the sample characteristic function and estimate the unknown parameters such that the distance between the sample and theoretical characteristic functions is minimized.
2. *Numerical approximation of the density function approach:* Approximate the density function using the one-to-one correspondence relation between the characteristic function and the density.

Sample Characteristic Function Approach

Developed by Press (1972), this approach is based on the comparison of the theoretical characteristic function with the sample characteristic function. In the first step of the procedure, for a given sample of n observations x_1, $x_2, \ldots, x_n$, the sample characteristic function for a value of t is calculated as

$$\hat{\phi}(t) = \frac{1}{n}\sum_{k=1}^{n} e^{itx_k}.$$

---

[8]See Chapter 6 for a discussion of the maximum likelihood method.

In the second step, mathematical optimization software is used to fit the theoretical characteristic function to the sample one. The estimates $(\hat{\alpha}, \hat{\beta}, \hat{\sigma}, \hat{\mu})$ are found so that the distance between the sample and theoretical characteristic functions is minimized.[9]

Numerical Approximation of the Density Function Approach

Suggested by DuMouchel (1971, 1973), this approach is based on the numerical approximation of the density function and then using the MLE to evaluate the unknown parameters. In the first step of the procedure, the density function is obtained from the characteristic function using the Fourier inversion method (see the appendix to this chapter). This task can be performed using the Fast Fourier Transform (FFT) algorithm.[10] In the second step, the MLE of the unknown parameters can be performed using a numerical optimization software, resulting in the choice of the parameter set $(\hat{\alpha}, \hat{\beta}, \hat{\sigma}, \hat{\mu})$ that maximizes the likelihood function.

USEFUL TRANSFORMATIONS OF ALPHA-STABLE RANDOM VARIABLES

For $\alpha > 1$ or $|\beta| < 1$, the alpha-stable distribution can take values on $(-\infty, +\infty)$. Such distribution can be useful for modeling data that can take both negative and positive values. It would be unwise, however, to directly apply this distribution to operational loss data that take only positive values. In this light, we suggest using one of three transformations of the alpha-stable distribution: symmetric alpha-stable distribution, log-alpha-stable distribution, and truncated alpha-stable distribution.

Symmetric Alpha-Stable Random Variable

The symmetric alpha-stable distribution is symmetric and centered around zero. To apply it to the operational loss severity data, one can do a simple transformation to the original data set: $Y = [-X; X]$. Then only two parameters need to be estimated: α and σ (β and μ equal zero).

---

[9]A detailed description of this approach can be found in Kogon and William (1998).
[10]For details on this approach, see Menn and Rachev (2006) and Nolan (1997). Numerical evaluation of $f(x)$ has been implemented in a software package STABLE available at no cost at http://academic2.american.edu/~jpnolan/stable/stable.html.

Log-Alpha-Stable Random Variable

It is often convenient to work with the natural logarithm transformation of the original data.[11] A random variable X is said to follow a log-alpha-stable distribution if the natural logarithm of the original data follows an alpha-stable distribution. Fitting log-alpha-stable distribution to data is appropriate when there is reason to believe that the data are very heavy-tailed, and the regular alpha-stable distribution may not be sufficient to capture the heavy tails.

Truncated Alpha-Stable Random Variable

Another scenario would involve a restriction on the density, rather than a transformation of the original data set. The support of the alpha-stable distribution can be restricted to the positive half-line in order to avoid the possibility of having a positive probability of values below zero in the case when $\beta < 1$. Then, the estimation part would involve fitting a left-truncated stable distribution of the form

$$f(x) = \frac{g(x)}{1 - G(0)} \times \mathbb{I}_{x>0},$$

where $\mathbb{I}_{x>0}$ is 1 if $x > 0$ and is 0 if $x \leq 0$; $g(x)$ is the density of the alpha-stable distribution; and $G(0)$ is its cumulative distribution function evaluated at zero. Fitting the left-truncated distribution to the data means fitting the right tail of the distribution. In operational risk modeling, left-truncated distributions are particularly relevant because losses take only positive amounts.[12]

APPLICATIONS TO OPERATIONAL LOSS DATA

Currently, applications of alpha-stable distribution to the operational risk data are limited. Recent work by Medova and Kuriacou (2001) pioneered the discussions of using this distribution to model operational losses. Applicability of the distribution was justified by the observation of high variability in the operational loss data (and the resulting heavy tail), and the stability

---

[11] A typical example is the lognormal distribution: if X follows a lognormal distribution, then $\log X$ follows a normal distribution with the same location and scale parameters μ and σ.

[12] See also Chapter 9 for a discussion of truncated distributions.

property desirable for practical implementation purposes. Basic properties of alpha-stable random variable are discussed in the study. Unfortunately, the model was not tested with actual operational loss data by Medova and Kuriacou (2001). However, two studies that do test operational loss data are described next.

Chernobai, Menn, Rachev, and Trück Study of 1980–2002 Public Loss Data

We present results of an empirical application of the alpha-stable distribution to modeling operational loss data. Chernobai, Menn, Rachev, and Trück (2005) examine a publicly available data set, identical to the one in the Chernobai, Menn, Rachev, and Trück study presented in Chapter 5. The data consist of five loss types: relationship, human, processes, technology, and external. Visual inspection of the sample (histograms are omitted in this chapter) reveals the leptokurtic nature of the data: A very high peak is observed close to zero, and an extended right tail indicates the right-skewness and high dispersion of the data values. This suggests that fitting an alpha-stable distribution may be a reasonable approach.

The data are subject to minimum recording thresholds of $1 million in nominal value. Therefore, conditional left-truncated loss distribution was fitted to the data using the method of restricted maximum likelihood.[13] Parameter estimates, together with goodness-of-fit statistic values (Kolmogorov-Smirnov (KS) and the quadratic class Anderson-Darling (AD)[14]) and the corresponding p-values[15] (in square brackets) for several distributions are summarized in Table 7.1.[16]

On the basis of the KS and AD statistic values, log-Weibull, Weibull, or lognormal densities describe best the loss data (the statistics are the lowest for these models in most cases). However, an examination of the p-values reveals that in 23 out of 30 cases either log-alpha-stable or symmetric alpha-stable, or even both, resulted in the highest p-values, suggesting

---

[13]See Chapter 9 for detailed discussion of the methodology.

[14]See Chapter 10 in which various goodness-of-fit tests are discussed. To account for the difference in sample sizes, the scaling factors $\sqrt{n}$ and n are used in the calculations of the KS and the AD statistics, accordingly.

[15]Higher p-values indicate a better fit. The p-values presented in this study are based on a composite goodness-of-fit test.

[16]More detailed analysis with a wider class of distributions and comprehensive goodness-of-fit tests can be found in Chernobai, Menn, Rachev, and Trück (2005).

TABLE 7.1 Parameter estimates and goodness-of-fit statistic values in Chernobai, Menn, Rachev, and Trück study

	Relationship	Human	Processes	Technology	External
Exponential					
β	$11.25 \cdot 10^{-9}$	$17.27 \cdot 10^{-9}$	$3.51 \cdot 10^{-9}$	$13.08 \cdot 10^{-9}$	$9.77 \cdot 10^{-9}$
KS	11.0868 [≈0]	14.0246 [≈0]	7.6043 [≈0]	3.2160 [≈0]	6.5941 [≈0]
AD	344.4 [≈0]	609.1 [≈0]	167.6 [≈0]	27.84 [≈0]	128.35 [≈0]
Lognormal					
μ	16.1911	15.4627	17.1600	15.1880	15.7125
σ	2.0654	2.5642	2.3249	2.7867	2.3639
KS	0.8056 [0.082]	0.8758 [0.032]	0.6854 [0.297]	1.1453 [≈0]	0.6504 [0.326]
AD	0.7554 [0.043]	0.7505 [0.408]	0.4624 [0.223]	1.3778 [≈0]	0.5816 [0.120]
Weibull					
β	0.0032	0.0240	0.0021	0.0103	0.0108
τ	0.3538	0.2526	0.3515	0.2938	0.2933
KS	0.5553 [0.625]	0.8065 [0.103]	0.6110 [0.455]	1.0922 [≈0]	0.4752 [0.852]
AD	0.7073 [0.072]	0.7908 [0.112]	0.2069 [0.875]	1.4536 [≈0]	0.3470 [0.519]
log-Weibull					
β	$0.27 \cdot 10^{-8}$	$30.73 \cdot 10^{-8}$	$0.11 \cdot 10^{-8}$	$11.06 \cdot 10^{-8}$	$2.82 \cdot 10^{-8}$
τ	7.0197	7.0197	7.1614	5.7555	6.2307
KS	0.5284 [0.699]	0.9030 [0.074]	0.5398 [0.656]	1.1099 [≈0]	0.6893 [0.296]
AD	0.4682 [0.289]	0.7560 [0.392]	0.1721 [0.945]	1.5355 [≈0]	0.4711 [0.338]
Log-alpha-stable					
α	1.9340	1.4042	2.0000	2.0000	1.3313
β	−1	−1	0.8195	0.8040	−1
σ	1.5198	2.8957	1.6476	1.9894	2.7031
μ	15.9616	10.5108	17.1535	15.1351	10.1928
KS	1.5929 [0.295]	9.5186 [0.319]	0.6931 [0.244]	1.1540 [≈0]	7.3275 [0.396]
AD	3.8067 [0.290]	304.6 [0.215]	0.4759 [0.202]	1.3646 [≈0]	194.7 [0.284]
Symmetric alpha-stable					
α	0.6592	0.6061	0.5748	0.1827	0.5905
σ	$1.0 \cdot 10^{7}$	$0.71 \cdot 10^{7}$	$1.99 \cdot 10^{7}$	$0.17 \cdot 10^{7}$	$0.71 \cdot 10^{7}$
KS	1.1634 [0.034]	1.1628 [0.352]	1.3949 [0.085]	2.0672 [0.085]	0.7222 [0.586]
AD	4.4723 [0.992]	11.9320 [0.436]	6.5235 [0.964]	19.6225 [≈1]	1.7804 [0.841]

the best fit. This supports the conjecture that the overall distribution of operational losses[17] are very heavy-tailed and are well described by the variations of the alpha-stable distribution.

[17]Another approach would be to split each data set into two parts: the main body of the data and the right tail. Some empirical evidence suggests that the two parts of the data follow different laws. Extreme Value Theory is an approach that can be used for such analysis. We describe this approach in Chapter 8.

Chernobai and Rachev Study of 1950–2002 Public Loss Data

In the second study, alpha-stable distribution was fitted to the interarrival times.[18] This study is different from the previous study discussed in that here the alpha-stable distribution is applied to the intervals of time between the events rather than the distribution of the losses themselves. A heavy-tailed interarrival times distribution may indicate that there are clusters of loss events in time that would violate the simple Poisson assumption on the arrival process.

Table 7.2 reports the KS goodness-of-fit statistics[19] for several distributions fitted to the times between the occurrences of events for which the exact dates were known. It is clear from the table that, based on the low KS statistic values, the alpha-stable distribution fits the data very well compared with alternative candidate distributions. In particular, the exponential distribution shows a poor fit, allowing one to conclude that the frequency distribution does not follow a homogeneous Poisson process.[20]

TABLE 7.2 Kolmogorov-Smirnov statistic values for a class of loss distributions in the Chernobai and Rachev Study

	Relationship	Human	Processes	Technology	External
One-Sided Distributions					
Exponential	0.3447	0.2726	0.2914	0.2821	0.3409
Lognormal	0.3090	0.2550	0.2575	0.2821	0.3409
Alpha-stable	0.1020	0.0944	0.1090	0.1153	0.1013
Pareto	0.3090	0.2222	0.2649	0.2821	0.3409
Two-Sided Distributions					
Student t	0.3083	0.3070	0.3623	0.4077	0.3523
Cauchy	0.2643	0.2630	0.3252	0.3924	0.3157
Sym. alpha-stable	0.1234	0.1068	0.0899	0.0931	0.1084

---

[18] For details of the study, see Chernobai and Rachev (2004).

[19] The KS values are not adjusted to account for sample size differences. The sample sizes for the relationship, human, processes, technology, and external data types are 554, 597, 199, 31, and 160, respectively.

[20] Recall that a standard homogeneous Poisson process implies that the distribution of the interarrival times is exponential with the same intensity parameter.

SUMMARY OF KEY CONCEPTS

- Alpha-stable distributions possess attractive features making them applicable to operational risk modeling: (1) high flexibility due to four parameters; (2) stability under linear transformations, and (3) the power-law tail decay that captures heavy tails.
- In general, a closed-form expression of the density does not exist, which complicates the analysis. However, the existence of a closed-form characteristic function enables one to use the characteristic function to estimate the unknown parameters of the distribution with the use of a numerical optimization software. Two methodologies can be employed: (1) sample characteristic function approach and (2) numerical approximation of the density function approach.
- Variations of the alpha-stable distributions may be considered before being applied to the operational loss data. They include symmetric alpha-stable distribution, log-alpha-stable distribution, and left-truncated alpha-stable distribution.
- Applications of the alpha-stable distribution to actual operational loss data provide empirical evidence that the operational loss data are severely heavy-tailed and are well captured by the variations of the alpha-stable distributions.

APPENDIX: CHARACTERISTIC FUNCTIONS

Every distribution can be uniquely described by its characteristic function. Although the density of a distribution may not always exist in a closed form, the characteristic function always exists and completely determines the distribution. Therefore, important properties of a random variable may be deducted from the behavior of its characteristic function. In Table 7.3 we present the expressions of the characteristic functions for some common discrete and continuous distribution functions.[21]

---

[21] Simple closed forms of the characteristic functions for some common distributions do not exist. In particular, this is disappointing in the case of the lognormal distribution that is commonly suggested for use with operational loss data. This makes working with lognormal distribution difficult. Some approximations can be used; see for example, Thorin and Wikstad (1977) and Leipnik (1991). Leipnik (1991) showed the characteristic function of the lognormal distribution to be of the form

$$\varphi_X(t) = \sqrt{\frac{\pi}{2\sigma^2}} e^{-\frac{(\log t + \mu + \frac{\pi i}{2})^2}{2\sigma^2}} \sum_{\ell=0}^{\infty} (-1)^\ell d_\ell (2\sigma^2)^{-\frac{\ell}{2}} H_\ell \left(\frac{\log t + \mu + \frac{\pi i}{2}}{\sigma\sqrt{2}} \right),$$

TABLE 7.3 Characteristic functions of common discrete and continuous distributions

Name	$f(x)$ or $P(X=x)$	Characteristic Function
1. *Discrete Distributions*		
Binomial	$P(X=x) = \binom{n}{x} p^x (1-p)^{n-x}$	$\phi(t) = (1 - p + pe^{it})^n$
Geometric	$P(X=x) = (1-p)^{x-1} p$	$\phi(t) = \dfrac{p}{e^{-it} - 1 + p}$
Poisson	$P(X=x) = \dfrac{e^{-\lambda}\lambda^x}{x!}$	$\phi(t) = e^{\lambda(e^{it}-1)}$
Neg. binomial	$P(X=x) = \binom{n+x-1}{x} p^x (1-p)^n$	$\phi(t) = \left(\dfrac{p}{e^{-it} - 1 + p}\right)^n$
2. *Continuous Distributions*		
Normal	$f(x) = \dfrac{1}{\sqrt{2\pi}\sigma} e^{-\frac{(x-\mu)^2}{2\sigma^2}}$	$\phi(t) = e^{i\mu t - \frac{1}{2}\sigma^2 t^2}$
Exponential	$f(x) = \lambda e^{-\lambda x}$	$\phi(t) = \dfrac{\lambda}{\lambda - it}$
Gamma	$f(x) = \dfrac{\beta^\alpha}{\Gamma(\alpha)} x^{\alpha-1} e^{-\beta x}$	$\phi(t) = \left(\dfrac{\beta}{\beta - it}\right)^\alpha$
Weibull	$f(x) = \alpha\beta x^{\alpha-1} e^{-\beta x^\alpha}$	Complicated
Beta	$\dfrac{\Gamma(\alpha+\beta)}{\Gamma(\alpha)\Gamma(\beta)} x^{\alpha-1}(1-x)^{\beta-1}$	$\phi(t) = \dfrac{\Gamma(\alpha+\beta)}{\Gamma(\alpha)} \sum\limits_{k=0}^{\infty} \left[\dfrac{\Gamma(\alpha+k)}{\Gamma(\alpha+\beta+k)} \dfrac{(-it)^k}{k!}\right]$
Lognormal	$\dfrac{1}{\sqrt{2\pi}\sigma x} e^{-\frac{(\log x - \mu)^2}{2\sigma^2}}$	Complicated
Pareto	$f(x) = \dfrac{\alpha\beta^\alpha}{x^{\alpha+1}}$	$\phi(t) = \alpha(-i\beta t)^\alpha \Gamma(-\alpha, -i\beta t)$
Burr	$f(x) = \gamma\alpha\beta^\alpha \dfrac{x^{\gamma-1}}{(\beta + x^\gamma)^{\alpha+1}}$	Complicated
Alpha-stable	Does not exist	$\phi(t) = \begin{cases} \exp\left(-|\sigma t|^\alpha (1 - i\beta(\text{sign } t)\tan\frac{\pi\alpha}{2}) + i\mu t\right), \\ \quad \alpha \neq 1 \\ \exp\left(-\sigma|t|(1 + i\beta\frac{2}{\pi}(\text{sign } t)\ln|t|) + i\mu t\right), \\ \quad \alpha = 1 \end{cases}$

Definition of Characteristic Functions

A characteristic function is the function that performs a mapping from the real plane to the complex plane: $\phi : \Re \longmapsto \mathbb{C}$. A characteristic function of the distribution function $F(x)$ around a particular point t $(-\infty < t < +\infty)$ for a random variable X is the expectation of a transformed variable e^{itX}, in which i is the complex number $\sqrt{-1}$:

$$\phi(t) := \mathbb{E}[e^{itX}] = \int_{-\infty}^{+\infty} e^{itx}\, dF(x).$$

---

where $d_0 = 1$, $d_{n+1} = \dfrac{\gamma d_n + \sum_{k=1}^{n} (-1)^k \zeta(k+1) d_{n-k}}{n+1}$, $n \geq 0$, in which γ is the Euler's constant, $\zeta(r) = \sum_{n=1}^{\infty} n^{-r}$ is the zeta function, and H_ℓ are the Hermite polynomials.

If X is a continuous random variable with density $f(x)$, then

$$\phi(t) = \int_{-\infty}^{+\infty} e^{itx} f(x) dx,$$

and if X is discrete with probability mass function $p_n = P(X = x_n)$, $n = 1, 2, \ldots, \sum_{n=1}^{+\infty} p_n = 1$, then

$$\phi(t) = \sum_{n=1}^{+\infty} e^{itx_n} p_n.$$

Some Properties of Characteristic Functions

Useful properties of characteristic functions can be found in standard textbooks on probability.[22] We present several properties that are important in practical applications.

- Denote $\phi^{(k)}(0)$ the kth derivative of the characteristic function evaluated around zero. Then, if $\mathbb{E}[X^k] < \infty$, the kth raw moment of X can be obtained by

$$\mathbb{E}[X^k] = \frac{\phi^{(k)}(0)}{i^k}.$$

- If a and b are real constants and $Y = aX + b$, then

$$\phi_Y(t) = e^{itb} \times \phi_X(at).$$

- If X and Y are independent random variables with corresponding characteristic functions $\phi_X(t)$ and $\phi_Y(t)$, then the characteristic function of $X + Y$ is

$$\phi_{X+Y}(t) = \phi_X(t) \times \phi_Y(t).$$

- Random variables X and Y are independent if and only if the joint characteristic function is of the following form:

$$\phi_{X,Y}(s, t) = \phi_X(s) \times \phi_Y(t).$$

---

[22] See, for example, Grimmett and Stirzaker (2001) and Ushakov (1999).

Relation to Distribution Functions

As stated earlier, there is a one-to-one correspondence between the distribution function and the characteristic function. The following relation[23] allows one to recover the density from the characteristic function:

$$f(x) = \frac{1}{2\pi} \int_{-\infty}^{+\infty} e^{-itx} \phi(t) dt.$$

REFERENCES

BIS (2001), "Working Paper on the Regulatory Treatment of Operational Risk," www.BIS.org.

BIS (2006), "International Convergence of Capital Measurement and Capital Standards," www.BIS.org.

Brown, R. J. (2005), *Private Real Estate Investment: Data Analysis and Decision Making*, Elsevier Academic Press, San Diego.

Chernobai, A., Menn, C., Rachev, S. T., and Trück, S. (2005), Estimation of Operational Value-at-Risk in the Presence of Minimum Collection Thresholds, Technical report, University of California at Santa Barbara.

Chernobai, A., and Rachev, S. T. (2004), Stable Modelling of Operational Risk, in M. G. Cruz, ed., "Operational Risk Modelling and Analysis. Theory and Practice," RISK Books, London, pp. 139–169.

Cizek, P., Härdle, W., and Weron, R., eds (2005), *Statistical Tools for Finance and Insurance*, Springer, Heidelberg.

DuMouchel, W. (1971), Stable Distributions in Statistical Inference, PhD thesis, Yale University.

DuMouchel, W. (1973), "Stable Distributions in Statistical Inference: 1. Symmetric Stable Distribution Compared to Other Symmetric Long-Tailed Distributions," *Journal of the American Statistical Association* 68, pp. 469–477.

Fama, E. F. (1963), "Mandelbrot and the Stable Paretian Hypothesis," *Journal of Business* 36, pp. 420–429.

Fama, E. F. (1965a), "Portfolio Analysis in a Stable Paretian Market," Management Science, January.

Fama, E. F. (1965b), "The Behavior of Stock-Market Prices," *Journal of Business* 38(1), pp. 34–105.

Grimmett, G., and Stirzaker, D. (2001), *Probability and Random Processes*, Oxford University Press, New York.

Kogon, S. M., and William, B. W. (1998), "Characteristic Function Based Estimation of Stable Distribution Parameters," in R. J. Adler, R. E. Feldman and M. S. Taqqu, eds, *A Practical Guide to Heavy Tails: Statistical Techniques and Applications*, Birkhäuser, Boston, pp. 311–336.

---

[23]This relation is followed from the Fourier inversion theorem.

Leipnik, R. B. (1991), "On Lognormal Random Variables: I—the Characteristic Function," *Journal of the Australian Mathematical Society, Series B* 32, pp. 327–347.

Medova, E. A., and Kuriacou, M. N. (2001), Extremes in Operational Risk Management, Technical report, Center for Financial Research, University of Cambridge.

Menn, C., and Rachev, S. T. (2006), "Calibrated FFT-Based Density Approximations for Alpha-Stable Distributions," *Computational Statistics and Data Analysis* 50, pp. 1891–1904.

Nolan, J. P. (1997), "Numerical Calculation of Stable Densities and Distribution Functions," *Communications in Statistics—Stochastic Models* 13, pp. 759–774.

Press, S. J. (1972), "Estimation of Univariate and Multivariate Stable Distributions," *Journal of the American Statistical Association* 67, pp. 842–846.

Rachev, S. T., ed. (2003), *Handbook of Heavy Tailed Distributions in Finance*, Elsevier, Amsterdam.

Rachev, S. T., Menn, C., and Fabozzi, F. J. (2005), *Fat-Tailed and Skewed Asset Return Distributions: Implications for Risk Management, Portfolio Selection, and Option Pricing*, John Wiley & Sons Hoboken, New Jersey.

Rachev, S. T., and Mittnik, S. (2000), *Stable Paretian Models in Finance*, John Wiley & Sons, New York.

Samorodnitsky, G., and Taqqu, M. S. (1994), *Stable Non-Gaussian Random Processes: Stochastic Models with Infinite Variance*, Chapman & Hall, London.

Stoyanov, S., and Racheva-Iotova, B. (2004a), "Univariate Stable Laws in the Field of Finance—Approximation of Density and Distribution Functions," *Journal of Concrete and Applicable Mathematics* 2(1).

Stoyanov, S., and Racheva-Iotova, B. (2004b), "Univariate Stable Laws in the Field of Finance—Parameter Estimation," *Journal of Concrete and Applicable Mathematics* 2(4).

Thorin, O., and Wikstad, N. (1977), "Calculation of Ruin Probabilities when the Claim Distribution is Lognormal," *Astin Bulletin* 9, pp. 231–246.

Ushakov, N. G. (1999), *Selected Topics in Characteristic Functions*, VSP, Utrecht.

Zolotarev, V. M. (1986), *One-dimensional Stable Distributions*, Translations of Mathematical Monographs, vol. 65., American Mathematical Society, Providence, RI.

CHAPTER **8**

Extreme Value Theory

A risk manager is often concerned with the distribution of the losses that are of low frequency and of high severity. Such types of losses lie in the upper tail of the loss distribution. The field of study that treats the distribution of very high quantiles of data is *extreme value theory* (EVT). The first model, *block maxima model*, examines the behavior of the maxima in equally spaced time blocks. A common application of EVT in modeling operational risk is using it to analyze the behavior of losses that exceed a certain high threshold (*peak over threshold model*). In this chapter, we give some theoretical background and properties of distributions used in EVT modeling. Advantages and limitations of EVT as a risk modeling tool will be presented. We then discuss some empirical studies.

BLOCK MAXIMA MODEL

Consider time series of operational loss data divided into independent blocks (e.g., one block equals one year) of the same size. The block maxima model focuses on the distribution of the largest events taken from each block. See Figure 8.1.

For very large extreme loss observations x, the limiting distribution of such normalized maxima is the *generalized extreme value* (GEV) distribution:

$$
F(x) = \begin{cases} \exp\left\{-(1 + \xi\frac{x-\mu}{\beta})^{-\frac{1}{\xi}}\right\} & \text{if } \xi \neq 0, \\ \exp\left\{-e^{-\frac{x-\mu}{\beta}}\right\} & \text{if } \xi = 0, \end{cases}
$$

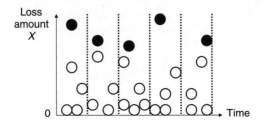

FIGURE 8.1   Block maxima model.

where $1 + \xi\frac{x-\mu}{\beta} > 0$ and

$$
\begin{aligned}
x > \mu - \frac{\beta}{\xi} &\qquad \text{if} \quad \xi > 0, \\
x < \mu - \frac{\beta}{\xi} &\qquad \text{if} \quad \xi < 0, \\
-\infty < x < +\infty &\qquad \text{if} \quad \xi = 0,
\end{aligned}
$$

x refers to the maxima, $-\infty < \mu < +\infty$, and $\beta > 0$. μ is the location parameter (often assumed to be 0), β is the scale parameter, and ξ is the shape parameter.

The inverse of the GEV distribution has a simple form $F^{-1}(p) = \mu - \beta \log(-\log p)$ for $\xi = 0$ and $F^{-1}(p) = \mu - \beta(1 - (-\log p)^{-\xi})/\xi$ for $\xi \neq 0$, $p \in (0, 1)$. Therefore, a GEV random variate can be simulated using the inverse transform method by $X = \mu - \beta\log(-\log U)$ for $\xi = 0$ and $X = \mu - \beta(1 - (-\log U)^{-\xi})/\xi$ for $\xi \neq 0$, where U is distributed uniformly on the $(0, 1)$ interval.

PEAK OVER THRESHOLD MODEL

In the *peak over threshold* (POT) model, the focus of the statistical analysis is put on the observations that lie above a certain high threshold (see Figure 8.2).

Generalized Pareto Distribution

Let X be a random variable representing operational losses with cumulative distribution function F. Let u be a certain high threshold. Then F_u is the distribution of losses above this threshold and is called the *conditional excess distribution function* (see the bottom of Figure 8.3 for an illustration):

$$
F_u(x) = P(X - u \leq x | X > u) = \frac{F(u + x) - F(u)}{1 - F(u)}.
$$

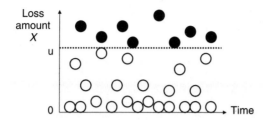

FIGURE 8.2   Peak over threshold model.

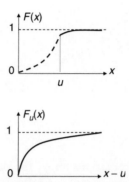

FIGURE 8.3   Illustration of conditional excess distribution.

We skip some technical details and state the final result. For a sufficiently large threshold u, the conditional excess distribution function F_u of such extreme observations is summarized by the generalized Pareto distribution (GPD).[1] The cumulative distribution function of GPD is as follows:

$$
F(x) = \begin{cases} 1 - \left(1 + \xi \frac{x-\mu}{\beta}\right)^{-\frac{1}{\xi}} & \text{if } \xi \neq 0, \\ 1 - e^{-\frac{x-\mu}{\beta}} & \text{if } \xi = 0, \end{cases}
$$

where

$$
\begin{aligned} x &\geq \mu & \text{if } \xi \geq 0, \\ \mu &\leq x \leq \mu - \tfrac{\beta}{\xi} & \text{if } \xi < 0, \end{aligned}
$$

---

[1] For details on EVT and the POT model, see, for example, Pickands (1975) and Embrechts, Klüppelberg, and Mikosch (1997).

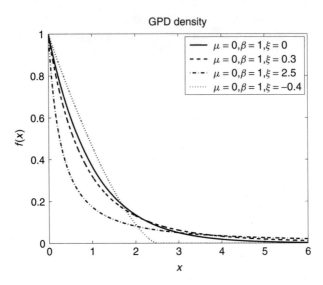

FIGURE 8.4 Illustration of the GPD density with varying shape parameter ξ.

x refers to the extreme observations above the threshold, $-\infty < \mu < +\infty$, and $\beta > 0$. μ is the location parameter (often assumed to be 0), β is the scale parameter, and ξ is the shape parameter. When $\xi > 0$, we have a heavy-tailed distribution,[2] $\xi = 0$ refers to the exponential distribution, and $\xi = -1$ corresponds to the uniform distribution. Figure 8.4 illustrates examples of the GPD density for some values of ξ.[3]

Raw moments are calculated as

$$\mathbb{E}(X^k) = \frac{\beta^k}{\xi^{k+1}} \frac{\Gamma(1/\xi - k)}{\Gamma(1 + 1/\xi)} k!, \quad \text{for} \quad \xi < 1/k,$$

and so the population mean and the variance are calculated by

$$\text{mean}(X) = \mu + \frac{\beta}{1 - \xi}, \quad \text{for} \quad \xi < 1,$$

$$\text{var}(X) = \frac{\beta^2}{(1 - \xi)^2 (1 - 2\xi)} \quad \text{for} \quad \xi < 1/2.$$

---

[2]The GPD with $\xi > 0$ is a reparameterized Pareto distribution. See Chapter 6 for a discussion of the Pareto and other loss distributions.

[3]More illustrative examples can be found in Chapter 3 in Embrechts, Klüppelberg, and Mikosch (1997).

The inverse of the GPD distribution has a simple form $F^{-1}(p) = \mu - \beta \log(1 - p)$ for $\xi = 0$ and $F^{-1}(p) = \mu - \beta(1 - p^{-\xi})/\xi$ for $\xi \neq 0$, $p \in (0, 1)$. Therefore, a GPD random variate can be simulated using the inverse transform method by $X = \mu - \beta\log(1 - U)$ for $\xi = 0$ and $X = \mu - \beta(1 - U^{-\xi})/\xi$ for $\xi \neq 0$, where U is distributed uniformly on the $(0, 1)$ interval.

Choosing the High Threshold

As we have discussed, data follow the GPD distribution when they exceed a certain threshold u. How does one decide on the choice of the threshold? The choice of the threshold essentially involves solving an optimization problem. On the one hand, GPD is designed to fit extreme events, so in order not to violate the asymptotic basis of the model, this should result in a limited sample size. On the other hand, if the number of upper-tail observations is chosen too small, then the choice of the threshold may result in estimators with a high variance. Unfortunately, this appears to be a difficult task and no commonly accepted analytic solution exists at this time. Nevertheless, practitioners and researchers often rely on the visual observation of the *mean excess plot*.[4]

The *mean excess function* is defined as the mean of all differences between the values of the data exceeding u and u, for different values of u:

$$e(u) = \mathbb{E}[X - u | X > u].$$

Plotting the mean excess function against various threshold levels u will result in the mean excess plot. As an example, Figure 8.5 illustrates the mean excess plot of the external type operational loss data that was analyzed in the empirical part of Chapter 6.

For the GPD, the mean excess function is

$$e(u) = \frac{\beta}{1 - \xi} + \frac{\xi}{1 - \xi}u,$$

which means that for $0 < \xi < 1$ and $\beta + \xi u > 0$, the mean excess plot should look like an upward-sloping straight line: The heavier the tail of the loss distribution (i.e., the closer ξ is to 1), the steeper the plot. An upward-sloping mean excess plot indicates a Pareto-like distribution. Similarly, a horizontal mean excess plot would indicate that the distribution is exponential.

---

[4]Other methods for finding high thresholds are described in Coles (2001), Danielson and DeVries (1997), Pictet, Dacorogna, and Muller (1996), Jansen and DeVries (1991), and Beirlant, Teugels, and Vynckier (1996).

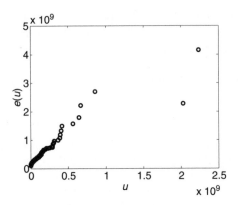

FIGURE 8.5   Mean excess plot for external operational loss data.

For $\xi < 0$, the distribution is very thin-tailed (and has a bounded support) and the plot is downward-sloping. In the example illustrated in Figure 8.5, the distribution is clearly heavy-tailed. Multiple examples of mean excess plots can be found in Embrechts, Klüppelberg, and Mikosch (1997), McNeil and Saladin (1997), and Medova and Kuriacou (2001), among others.

    Thus, the general rule of thumb for choosing u is to choose u so that the mean excess plot is roughly linear for $x \geq u$. A drawback of such methodology is that the unknown parameters are very sensitive to the choice of the threshold.

Value-at-Risk under Peak over Threshold Model

One can easily calculate the value-at-risk (VaR)[5] under the POT model using the conditional mean excess function and the expression for the inverse of the GPD function that were presented earlier. If one uses the empirical distribution function for the losses below the threshold, then $(n - N_u)/n$ losses are below the threshold u and N_u losses are above the threshold u, where n is the total number of loss events in a one-year period. One hence arrives at the expression for VaR at the $1 - \alpha$ confidence level, as follows:[6]

$$\widehat{\text{VaR}}_{1-\alpha} = u - \frac{\hat{\beta}}{\hat{\xi}}\left(1 - \left(\frac{N_u}{n(1 - \alpha)}\right)^{\hat{\xi}}\right).$$

---

[5]The notions of VaR and CVaR are reviewed in Chapter 11.
[6]For details, see, for example, Embrechts, Furrer, and Kaufmann (2003).

Similarly, the conditional value-at-risk (CVaR) at the $1 - \alpha$ confidence level can be found using[7]

$$\widehat{\text{CVaR}}_{1-\alpha} = \widehat{\text{VaR}}_{1-\alpha}\left(\frac{1}{1-\hat{\xi}} + \frac{\hat{\beta}-\hat{\xi}u}{(1-\hat{\xi})\widehat{\text{VaR}}_{1-\alpha}}\right).$$

ESTIMATING THE SHAPE PARAMETER

Operational loss data sets often lack a sufficient number of observations in the upper tail. Hence, the estimation of the parameters of the GPD and GEV distribution may be complicated. In particular, it is important to accurately estimate the shape parameter ξ. The parametric Maximum Likelihood estimator (discussed in Chapter 6) may be convenient but not optimal. Instead, two nonparametric estimators can be used: the Hill estimator and the Pickands estimator.[8]

Hill Estimator

Suppose that $X_{(1)} \geq X_{(2)} \geq \ldots \geq X_{(n)}$ is the ordered data (i.e., order statistics). The Hill estimator[9] of the shape parameter ξ is estimated by

$$\hat{\xi}^{\text{H}} = \frac{1}{k}\sum_{j=1}^{k}\ln X_j - \ln X_{(k)}.$$

Suppose we have a data sample[10] consisting of 12 extreme observations (in thousands of dollars):

$$x = \{600, 400, 260, 250, 240, 165, 120, 115, 86, 83, 75, 52\}.$$

Then, for values of k from 1 to 12, the Hill estimator produces the shape parameter estimates

$$\hat{\xi} = \{0, 0.2027, 0.4223, 0.3462, 0.3096, 0.5702, 0.7617, 0.7038, 0.8839,$$

$$0.8274, 0.8444, 1.1097\}.$$

Figure 8.6 illustrates the Hill plot.

---

[7]For details, see, for example, Chavez-Demoulin and Embrechts (2004).
[8]Financial time series, such as daily log-returns, often exhibit tail behavior with the shape parameter between one-fourth and one-third.
[9]The Hill estimator was introduced by Hill (1975).
[10]A similar example can be found in Cruz (2002), Chapter 4.

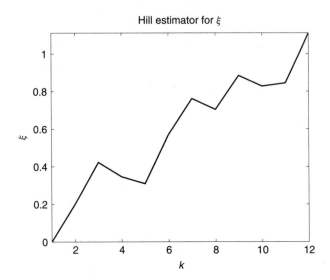

FIGURE 8.6 Hill plot for an exemplary data sample.

The Hill estimator is particularly useful for distributions with a power tail decay.[11] Some asymptotic properties of the Hill estimator can be found in Embrechts, Klüppelberg, and Mikosch (1997).

Pickands Estimator

The Pickands estimator[12] of the shape parameter ξ is estimated by

$$\hat{\xi}^{\mathrm{P}} = \frac{1}{\ln 2} \ln \frac{X_{(k)} - X_{(2k)}}{X_{(2k)} - X_{(4k)}}.$$

Clearly, the Pickands estimator requires a higher number of extreme observations than the Hill estimator. For the same example that we used to illustrate the Hill estimator, with a sample $x = 600, 400, 260, 250, 240, 165, 120, 115, 86, 83, 75, 52$ (in thousands of dollars), we obtain the Pickands estimates corresponding to the threshold level u equal to each of the top three observations of $\hat{\xi} = \{0.4150, 0.1520, -0.2503\}$.

Some asymptotic properties of the Pickands estimator can be found in Dekkers and de Haan (1989) and Embrechts, Klüppelberg, and Mikosch (1997).

---

[11] See Chapter 6, in which we discussed some tail properties.
[12] The Pickands estimator was introduced by Pickands (1975). Extensions of Pickands estimator are given in Rachev and Mittnik (2000).

ADVANTAGES AND LIMITATIONS OF EXTREME VALUE THEORY

We follow primarily Diebold, Schuermann, and Stroughair (1998) and Embrechts (2000) to list some advantages and limitations of EVT in modeling operational risk.

The advantages are as follows:

- EVT provides theoretical properties of the limiting distribution of extreme events. Hence, it provides direct treatment of the events of low frequency and high severity, both near the boundary of the range of observed data, and beyond.
- POT model can be used to deal with catastrophic losses that lie beyond a high threshold such as VaR.
- Both theoretical and computational tools are available. The tail of loss distribution has a functional form determined *a priori*.
- Nonparametric estimators of the shape parameter—Hill estimator and Pickands estimator—possess nice asymptotic properties.

Some pitfalls of EVT can be summarized as follows.

- In the POT model, interpretations and estimations are based on a small sample of observations.[13] This may lead to biased estimators that are very sensitive to the choice of the high threshold.
- The choice of the high threshold in the POT model that determines extreme losses is based primarily on the visual examination of the mean excess plot. More rigorous techniques must be developed.
- The analysis based on EVT relies on the distributional properties of extreme losses and puts little weight on the properties of low- and medium-scale observations.

EMPIRICAL STUDIES WITH OPERATIONAL LOSS DATA

In this section we present some applications of EVT to operational loss data. Most empirical studies investigate the POT model.[14] The majority

---

[13] The Hill estimator can be used to estimate the shape parameter of the alpha-stable distribution. However, Rachev and Mittnik (2000) showed that the minimum sample size required for the Hill estimator to produce reasonable results is 500,000 data points, even if the sample is taken from an alpha-stable distribution with the shape parameter $\alpha = 1.8$ (i.e., the distribution of the data is not very heavy-tailed but is close to Gaussian). See Chapter 7 on the alpha-stable distributions.

[14] Other studies not presented here include those by Lewis (2004), Di Clemente and Romano (2004), Medova (2002), Ebnöther, Vanini, McNeil, and

of studies conclude that the shape parameter ξ of the GPD exceeds unity, suggesting that both the first and the second moments of the loss distribution are infinite.[15]

Cruz Study of Fraud Loss Data

Cruz (2002) applied the block maxima model to fraud data from an undisclosed source, for a period of five years from 1992 to 1996. He used the Hill estimator to estimate the shape parameter and the probability weighted moments estimator to estimate μ and β. Table 8.1 reports parameter estimates and goodness-of-fit statistics (Kolmogorov-Smirnov statistic is denoted by KS and Kuiper statistic[16] is denoted by V). In 1994 and 1996, ξ exceeds 1, indicating a very heavy-tailed GEV distribution (with infinite first moment).

Cruz also tested the block maxima model using legal loss data for a business unit. He applied the same technique for parameter estimation. Sample descriptive statistics and the GEV parameter estimates are shown in Table 8.2. Comparing the fit of the GEV distribution with Pareto, Weibull, and exponential distributions applied to the entire data set, Cruz concluded that GEV resulted in a superior fit.

Moscadelli Study with 2002 LDCE Data

Moscadelli (2004) explores the data collected by the Risk Management Group (RMG) of the Basel Committee in June 2002's Operational Risk Loss Data Collection Exercise (LDCE).[17]

Antolinez-Fehr (2001), Chapelle, Crama, Hübner, and Peters (2005), de Fontnouvelle, DeJesus-Rueff, Jordan, and Rosengren (2003a,b), Embrechts, Furrer, and Kaufmann (2003), Embrechts, Kaufmann, and Samorodnitsky (2004), Medova and Kuriacou (2001), and Chavez-Demoulin, Embrechts, and Nešlehová (2005), among others. For general financial loss models, the POT model has been examined in Embrechts, Klüppelberg, and Mikosch (1997), McNeil (1996), McNeil (1999), McNeil and Saladin (1997), McNeil and Saladin (1998), McNeil and Frey (1999), Diebold, Schuermann, and Stroughair (1998), Embrechts, Resnick, and Samorodnitsky (1999), Embrechts (2000, 2004), Gilli and Këllezi (2003), Gettinby, Sinclair, Power, and Brown (2004), Huisman, Koedijk, Kool, and Palm (2001), Marinelli, d'Addona, and Rachev (2006), among others.

[15]This creates problems when estimating VaR and CVaR, as they may produce unrealistically high values. A possible solution would be to use robust estimators; see the discussion in Chapter 12.

[16]KS and V tests tend to put more weight on the central part of the distribution. KS, V, and other goodness-of-fit statistics will be discussed in Chapter 10.

[17]See Chapter 3 for a review of the Basel II Capital Accord. See also BIS (2003) on the description of the data.

TABLE 8.1 Estimates of the parameters of the GEV distribution and corresponding goodness-of-fit statistic values in the Cruz study with fraud loss data

	1992	1993	1994	1995	1996
1. GEV Parameter Estimates					
ξ	0.9593	0.9941	1.5658	0.6795	1.0706
β	147,105.40	298,067.91	612,300.60	97,262.00	216,539.66
μ	410,279.77	432,211.40	1,101,869.17	215,551.84	445,660.38
2. Goodness-of-Fit Statistics					
KS test	0.110	0.090	0.287	0.105	0.156
V test	0.112	0.175	0.352	0.150	0.251

Source: Cruz (2002, p. 82), with modifications.

TABLE 8.2 Sample descriptive statistics and GEV parameter estimates in the Cruz study with legal loss data

1. Sample Descriptive Statistics		2. GEV Parameter Estimates	
mean	439,725.99	ξ	0.60
st.deviation	538,403.93	β	305,088.17
skewness	4.42	μ	1,085,091.15
kurtosis	23.59		

Source: Cruz (2002, p. 84), with modifications.

Moscadelli (2004) applies the POT model to estimate the operational risk capital charge. The threshold level u was chosen based on an examination of the mean excess plot. Because it fairly resembled a straight line beginning from low values of u, Moscadelli chose the 90th empirical percentile as the average cutoff point above which the GPD model was applied. Table 8.3 shows the model parameters, goodness-of-fit test statistics, and the VaR estimates for the eight business lines. In all samples except BL7 and BL8, the mean of the GPD is infinite as a consequence of the value of ξ being above unity.

Moscadelli further carries out backtesting of his VaR models under the POT, lognormal, and Gumbel models (estimates of the latter two are omitted here) and concludes that the POT model is rarely violated in practice compared to the other models. This can be explained by the fact that the lognormal and Gumbel models tend to underestimate the heaviness in the tail of the loss distribution.

TABLE 8.3 Estimates of the threshold value, GPD parameters, goodness-of-fit statistic values, and value-at-risk measures in the Moscadelli study with 2002 LDCE data

	BL1	BL2	BL3	BL4	BL5	BL6	BL7	BL8
1. Sample Size and Threshold								
n	423	5,132	28,882	3,414	1,852	1,490	1,109	3,267
N_u	42	512	1,000	315	187	158	107	326
u (euro '000)	400.28	193.00	247.00	270.00	110.00	201.66	235.00	149.51
2. GPD Parameter Estimates (μ; equals u).								
ξ	1.19	1.17	1.01	1.39	1.23	1.22	0.85	0.98
β (euro '000)	774	254	233	412	107	243	314	124
3. Goodness-of-Fit Statistics								
KS test	0.099	0.027	0.020	0.058	0.028	0.064	0.060	0.033
AD test	0.486	0.508	0.675	1.541	0.247	0.892	0.217	0.291
4. Value-at-Risk								
95%VaR (euro '000)	1,222	463	176	668	230	501	511	272
99%VaR (euro '000)	9,743	3,178	826	6,479	1,518	3,553	2,402	1,229
99.9%VaR (euro '000)	154,523	47,341	8,356	159,671	25,412	58,930	17,825	11,539

Source: Moscadelli (2004, pp. 37, 40, and 49), with modifications.

De Fontnouvelle, Rosengren, and Jordan Study with 2002 LDCE Data

De Fontnouvelle, Rosengren, and Jordan (2005) examine the same data set analyzed by Moscadelli (2004). They limited their analysis to the data collected from six banks, and performed the analysis on a bank-by-bank basis, rather than pooling the data as was done in Moscadelli (2004). They focused on the data from four business lines:

BL2: Trading and Sales

BL3: Retail Banking

BL5: Payment and Settlement

BL7: Asset Management

and five event types:

ET1: Internal Fraud

ET2: External Fraud

ET3: Employment Practices and Workplace Safety

ET4: Clients, Products, and Business Practices

ET5: Execution, Delivery, and Process Management

De Fontnouvelle, Rosengren, and Jordan compared the GPD model with other loss distributions. Table 8.4 reports the estimates of the shape

TABLE 8.4 Estimates of the shape parameter ξ in the de Fontnouvelle, Rosengren, and Jordan study with LDCE data

	Bank 1*	Bank 2	Bank 3	Bank 4	Bank 5	Bank 6
All BL and ET	1.28	0.87	0.99	0.92	0.97	1.01
ET1	1.24	1.31		1.10		1.02
ET2	1.17	0.79	0.63	0.69	0.86	0.93
ET3	0.50	0.42		−0.15		0.50
ET4	1.36	1.25				1.46
ET5	1.42	0.71	0.94	1.00	0.96	0.93
BL2		0.68	1.18	0.49		0.42
BL3	1.15	1.09	0.55	0.94	0.99	0.93
BL5		1.06			1.07	1.03
BL7		0.49	0.96		0.37	1.64

*Blank spaces indicate insufficient data to perform the analysis.
Source: de Fontnouvelle, Rosengren, and Jordan (2005, p. 35).

parameter ξ for six banks (the estimates of u and β are not reported to preserve confidentiality of the banks). De Fontnouvelle, Rosengren, and Jordan argue that the parameter estimates suggest that the GPD is not a plausible assumption. They come to this conclusion because the estimate for the shape parameter exceeded unity in many instances, meaning that the estimates of expected aggregate loss and regulatory capital would be unreasonably high. As a result, they suggest employing different techniques to find the threshold level u: in particular, they suggest using a regression-type Hill estimator[18] that produces a reasonable shape parameter estimate of around 0.68.

Chavez-Demoulin and Embrechts Study of Operational Loss Data

Chavez-Demoulin and Embrechts (2004) analyze three types of operational loss data for a 10-year period.[19] The data were modified to preserve confidentiality. Table 8.5 reports the GPD parameter estimates and the corresponding values for VaR and CVaR. The threshold level of $u = 0.4$ was fixed for all three loss types. It is evident from the estimates of the shape parameter that the distribution for the Type 3 loss is less heavy-tailed than

TABLE 8.5   GPD Parameter Estimates, VaR, and CVaR Estimates for Three Loss Types in the Chavez-Demoulin and Embrechts Study

	Type 1	Type 2	Type 3
1. GPD Parameter Estimates			
u	0.4	0.4	0.4
ξ	0.7	0.7	0.3
β	1	1.8	1.3
2. VaR and CVaR			
99%VaR	40.4	48.4	11.9
99%CVaR	166.4	148.5	18.8

Source: Chavez-Demoulin and Embrechts (2004, p. 11), with modifications.

----

[18] See Huisman, Koedijk, Kool, and Palm (2001) for a discussion of the method.
[19] For detailed study with the same data set, see also Chavez-Demoulin, Embrechts, and Nešlehová (2005).

those of the other two types. The value of ξ was estimated to be less than unity for all three types, suggesting that the distribution possesses a finite mean—a property convenient in estimating CVaR:

Dutta and Perry Study of 2004 LDCE Operational Loss Data

Using data collected from the 2004 LDCE for U.S. banks,[20] Dutta and Perry (2006) investigate the implications of various distributional assumptions of operational loss data on the amount of regulatory capital estimated. A total of 23 institutions participated in this exercise. They narrowed down their data set to seven institutions reporting at least 1,000 observations of $10,000 or more of operational losses. To preserve confidentiality of the banks' data, the banks were identified as Bank A, B, C, D, E, F, and G, respectively.

Dutta and Perry use the Hill estimator to estimate the shape parameters of the loss distributions for each of the seven banks. They set the high threshold values at the top 5% and top 10% of the data. Later, they estimate the regulatory capital amount using a 99.9% confidence level. Table 8.6 reports the estimates of the shape parameter ξ and the capital estimates as a percentage of total assets. Because for more than half of the banks in their study (4 out of 7) the shape parameter exceeded unity, the resulting capital estimates were unreasonably high. For roughly half of all banks, the operational capital amounted to nearly a third of total assets, and for nearly a quarter of all banks, the operational capital exceeded 50% of the total value of assets. Moreover, the estimates appeared to be unstable and highly sensitive to the choice of the high threshold: for the same bank, different cutoff levels resulted in different Hill estimates of the shape parameter.

SUMMARY OF KEY CONCEPTS

- Extreme value theory (EVT) is a field of study in statistics that focuses on the properties and behavior of extreme events. Two models frequently used in operational risk modeling are (1) the block maxima model and (2) the peak over threshold (POT) model.
- The block maxima model can be used to characterize the behavior of the highest operational losses, each taken from an equal-size time interval. The limiting distribution describing such extreme events is the generalized extreme value (GEV) distribution.

---

[20]The 2004 LDCE is also known as Quantitative Impact Study 4 (QIS4). Unlike previous such studies, this study was conducted by several countries separately from each other. Descriptions of QIS2, QIS3, QIS4, and QIS5 are presented in Chapter 3.

TABLE 8.6 Hill estimates of the shape parameter ξ for the cutoff levels 5% and 10% and summary statistics of the regulatory operational risk capital estimates as percentage of total assets

	Threshold: 5%	Threshold: 10%
1. Hill Estimates of ξ		
Bank A	1.03	1.07
Bank B	0.92	0.89
Bank C	1.12	1.01
Bank D	1.28	1.20
Bank E	1.10	1.06
Bank F	0.83	0.98
Bank G	0.79	0.91
2. Sample Statistics of Capital Estimates (% of total assets)		
25th percentile	5.83	11.88
median	33.57	23.04
75th percentile	48.20	45.19

Source: Dutta and Perry (2006, p. 37).

- The POT model targets the behavior of the losses that lie beyond a high threshold. The limiting distribution describing such extreme events is the generalized Pareto distribution (GPD). Several approaches are suggested for determining the high threshold level, with the most common approach based on the visual examination of the mean excess plot.
- Estimating the shape parameter of the GEV distribution and GPD is complicated due to limited sample sizes of extreme operational losses. Therefore, maximum likelihood procedures may not be optimal. Common nonparametric estimators of the shape parameter include the Hill estimator and the Pickands estimator.
- Advantages of the EVT include focusing the analysis on the low frequency/high severity and catastrophic events, availability of analytic expression for the loss distribution, and easily available techniques for the estimation of the model parameters. Pitfalls include the possibility of bias in the model parameters due to small data samples, no commonly available analytic procedures for determining the high threshold in the POT model, and little attention devoted to the properties of low- and medium-scale operational losses.

■ Empirical studies of operational loss data indicate that the shape parameter often exceeds unity in magnitude. This means that, apart from the infinite variance, the resulting estimates of the aggregate expected loss and the regulatory capital charge may be unrealistically high.

REFERENCES

Beirlant, J., Teugels, J., and Vynckier, P. (1996), *Practical Analysis of Extreme Values*, Leuven University Press, Belgium.

BIS (2003), "The 2002 Loss Data Collection Exercise for Operational Risk: Summary of the Data Collected," www.BIS.org.

Chapelle, A., Crama, Y., Hübner, G., and Peters, J. (2005), Measuring and Managing Operational Risk in the Financial Sector: An Integrated Framework, Technical report, National Bank of Belgium.

Chavez-Demoulin, V. and Embrechts, P., (2004), Advanced Extremal Models for Operational Risk, Technical report, ETH Zürich.

Chavez-Demoulin, V., Embrechts, P. and Nešlehová, J. (2005), Quantitative Models for Operational Risk: Extremes, Dependence, and Aggregation, Technical report, ETH Zürich.

Coles, S. (2001), *An Introduction to Statistical Modeling of Extreme Events*, Springer-Verlag, London.

Cruz, M. G. (2002), *Modeling, Measuring and Hedging Operational Risk*, John Wiley & Sons, New York, Chichester.

Danielson, J., and DeVries, C. (1997), "Robust Tail Index and Quantile Estimation," *Journal of Empirical Finance* 4, pp. 23–32.

de Fontnouvelle, P., DeJesus-Rueff, V., Jordan, J., and Rosengren, E. (2003a), Using Loss Data to Quantify Operational Risk, Technical report, Federal Reserve Bank of Boston.

de Fontnouvelle, P., DeJesus-Rueff, V., Jordan, J., and Rosengren, E. (2003b), Capital and Risk: New Evidence on Implicatins of Large Operational Losses, Technical report, Federal Reserve Bank of Boston.

de Fontnouvelle, P., Rosengren, E., and Jordan, J. (2005), Implications of Alternative Operational Risk Modeling Techniques, Technical report, Federal Reserve Bank of Boston and Fitch Risk.

Dekkers, A. L. M., and de Haan, L. (1989), "On the Estimation of the Extreme-Value Index and Large Quantile Estimation," *Annals of Statistics* 17, pp. 1795–1832.

Di Clemente, A., and Romano, C. (2004), "A Copula-Extreme Value Theory Approach for Modelling Operational Risk", in M. G. Cruz, ed., *Operational Risk Modelling and Analysis. Theory and Practice*, RISK Books, London, pp. 189–208.

Diebold, F. X., Schuermann, T., and Stroughair, J. D. (1998), Pitfalls and Opportunities in the Use of Extreme Value Theory in Risk Management, Technical report, Wharton School, University of Pennsylvania.

Dutta, K., and Perry, J. (2006), A Tale of Tails: An Empirical Analysis of Loss Distribution Models for Estimating Operational Risk Capital, Technical Report 06-13, Federal Reserve Bank of Boston.

Ebnöther, S., Vanini, P., McNeil, A. J. and Antolinez-Fehr, P. (2001), Modeling Operational Risk, Technical report, ETH Zürich.

Embrechts, P. (2000), "Extreme Value Theory: Potential and Limitations as an Integrated Risk Management Tool," *Derivatives Use, Trading and Regulation* 6, pp. 449–456.

Embrechts, P. (2004), "Extremes in Economics and Economics of Extremes", in B. Finkenstädt and H. Rootzén, eds, *Extreme Values in Finance, Telecommunications and the Environment*, Chapman & Hall, London, pp. 169–183.

Embrechts, P., Furrer, H., and Kaufmann, R. (2003), "Quantifying Regulatory Capital For Operational Risk," *Derivatives Use, Trading, and Regulation* 9(3), pp. 217–233.

Embrechts, P., Kaufmann, P., and Samorodnitsky, G. (2004), "Ruin Theory Revisited: Stochastic Models for Operational Risk", in C. Bernadell, P. Cardon, J. Coche, F. X. Diebold and S. Manganelli, eds, *Risk Management for Central Bank Foreign Reserves*, European Central Bank, Frankfurt, pp. 243–261.

Embrechts, P., Klüppelberg, C., and Mikosch, T. (1997), *Modeling Extremal Events for Insurance and Finance*, Springer-Verlag, Berlin.

Embrechts, P., Resnick, S. I., and Samorodnitsky, G. (1999), "Extreme Value Theory as a Risk Management Tool," *North American Actuarial Journal* 3, pp. 30–41.

Gettinby, G. D., Sinclair, C. D., Power, D. M. and Brown, R. A. (2004), "An Analysis of the Distribution of Extreme Share Returns in the UK from 1975 to 2000," *Journal of Business Finance and Accounting* 31(5,6), pp. 607–645.

Gilli, M., and Këllezi, E. (2003), An Application of Extreme Value Theory for Measuring Risk, Technical report, University of Geneva and FAME.

Hill, B. M. (1975), "A Simple General Approach to Inference About the Tail of the Distribution," *Annals of Statistics* 3, pp. 1163–1174.

Huisman, R., Koedijk, K. G., Kool, C. J. M. and Palm, F. (2001), "Tail-Index Estimates in Small Samples," *Journal of Business and Economic Statistics* 19(1), pp. 208–216.

Jansen, D. W., and DeVries, C. (1991), "On the Frequency of Large Stock Returns: Putting Booms and Busts into Perspective," *Review of Economics and Statistics* 73, pp. 18–24.

Lewis, N. (2004), *Operational Risk with Excel and VBA*, John Wiley & Sons, Hoboken, New Jersey.

Marinelli, C., d'Addona, S., and Rachev, S. T. (2006), A Comparison of Some Univariate Models for Value-at-Risk and Expected Shortfall, Technical report, Universität Bonn.

McNeil, A. J. (1996), Estimating the Tails of Loss Severity Distributions Using Extreme Value Theory, Technical report, ETH Zürich.

McNeil, A. J. (1999), Extreme Value Theory for Risk Managers, Technical report, ETH Zürich.

McNeil, A. J., and Frey, R. (1999), Estimation of Tail-Related Risk Measures for Heteroscedastic Financial Time Series: an Extreme Value Approach, Technical report, ETH Zürich.

McNeil, A. J., and Saladin, T. (1997), The Peaks over Thresholds Method for Estimating High Quantiles of Loss Distributions, Technical report, ETH Zürich.

McNeil, A. J., and Saladin, T. (1998), Developing Scenarios for Future Extreme Losses using the POT Model, Technical report, ETH Zürich.

Medova, E. A. (2002), Operational Risk Capital Allocation and Integration of Risks, Technical report, Center for Financial Research, University of Cambridge.

Medova, E. A. and Kuriacou, M. N. (2001), Extremes in Operational Risk Management, Technical report, Center for Financial Research, University of Cambridge.

Moscadelli, M. (2004), The Modelling of Operational Risk: Experience with the Analysis of the Data Collected by the Basel Committee, Technical report, Bank of Italy.

Pickands, J. I. (1975), "Statistical Inference Using Extreme Order Statistics," *Annals of Statistics* 3, pp. 119–131.

Pictet, O., Dacorogna, M. and Muller, U. (1996), *Hill, Bootstrap and Jackknife Estimators for Heavy Tails*, Olsen & Associates.

Rachev, S. T., and Mittnik, S. (2000), *Stable Paretian Models in Finance*, John Wiley & Sons, New York.

CHAPTER 9

Truncated Distributions

I n an ideal scenario, the data collection process results in all operational
loss events being detected and duly recorded. However, the data recording
is subject to lower recording thresholds, so that only data above a certain
amount enter databases. In this sense, the data available for estimation
appear to be left-truncated. Left-truncation of the data must be appropriately
addressed in the estimation process, in order to determine a correct capital
charge.

In this chapter we discuss a methodology for the estimation of the
parameters of the severity and frequency distributions when some operational loss data are missing from the data set. We further explore the
implications of using a wrong approach (under which the truncation is
ignored) and correct approaches (under which the truncation is adequately
treated) on the resulting capital charge and present results of related empirical studies.

REPORTING BIAS PROBLEM

In the 2002 LDCE (Quantitative Impact Study 3) by the Basel Committee,
89 participating banks were asked to report information about the minimum cutoff levels that they used when recording operational loss data.
Table 9.1 reports the results. The majority of the banks set the cutoff level
at euro 10,000.

While for internal databases the minimum collection threshold is set
at approximately euro 10,000, for public (or external) databases and
consortiums, the minimum collection threshold is set at approximately \$1
million.[1]

---

[1]For example, the British Bankers Association (BBA) operational risk database has
a threshold of \$500,000 for retail and \$1 million for wholesale.

TABLE 9.1 Minimum cutoff thresholds used by 2002 LDCE participating banks. The information is based on 77 banks who provided information on the cutoff thresholds.

Minimum Cutoff Threshold (in Euro)	No. of Banks
Below 10,000 for all business lines	5
10,000:	59
For all business lines	57
For some business lines	2
Above 10,000:	13
For all business lines[a]	12
For some business lines[b]	1

[a]The cutoff thresholds ranged between euro 11,347 and euro 570,000.
[b]The minimum loss amounts ranged between euro 1,000 and euro 53,000.
Source: BIS (2003, p. 5), with modifications. Permission to use this table was obtained from the Basel Committee on Banking Supervision. The original table is available free of charge from the BIS website (www.BIS.org).

Such thresholds in the data-collecting process create a *reporting bias*. There are several reasons for setting such minimum threshold.

1. Data recording may be costly. When the threshold is decreased linearly, the costs of recording data increase exponentially. Furthermore, a large number of small losses may be recorded with mistakes that can result in additional operational losses.
2. Smaller losses are easier to hide, while it is harder to hide larger losses. For example, a trader who has committed a trading error may falsify document and succeed in making small-magnitude losses go unnoticed by bank management. However, large amounts are much more difficult to hide.
3. Poor operational loss data recording practices in past years may have been such that smaller losses could be left unrecorded, while larger losses were properly reported and recorded.

TRUNCATED MODEL FOR OPERATIONAL RISK

In the presence of missing data, the recorded operational losses follow a *truncated* compound Poisson process.[2]

---

[2]Compound models for operational risk are reviewed in Chapter 11.

Data Specification

Let us denote the minimum threshold above which losses are being recorded in a bank's internal databases by H. If one constructs a histogram of the observed loss data, it would represent only the right tail of the loss distribution rather than the entire (or true) distribution. We identify two distinct approaches—misspecified and correctly specified—that one can use:

1. *Naive approach.* Under the naive misspecified approach, one would treat the observed data as complete and fit an *unconditional* loss distribution directly to the observed data (e.g., using the maximum likelihood procedure explained in Chapter 6). The observed frequency is treated as the true frequency distribution.
2. *Conditional approach.* Under the conditional approach one correctly specifies the distribution by noting the fact that the data are recorded only above H. The frequency of the observed data is below the true frequency of loss events, and needs to be rescaled.

The first approach, naive approach, is incorrect because it ignores the missing data in the lower quantiles of the loss distribution (between 0 and H), and both the severity and frequency distributions are misspecified.

The second approach, conditional approach, relies on three main assumptions:

1. There is no prior information (neither regarding the frequency nor the severity) on the missing data.
2. Missing data and recorded data belong to the same family of distributions with identical parameters.
3. Loss magnitudes are independent from the frequency of loss occurrence and can be treated as two independent random processes.

Under the conditional approach, one needs to fit directly the right tail of the distribution by conditioning on the fact that the recorded data begin from H rather than 0. Given that the recorded data are at least H in magnitude, using the law of conditional probabilities, the density of the loss amounts can be represented as

$$f(x|X \geq H) = \frac{f(x; X \geq H)}{P(X \geq H)} \cdot I_{\{x \geq H\}},$$

where

$$I_{\{x \geq H\}} = \begin{cases} 1 & \text{if } x \geq H \\ 0 & \text{if } x < H \end{cases}.$$

After fitting the conditional density, the obtained parameters can be used to extrapolate the truncated density to cover the lower quantiles of the loss distribution, and to express the unconditional density for the complete data sample, which is composed of the recorded and missing data. Figure 9.1 illustrates an exemplary histogram of operational loss data with fitted naive

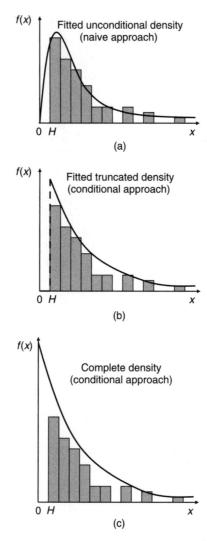

FIGURE 9.1   Fitted densities under (a) naive approach; (b) conditional approach; (c) and complete density.

density (part a), conditional (truncated) density (part b), and the complete correctly specified density (part c).

The frequency of the recorded loss process is less than the true frequency of loss occurrence.[3] Under the conditional approach, given that the frequency process of the operational losses at least H in scale follows a Poisson process with the observed intensity rate (which is also the average number of loss events) $\lambda(t)^{\text{observed}}$, and using again the law of conditional probabilities, the observed intensity rate can then be corrected for the reporting bias in the following way:

$$\lambda(t)^{\text{true}} = \frac{\lambda(t)^{\text{observed}}}{P(X \geq H)}.$$

Parameter Estimation

Two methodologies can be used to find the unknown parameters of the severity distribution: constrained maximum likelihood function and expectation-maximization algorithm.

Constrained Maximum Likelihood Function Approach   In the constrained maximum likelihood function approach, one can obtain the parameters of the loss distribution by directly maximizing the likelihood function. If the observed data sample $x = \{x_1, x_2, \ldots, x_n\}$ constitute an independent and identically distributed left-truncated sample, then the likelihood function is expressed as:

$$L_\gamma(x|X \geq H) = \prod_{j=1}^{n} \frac{f_\gamma(x_j; X \geq H)}{P_\gamma(X \geq H)},$$

where γ is the parameter set that defines the density. The estimated parameters ($\hat{\gamma}_{\text{MLE}}$) can be then used to find $P_{\hat{\gamma}\text{MLE}}(x \geq H)$ that is used to rescale the intensity rate function in the frequency distribution.

Expectation-Maximization Algorithm Approach   This expectation-maximization (EM) algorithm approach, advocated by Dempster, Laird, and Rubin (1977), is aimed at estimating the unknown parameters by maximizing the expected likelihood function using available information on the observed and missing data.

---

[3]See Chapter 5 where we discuss operational frequency distributions.

The EM algorithm is a two-step iterative procedure. In the initial step, given an initial guess value $\gamma^{(0)}$ for the unknown parameter set γ, the missing data values in the log-likelihood function are replaced by their expected values. This leads to the guess value for the expected complete log-likelihood function (*expectation* step), which is further maximized with respect to the parameter values (*maximization* step). The solution is then used as the initial guess in the next iteration of the algorithm, and the expectation step and the maximization step are repeated, and so on. The EM algorithm can be thus summarized as follows:

1. *Initial step*: Choose initial values $\gamma^{(0)}$. These can be used to estimate the initial guess value $m^{(0)}$ representing the number of missing data.
2. *Expectation step (E-step)*: Given $\gamma^{(0)}$, calculate the expected log-likelihood function of complete data. Mathematically, we need to calculate

$$\mathbb{E}_{\gamma^{(0)}}\left[\log L_{\gamma}\left(x^{\text{complete}}\right) \mid x^{\text{observed}}\right]$$

$$= m^{(0)}\mathbb{E}_{\gamma^{(0)}}\left[\log f_{\gamma}\left(x^{\text{missing}}\right)\right] + \sum_{j=1}^{n} \log f_{\gamma}\left(x_{j}^{\text{observed}}\right).$$

3. *Maximization step (M-step)*: Find the parameter set γ that maximizes the expected log-likelihood function from the previous step and set it equal to the guess value in the next step $\gamma^{(1)}$. Mathematically, we need to estimate

$$\gamma^{(1)} := \arg\max_{\gamma} \mathbb{E}_{\gamma^{(0)}}\left[\log L_{\gamma}\left(x^{\text{complete}}\right) \mid x^{\text{observed}}\right].$$

4. *Iteration*: Repeat E-step and M-step—the sequence $\{\gamma^{(k)}\}_{k>0}$ will converge to the desired maximum likelihood estimates of the parameters $(\hat{\gamma}_{\text{MLE}})$ of the distribution of the complete data sample.

Because in every round of the EM-algorithm the unknown parameters are replaced with the values that are closer to the true values, at every round the value of the likelihood function increases relative to the previous round.

The estimated parameters of the severity distribution can then be used in $P_{\hat{\gamma}_{\text{MLE}}}(X \geq H)$ to rescale the intensity rate function in the frequency distribution.

Comparison of Naive and Conditional Approaches: Lognormal Example   Many empirical studies found in operational risk literature ignore the missing data and use the naive approach. What are the implications of using the naive approach on the operational capital charge? We illustrate the implications using a simple example with lognormally distributed losses.

Our first question is the impact of using the wrong approach on the parameter estimates. Suppose we estimate the parameters of lognormal distribution to be $\hat{\mu}$ and $\hat{\sigma}$ and the observed intensity rate of the Poisson process is $\hat{\lambda}(t)$ under the naive approach, while the correct parameters (for the complete data) are μ, σ, and $\lambda(t)$, respectively. Then, simple calculations will produce the following bias estimates (i.e., the difference between the estimated parameter value and the true value):

$$\text{bias}(\hat{\mu}) = \sigma \cdot \frac{\varphi\left(\dfrac{\log H - \mu}{\sigma}\right)}{1 - \Phi\left(\dfrac{\log H - \mu}{\sigma}\right)} \qquad > 0$$

$$\text{bias}(\hat{\sigma}^2) = \sigma^2 \left(\frac{\log H - \mu}{\sigma} \cdot \frac{\varphi\left(\dfrac{\log H - \mu}{\sigma}\right)}{1 - \Phi\left(\dfrac{\log H - \mu}{\sigma}\right)} \right.$$

$$\left. - \left(\frac{\varphi\left(\dfrac{\log H - \mu}{\sigma}\right)}{1 - \Phi\left(\dfrac{\log H - \mu}{\sigma}\right)} \right)^2 \right) \qquad < 0$$

since $\log H$ has typically small values in practical applications

$$\text{bias}(\hat{\lambda}(t)) = -\lambda(t) \cdot \Phi\left(\frac{\log H - \mu}{\sigma}\right) \qquad < 0,$$

where $\varphi(\cdot)$ and $\Phi(\cdot)$ are the density and distribution function of the standard normal distribution. Clearly, the location parameter $\hat{\mu}$ is overestimated, and the scale parameter $\hat{\sigma}$ and the intensity rate $\hat{\lambda}(t)$ are underestimated under the naive approach.

A simple example can portray how the magnitude of the bias of the estimated parameters increases with an increased fraction of missing data. For an exemplary minimum recording threshold of $H = 50$, and the true parameters μ_0 and σ_0, Table 9.2 reveals the corresponding fractions of missing data. Figure 9.2 shows the effects of the biases by illustrating the ratios of the parameters estimated under the naive approach to the true parameter values, μ_0, σ_0, and λ_0. The distance between the ratio and unity represents the relative bias for each case. The ratio being equal to unity indicates the absence of any bias. Clearly, the bias estimate increases with an increased fraction of missing data. The conditional approach (figures are omitted here) resulted in correct parameter estimates, yielding the ratios equal to one.

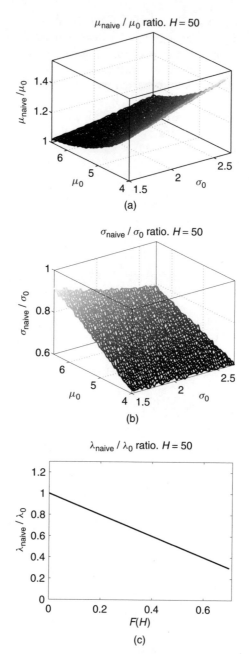

FIGURE 9.2   Illustration of the effects of reporting bias on parameters of lognormal distribution, estimated using the naive approach.

TABLE 9.2 Fraction of missing data estimated using conditional approach when the losses follow a lognormal distribution with true parameters μ_0 and σ_0 and have a nominal cutoff threshold of $H = 50$

	$\mu_0 = 4$	$\mu_0 = 5$	$\mu_0 = 6.5$
$\sigma_0 = 1.5$	0.48	0.23	0.04
$\sigma_0 = 2$	0.48	0.29	0.10
$\sigma_0 = 2.7$	0.49	0.34	0.17

Our second question is the impact of using the wrong approach on the estimates of the expected aggregate operational loss (EL), value-at-risk (VaR), and conditional value-at-risk (CVaR).[4] For the same example as before, with $\lambda = 100$ and $\alpha = 0.05$, Figure 9.3 demonstrates the ratios of EL, VaR, and CVaR estimated under the naive approach to the true corresponding measures. The conditional approach (figures are omitted here) resulted in correct estimates for the three measures producing the ratios equal to one. It is clear that if the naive approach is used to calculated the risk measures, they would be underestimated.[5] Serious consequences of using the wrong approach would be a mismatch between the true exposure to operational risk and the estimated capital charge: amount of funds set aside by a financial institution may be insufficient to cover operational losses.

An important consequence follows from the methodology just described. If the conditional approach is used to estimate the parameters of the loss and frequency distribution, then the capital charge must be invariant to the choice of the initial threshold level. This, of course, relies on the assumption that the true distribution of loss severity and frequency is correctly identified.

EMPIRICAL STUDIES WITH OPERATIONAL LOSS DATA

The majority of empirical studies with operational loss data use the naive approach to estimate the unknown parameters of the loss and frequency distributions, under which the missing data problem is overlooked and not

---

[4]The bias estimates for EL, VaR, and CVaR cannot be expressed in a simple closed form. For details, see Chernobai, Menn, Rachev, and Trück (2005a,b).
[5]For more details on this theoretical study see Chernobai, Menn, Rachev, and Trück (2005a,b) and Moscadelli, Chernobai, and Rachev (2005).

EL_{naive}/EL_0 ratio. Initial threshold = 50

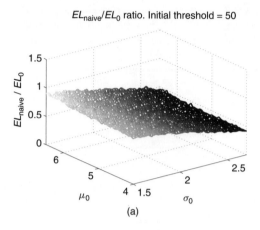

(a)

$VaR_{\mathrm{naive}}/VaR_0$ ratio. Initial threshold = 50

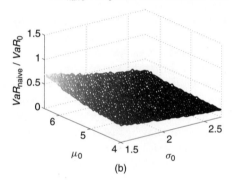

(b)

$CVaR_{\mathrm{naive}}/CVaR_0$ ratio. Initial threshold = 50

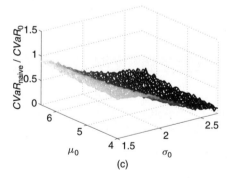

(c)

FIGURE 9.3 Illustration of the effects of reporting bias on EL, VaR, and CVaR when losses follow a lognormal distribution and parameters are estimated using the naive approach.

adequately addressed.[6] A common misconception is that using the naive approach can severely overestimate the capital charge. We give an overview of some empirical studies that are related to modeling truncated operational loss data.

Lewis and Lantsman Study with Unauthorized Trading Data

Lewis and Lantsman (2005) examine publicly reported unauthorized trading operational loss data obtained from the OpVar database (marketed by OpVantage) for the 1980 to 2001 period. They defined *material* unauthorized trading losses as those events resulting in direct financial losses greater than $100,000. They explain the necessity for the threshold by poor data reporting practices prior to 1990. Lewis and Lantsman use truncated loss distribution to model the severity and the observed frequency distribution to model the frequency of the losses. By doing so, they leave small and medium-magnitude losses out of the estimation process, basically assuming that only larger-magnitude losses contribute to the loss process.

Baud, Frachot, and Roncalli Study with Crédit Lyonnais Loss Data

Baud, Frachot, and Roncalli (2002b) explore truncated operational loss data. In particular, they discuss the importance of this issue when data coming from various institutions are pooled together in public databases. Because different institutions may have different threshold levels, in addition to a fixed threshold they consider the possibility of a random threshold.[7]

To preserve confidentiality of the Crédit Lyonnais operational loss data, they simulate several databases, which they use for the analysis. They simulate three data sets from the lognormal distribution with parameters $\mu = 8$ and $\sigma = 2$. The third data set (see Table 9.3) is composed of three pooled data sets of different size and different truncation level H. Comparison of

---

[6]One example is the Moscadelli (2004) study of the 2002 LDCE data. He points out the minimum collection threshold of approximately euro 10,000, but nevertheless states that it is not necessary to focus on the correct modeling of low and medium magnitude losses since it is the upper quantiles that determine the capital charge. Hence, according to Moscadelli, the truncation in the data can be ignored. In his study, he fits unconditional loss distributions to the data.

[7]Baud, Frachot, and Roncalli (2002b) also suggest using this methodology to pool internal and external data. The methodology for pooling internal and external data, together with its empirical application, are presented later in this chapter.

TABLE 9.3 Description of data sets, parameter estimates, and capital charge estimates in the Baud, Frachot, and Roncalli study

Data Set	No. of Losses	H (Euro '000)	μ_{naive}	σ_{naive}	VaR$_{naive}$ (Euro '000,000)	VaR$_{actual}$ (Euro '000,000)
1	2,000	10	10.39	0.97	32.9	37.8
2	2,500	15	10.75	0.95	45.9	37.8
	1,000	10				
3	1,500	20	11.25	1.00	80.1	37.8
	2,500	50				

Source: Baud, Frachot, and Roncalli (2002b, p. 6), with modifications.

the parameter estimates under the naive approach for data sets 1 and 2 in Table 9.3, supports our earlier discussion that a higher threshold level results in greater bias of the lognormal distribution parameters.

The last two columns compare the one-year 99.9% VaR estimates under the naive approach with the true VaR. It is notable that in this empirical study computations were performed under the assumption that the loss occurrence process follows a Poisson process with intensity rate 500, and no adjustments to the frequency were performed to differentiate the naive and actual scenarios.[8] For this reason, it was concluded from this empirical study that using the naive estimation procedure overestimates the capital charge, in contrast to what was demonstrated earlier in this chapter.

One can draw an important conclusion from this empirical study: The contribution of the frequency distribution to the capital charge is very significant in a sense that, when the frequency distribution is correctly specified (see our earlier theoretical discussions), then (at least for the lognormal example) the naive approach tends to underestimate the capital charge.

Chernobai, Menn, Rachev, and Trück Study with 1980–2002 Public Operational Loss Data

Chernobai, Menn, Rachev, and Trück (2005a) discussed theoretical implications of using the naive approach for the operational risk modeling. In Chernobai, Menn, Rachev, and Trück (2005b), they applied the methodology to 1980–2001 operational loss data from a public database.

---

[8]In Frachot, Moudoulaut, and Roncalli (2003) present the adjustment procedure for the frequency parameter, similar to the one previously discussed in this chapter.

The data consist of five loss types: relationship, human, processes, technology, and external. The focus of this empirical study was to compare the results obtained under the naive and conditional methodologies.

Table 9.4 demonstrates the results of the empirical study.[9] For every distribution considered, quantities of interest were estimated using the misspecified naive approach (first row) and correctly specified conditional approach (second row). The quantities of interest are: (1) maximum likelihood parameter estimates; (2) fraction of missing data under the estimated parameters; (3) estimate of log-likelihood function; (4) one-year expected aggregate loss; (5) one-year 95% VaR; and (6) one-year 95% CVaR. It is evident from Table 9.4 that a considerable fraction of data appears to be missing (as represented by $F(H)$ under the conditional approach). The log-likelihood function is higher under the conditional approach, indicating a better fit of the distributions to the data. Furthermore, ignoring the missing data results in (often significant) underestimation of the expected aggregate loss, VaR, and CVaR, whenever the wrong approach is used, in some instances up to five times.[10]

---

[9]In the actual study, a large number of distributions were analyzed; here we reproduce the results for three distributions—lognormal, Weibull, and symmetric alpha-stable—for the purpose of saving space. See Chernobai, Menn, Rachev, and Trück (2005b) for details.

[10]The estimates of EL and CVaR were infinite (denoted by "-" in the table) whenever the first moment of the loss distribution was infinite. One way to fix this problem would be to fit doubly truncated loss distribution to the data, by defining the upper bound U for the loss amount. In this case, the conditional distribution must be specified as

$$f_\gamma(x \mid H \leq X < U) = \frac{f_\gamma(x; H \leq X < U)}{F_\gamma(U) - F_\gamma(H)} \mathbb{I}_{H \leq x < U},$$

which results in the maximum likelihood parameters $\hat{\gamma}_{\text{MLE}}$. Then the unconditional distribution becomes

$$f_{\hat{\gamma}_{\text{MLE}}}(x \mid X < U) = \frac{f_{\hat{\gamma}_{\text{MLE}}}(x; X < U)}{F_{\hat{\gamma}_{\text{MLE}}}(U)} \mathbb{I}_{x < U}.$$

The scaling factor for the frequency distribution becomes $(F_{\hat{\gamma}_{\text{MLE}}}(U) - F_{\hat{\gamma}_{\text{MLE}}}(H))^{-1}$. One possibility for U would be determining the worst potential loss or, alternatively, the total value of assets. See also Rosenberg and Schuermann (2004), footnote 15, for a brief discussion of a similar issue. They suggest Winsorizing loss data at the point equal to 1,000 standard deviations.

TABLE 9.4 Parameter estimates, log-likelihood values, and estimates of EL, 95% VaR, and 95% CVaR in the Chernobai, Menn, Rachev, and Trück study

		Relationship	Human	Processes	Technology	External
Lognormal	μ	16.6771	16.5878	17.5163	16.6176	16.5789
		16.1911	15.4627	17.1600	15.1880	15.7125
	σ	1.6956	1.8590	2.0215	1.9390	1.7872
		2.0654	2.5642	2.3249	2.7867	2.3639
	$F(H)$	0.05	0.07	0.03	0.07	0.06
		0.13	0.26	0.08	0.31	0.21
	$\log L$	−15812	−15144	−6383	−1253	−4329
		−15751	−15045	−6367	−1244	−4304
	EL	0.1105	0.1981	0.5662	0.0324	0.0157
		0.1634	0.4171	0.8457	0.0958	0.0327
	95% VaR	0.2832	0.4970	1.5508	0.1202	0.0613
		0.4662	1.2161	2.5610	0.2898	0.1126
	95% CVaR	0.4662	0.8534	3.1201	0.2970	0.1450
		0.9016	3.3869	5.7823	1.5439	0.3962
Weibull	β	$6.10 \cdot 10^{-5}$	0.0002	0.0001	$6.37 \cdot 10^{-5}$	$1.16 \cdot 10^{-4}$
		0.0032	0.0240	0.0021	0.0103	0.0108
	α	0.5528	0.4841	0.4938	0.5490	0.5175
		0.3538	0.2526	0.3515	0.2938	0.2933
	$F(H)$	0.12	0.15	0.09	0.12	0.14
		0.35	0.54	0.23	0.45	0.46
	$\log L$	−15923	−15274	−6412	−1257	−4361
		−15752	−15045	−6365	−1242	−4304
	EL	0.1065	0.1993	0.4170	0.0226	0.0151
		0.1284	0.2881	0.5131	0.0358	0.0208
	95% VaR	0.2203	0.4017	0.8800	0.0798	0.0613
		0.3187	0.7997	1.2761	0.1454	0.0885
	95% CVaR	0.2700	0.4945	1.0891	0.1159	0.0975
		0.4430	1.3232	1.8257	0.2958	0.2025
Symmetric alpha-stable	α	0.7377	0.6724	0.5902	0.1827	0.6820
		0.6592	0.6061	0.5478	0.1827	0.5905
	σ	$1.37 \cdot 10^7$	$1.11 \cdot 10^7$	$2.72 \cdot 10^7$	$0.17 \cdot 10^7$	$1.14 \cdot 10^7$
		$1.00 \cdot 10^7$	$0.71 \cdot 10^7$	$1.99 \cdot 10^7$	$0.17 \cdot 10^7$	$0.71 \cdot 10^7$
	$F(H)$	0.06	0.07	0.04	0.37	0.07
		0.08	0.12	0.05	0.37	0.13
	$\log L$	−77339	−72454	−29831	−5038	−20807
		−30308	−27583	−12042	−1449	−7800
	EL	—	—	—	—	—
		—	—	—	—	—
	95% VaR	2.1873	6.2811	38.7627	$4.9 \cdot 10^5$	0.1730
		4.5476	14.5771	74.9073	$7.1 \cdot 10^6$	0.4714
	95% CVaR	—	—	—	—	—
		—	—	—	—	—

Note: For each item in the second column, the estimates in the first row represent the naive approach and those in the second row the conditional approach.

Certainly, the true fraction of missing data and, hence, the correct amount of the capital charge, depend on the loss distribution that is selected for modeling the losses. Therefore, in-sample and out-of-sample goodness-of-fit tests become essential for this purpose.[11]

Not surprisingly, goodness-of-fit tests (results are omitted here) for this study resulted in near-zero *p*-values for most of the goodness-of-fit statistics whenever the naive approach was used, and in high *p*-values whenever the conditional approach was used. Again, this supports the idea that the naive approach is misspecified for the data in hand.

Pooling Internal and External Data: Chapelle, Crama, Hübner, and Peters Study

In Chapters 3 and 4, we explained why supplementing internal data with data obtained from external (public) databases may provide a solution to expand the database when available historic loss data are scarce. The methodology described earlier in this chapter may be utilized in order to pool internal and external data correctly when external data have a minimum cutoff threshold (usually, $1 million).

Baud, Frachot, and Roncalli (2002a) propose a statistical methodology to pool internal and external data. Let $f_\gamma(x)$ be the density of the internal data, $f_\gamma^*(x^*)$ be the density of the external data, and n and n^* be the length of the sample of the internal and external data, respectively. Homogeneity of the operational loss data is assumed in that the internal and external data of the same business line/event type combination are assumed to be drawn from the same class of distributions with the same parameter set γ. Because it is common that the external data are recorded only above some high fixed threshold H^* (such as $1 million, as discussed earlier), then the density of the external data can be expressed as

$$f_\gamma^*(x^*) = \frac{f_\gamma(x^*)}{1 - F_\gamma(H^*)} \cdot I_{\{x^* \geq H^*\}},$$

where

$$I_{\{x^* \geq H^*\}} = \begin{cases} 1 & \text{if } x^* \geq H^* \\ 0 & \text{if } x^* < H^* \end{cases}.$$

---

[11] Goodness-of-fit tests will be discussed in Chapter 10.

Then the estimate of the unknown parameter set γ can be found by maximizing the following log-likelihood function with respect to γ:

$$\log L_\gamma(x, x^*) = \sum_{j=1}^{n} \log f_\gamma(x_j) + \sum_{j=1}^{n^*} \log f_\gamma^*(x_j^*).$$

Because external data are considerably larger in magnitude than internal bank data, and because internal bank data vary in magnitude from bank to bank, it is necessary to rescale the external data before mixing it with the internal data. Shih, Samad-Khan, and Medapa (2000) provide a methodology for measuring the dependence between a bank size and operational losses that was described in Chapter 2. This procedure was applied both to rescale the external observations and the threshold H.[12]

Chapelle, Crama, Hübner, and Peters compare operational VaR estimates for two scenarios. In scenario 1, only the internal data are used for the analysis. In scenario 2, both internal and external data are used. The internal loss data in their study consisted of 3,000 observations for a large European bank. All losses were rescaled to preserve confidentiality of the bank. External loss data, obtained from the OpVar Loss Database (provided by FitchRisk), were rescaled to preserve confidentiality of the banks. Therefore, all data used in the study were measured in units rather than in monetary terms.

They mixed internal and external data for the retail banking business line and clients, products, and business practices event-type combination. The median and mean of the internal data for these business line/event type combinations were 29 and 178, respectively. The median and mean of the external data (before rescaling) were 183,484 and 1,440,525, respectively. Internal loss data were split into low- and medium-magnitude losses and large losses. The lognormal distribution (with location parameter $\mu = 0.94$ and scale parameter $\sigma = 2.74$) was fitted to low- and medium-magnitude losses (under the cutoff threshold of 544) and the GPD distribution (with scale parameter $\beta = 522$ and shape parameter $\xi = 0.736$) was fitted to large losses (between the threshold 544 until the threshold 21,170). The lognormal distribution (with location parameter $\mu = 9.04$ and scale parameter $\sigma = 1.53$) was used to model the external losses (above the threshold 21,170). The estimates of the capital charge for the two scenarios are reproduced in Table 9.5. Clearly, ignoring potential extreme losses may result in underestimation of the capital charge when VaR is estimated at high confidence levels (above 99.5); for lower confidence levels the reverse is true.

---

[12] See footnote 13 in Chapter 2.

TABLE 9.5 Estimates (in units) of the median, mean, and VaR in Chapelle, Crama, Hübner, and Peters study

	Scenario 1: Internal Data Only	Scenario 2: Internal and External Data
Median	63,876	60,446
Mean	81,504	69,528
95% VaR	167,443	96,079
99% VaR	375,584	210,295
99.5% VaR	539,823	515,781
99.9% VaR	1,439,834	1,829,351
99.95% VaR	1,866,989	2,394,707

Source: Chapelle, Crama, Hübner, and Peters (2005, p. 18), with modifications.

SUMMARY OF KEY CONCEPTS

- Operational loss data are subject to minimum collection threshold: banks' internal loss data below this threshold are left unrecorded. The threshold is usually set at approximately euro 10,000 for internal databases and approximately $1 million for public databases.
- The reasons for the existence of such thresholds are costly data recording, small losses being easy to hide, and poor data recording practices.
- Missing data in the databases create a reporting bias problem. Two approaches may be employed: naive approach and conditional approach.
- The naive approach relies on the assumption that the recorded data are complete. Under this approach, the loss distribution becomes misspecified and the frequency of losses is underestimated.
- Reporting bias can be fixed using the conditional approach that relies on certain assumptions on the loss process. It allows one to capture the portion of data that is missing from the databases and correctly estimate the unknown parameters, as well as the loss and frequency distributions.
- Theoretical studies reveal that using the naive approach may have serious financial consequences. It often results in severe underestimation of the capital charge.
- Empirical studies demonstrate that the issue of missing data is often inadequately addressed. Correct accounts of the problem support the theoretical findings that the expected aggregate loss, value-at-risk, and conditional value-at-risk are understated whenever a wrong approach is used. The risk measures may be understated by a multiple.

- Another application of the conditional approach is to pool internal and external data.

REFERENCES

Baud, N., Frachot, A., and Roncalli, T. (2002a), Internal Data, External Data, and Consortium Data for Operational Risk Measurement: How to Pool Data Properly, Technical report, Groupe de Recherche Opérationnelle, Crédit Lyonnais, France.

Baud, N., Frachot, A., and Roncalli, T. (2002b), How to Avoid Over-Estimating Capital Charge for Operational Risk, Technical report, Groupe de Recherche Opérationnelle, Crédit Lyonnais, France.

BIS (2003), "The 2002 Loss Data Collection Exercise for Operational Risk: Summary of the Data Collected," www.BIS.org.

Chapelle, A., Crama, Y., Hübner, G., and Peters, J. (2005), Measuring and Managing Operational Risk in the Financial Sector: An Integrated Framework, Technical report, National Bank of Belgium.

Chernobai, A., Menn, C., Rachev, S. T., and Trück, S. (2005a), "A Note on the Estimation of the Frequency and Severity Distribution of Operational Losses," *Mathematical Scientist* 30(2), pp. 87–97.

Chernobai, A., Menn, C., Rachev, S. T., and Trück, S. (2005b), Estimation of Operational Value-at-Risk in the Presence of Minimum Collection Thresholds, Technical report, University of California at Santa Barbara.

Dempster, A. P., Laird, N. M., and Rubin, D. B. (1977), "Maximum Likelihood from Incomplete Data via the EM Algorithm," *Journal of the Royal Statistical Society, Series B (Methodological)* 39(1), pp. 1–38.

Frachot, A., Moudoulaut, O., and Roncalli, T. (2003), Loss Distribution Approach in Practice, Technical report, Groupe de Recherche Opérationnelle, Crédit Lyonnais, France.

Lewis, C. M., and Lantsman, Y. (2005), What Is a Fair Price to Transfer the Risk of Unauthorised Trading? A Case Study on Operational Risk, in E. Davis, ed., *Operational Risk: Practical Approaches to Implementation*, RISK Books, London, pp. 315–355.

Moscadelli, M. (2004), The Modelling of Operational Risk: Experience with the Analysis of the Data Collected by the Basel Committee, Technical report, Bank of Italy.

Moscadelli, M., Chernobai, A., and Rachev, S. T. (2005), "Treatment of missing data in the field of operational risk: Effects on parameter estimates, EL, UL and CVaR measures," *Operational Risk*, June, pp. 28–34.

Rosenberg, J. V., and Schuermann, T. (2004), A General Approach to Integrated Risk Management with Skewed, Fat-Tailed Risks, Technical report, Federal Reserve Bank of New York.

Shih, J., Samad-Khan, A. J., and Medapa, P. (2000), "Is the Size of an Operational Risk Related to Firm Size?" *Operational Risk*, January.

CHAPTER 10

Testing for the Goodness of Fit

T he process of modeling operational losses is necessarily accompanied by *model risk*—the risk of selecting a wrong model. In operational risk modeling, correct model selection is critical because mistakes would have serious consequences on the amount of estimated VaR and the capital charge. An underestimated VaR would jeopardize the long-term ability of a bank to maintain a sufficient amount of capital in reserves to protect against catastrophic operational losses, while a severely overestimated VaR would limit the amount of funds available for investments. In both cases, a bank would be sending a bad signal to shareholders and other stakeholders.

Looking at the big picture, there are two types of procedures to test for the goodness of fit of the model:

1. In-sample goodness-of-fit tests.
2. Out-of-sample goodness-of-fit tests—that is, forecasting (backtesting).

Backtesting is an important procedure to test the validity of a chosen model and test its practical applicability.[1] We discuss backtesting of VaR models in Chapter 11. In practical applications, one cannot rely on one single test to determine which model is optimal, but instead should perform a variety of tests in model selection. In this chapter we focus on the in-sample goodness-of-fit tests. The mechanism of hypothesis testing is described in the appendix to this chapter.

VISUAL TESTS FOR THE GOODNESS OF FIT

Common visual tests for the goodness of fit include the quantile-quantile plot and the mean excess plot.

---

[1]It is not uncommon that in-sample goodness-of-fit tests and backtesting produce contradicting results. A careful interpretation of the test is necessary. See, for example, discussions in Chernobai, Menn, Rachev, and Trück (2005).

Quantile-Quantile Plots

Quantile-quantile (QQ) *plots* provide a convenient technique to visually investigate a data set. QQ-plots plot empirical quantiles against the quantiles of a hypothesized distribution fitted to the data. In an ideal scenario, if the distribution is chosen correctly, then the QQ-plot would coincide with a 45° line.

Suppose we plot empirical quantiles of some data against the quantiles of an exponential distribution (that has exponentially fast decaying right tail). Then we would make the following observations from the QQ-plot:

- If the data follow an exponential distribution, then the plot would almost coincide with a straight 45° line.
- If the data follow a heavy-tailed distribution, then the QQ-plot would capture it by curving downward below a 45° line.

Figure 10.1 illustrates QQ-plots of a heavy-tailed operational loss data sample against the exponential and Pareto quantiles. Clearly, the heavy-tailed Pareto distribution would be a better choice.

Mean Excess Plots

For a specified value of u, the *mean excess function* of X is the conditional average of the excesses of X over u, given that X is above u. It is mathematically defined as[2]

$$e(u) = \mathbb{E}[X - u | X > u].$$

The *sample mean excess function* is then calculated as

$$e_n(u) = \frac{\sum_{j=1}^{n}(x_j - u)_+}{\sum_{j=1}^{n} \mathbb{I}_{\{x_j > u\}}}.$$

The *mean excess plot* plots the values of $e_n(u)$ against various u values.

For heavy-tailed data, $e(u)$ typically tends to infinity with an upward-sloping mean excess plot. For example, for the lognormal and heavy-tailed Weibull ($\alpha < 1$) distribution, the second derivative is negative; for the Pareto distribution, it is zero. For the thin-tailed exponential distribution, the mean excess plot is horizontal. Figure 10.2 illustrates the mean excess plot of an

---

[2]For more discussion on the mean excess function, see, for example, Embrechts, Klüppelberg, and Mikosch (1997).

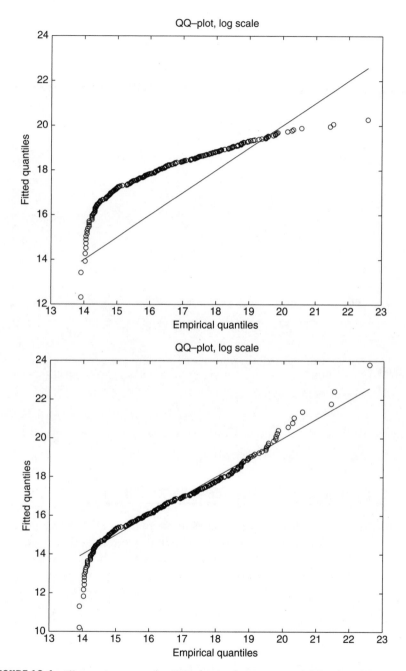

FIGURE 10.1 Illustrative example: QQ-plot against exponential (top) and Pareto (bottom) quantiles for an operational loss data sample.

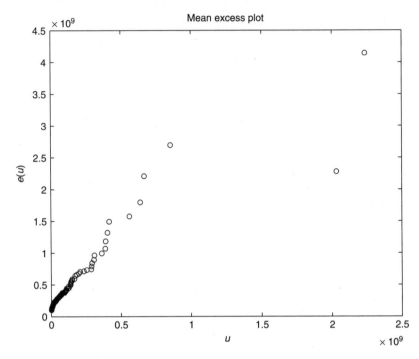

FIGURE 10.2   Illustrative example: mean excess plot of an operational loss data sample.

operational loss data sample.[3] The upward-sloping plot suggests a heavy upper tail.

COMMON FORMAL TESTS FOR THE GOODNESS OF FIT

In this section we discuss some common formal goodness-of-fit tests for discrete and continuous distributions. The first two tests—the chi-squared test and the likelihood ratio test—are grouped under chi-squared tests. The remaining tests are the empirical distribution function-based tests.

We wish to test whether the data sample follows a hypothesized distribution. For formal goodness-of-fit tests, the null and the alternative hypothesis are stated as[4]

---

[3] The same data sample was used earlier to produce the QQ-plots.

[4] The procedure for hypothesis testing is explained in the appendix to this chapter.

H_0 :   The data follow the specified distribution

H_1 :   The data do not follow the specified distribution

Chi-Squared Tests

Chi-squared tests are based on the asymptotic result on the chi-squared (χ^2) distribution of the underlying test statistic.

Pearson's Chi-Squared Test   The Pearson's chi-squared test is particularly useful for testing the goodness of fit of discrete probability distributions. For example, it can be applied to test the validity of a binomial or a Poisson model.[5]

Chi-squared test tests a null hypothesis that the relative frequencies of observed events follow a specified distribution. Essentially, the chi-squared test looks at the distances between the frequencies under the theoretical models and the actual frequencies. The first step in conducting the test is to divide the data into K classes. For example, with discrete distributions, the classes can correspond to the specific values. In the second step, the chi-square test statistic is calculated as the sum of the ratios each of which has the squared differences between each observed and the corresponding theoretical frequencies as the numerator and the theoretical frequencies as the denominator:

$$\chi^2 = \sum_{k=1}^{K} \frac{(n_k - \mathbb{E}n_k)^2}{\mathbb{E}n_k},$$

where n_k and $\mathbb{E}n_k$ are, respectively, the observed frequency and the expected (or theoretical) frequency defined by the null hypothesis, for each of the classes $k = 1, 2, \ldots, K$. In the last step, the statistic must be compared with the percentile of the χ^2 distribution at the prespecified confidence level, with degrees of freedom d equal to the number of classes minus 1. The null hypothesis is rejected if the statistic value exceeds the tabulated value.

One disadvantage of the chi-squared test is that it is sensitive to the choice of classes. Although it may be a good test for discrete distributions where each class corresponds to one value, one cannot avoid having to decide on the class size when working with continuous distributions. In addition, for the asymptotic χ^2 approximation to work, a sufficiently large sample size is required.

---

[5]For a detailed treatment of various chi-squared tests, see D'Agostino and Stephens (1986).

Likelihood Ratio Test   The *likelihood ratio* (LR) test is useful for continuous distributions. It compares the likelihood function under the parameters estimated using the *maximum likelihood estimation* (MLE) procedure[6] to the likelihood function under the true (null) parameters and determines whether it is likely that the sample belongs to the population characterized by the true parameters.

The test begins by estimating the LR test statistic:

$$LR(x) = \frac{\sup\limits_{\theta \in \Theta_0} L(x; \theta)}{\sup\limits_{\theta \in \Theta} L(x; \theta)}.$$

The numerator represents the supremum[7] of the restricted likelihood function in which parameters are restricted in value. The denominator represents the supremum of the unrestricted likelihood function, in which parameters are unrestricted in value and are estimated via MLE. The observed statistic $LR(x)$ is always between 0 and 1, and the less likely the null assumption, the smaller the ratio. One then needs to calculate this statistic:

$$\chi^2 = -2 \log LR(x).$$

Asymptotically, under the null hypothesis, the variable $-2\log LR$ is distributed χ^2_d, where the degrees of freedom d equal to the difference in dimensionality of Θ and Θ_0. The smaller the $LR(x)$ statistic, the larger the statistic $-2\log LR(x)$. The LR test rejects the null hypothesis if the statistic value exceeds the tabulated percentile of the χ^2 distribution, determined by α, with d degrees of freedom.

The LR test is useful in situations when one is confident that the population parameters specified under the null hypothesis are the true population parameters. It is notable that for the asymptotic χ^2 approximation to work, a sufficiently large sample size is required.

Empirical Distribution Function-Based Tests

Empirical distribution function-based (EDF) tests directly compare the empirical distribution function with the fitted distribution function.[8] To be

---

[6] See the Appendix to Chapter 6 for the discussion of the MLE procedure.

[7] Let E be a nonempty set. A number M is called an *upper bound* of the set E if and only if $a \leq M$ for all $a \in E$. A number S is called a *supremum* of the set E if and only if S is an upper bound of the set E and $S \leq M$ for all upper bounds M of E, that is, supremum is the smallest of all upper bounds.

[8] A definition of EDF is provided in Chapter 6.

precise, the tests are based on the vertical differences between the fitted and empirical distribution functions.[9]

These tests are broadly divided into two groups: supremum-type tests and quadratic-type tests. The first group includes tests such as the Kolmogorov-Smirnov test, Kuiper test, and Anderson-Darling test. The second group of tests includes the Cramér–von Mises test and the quadratic-type Anderson-Darling test. Limiting distributions of these test have been studied and necessary tables can be easily found in related textbooks. In subsequent descriptions of the test, we denote EDF by $F_n(x)$ and the fitted distribution function by $F(x)$. For the sample order statistics $x_{(1)} \leq x_{(2)} \leq \ldots \leq x_{(n)}$, we denote $z_{(j)} = F(x_{(j)})$, $j = 1, 2, \ldots, n$. A summary of the EDF statistics is provided in Table 10.1.

Kolmogorov-Smirnov Test   Kolmogorov-Smirnov (KS) test uses the largest vertical distance between $F_n(x)$ and $F(x)$ in the calculation of the test statistic. Let us denote D^+ as the largest difference between $F_n(x)$ and $F(x)$ and denote D^- as the largest difference between $F(x)$ and $F_n(x)$. Mathematically,

$$D^+ = \sup_x \{F_n(x) - F(x)\},$$

$$D^- = \sup_x \{F(x) - F_n(x)\}.$$

The KS statistic is calculated as:[10]

$$KS = \sqrt{n} \max\{D^+, D^-\}.$$

To directly compute the sample statistic value, it is necessary to use a suitable computing formula. The computing formula can be found by the use of the probability integral transformation method.[11] The computing formula for the KS statistic is

$$KS = \sqrt{n} \max \left\{ \sup_j \left\{ \frac{j}{n} - z_{(j)} \right\}, \ \sup_j \left\{ z_{(j)} - \frac{j-1}{n} \right\} \right\}.$$

---

[9] The literature on EDF-based tests includes Anderson and Darling (1952), Anderson and Darling (1954), D'Agostino and Stephens (1986), and Shorack and Wellner (1986).

[10] The factor $\sqrt{n}$ is often omitted in the literature. It is important to include it whenever one deals with multiple samples, as the factor allows standardization of the statistic to account for the difference in sample sizes.

[11] See D'Agostino and Stephens (1986) for the explanation of the probability integral transformation method.

TABLE 10.1 Summary of EDF statistics and their computing formulas

Statistic	Description and Computing Formula
KS	$KS = \sqrt{n}\sup_{x}\left\| F_n(x) - \widehat{F}(x) \right\|$ Computing formula: $KS = \sqrt{n}\max\left\{ \sup_{j}\left\{ \frac{i}{n} - z_{(j)} \right\}, \; \sup_{j}\left\{ z_{(j)} - \frac{i-1}{n} \right\} \right\}$
V	$V = \sqrt{n}\left(\sup_{x}\left\{ F_n(x) - \widehat{F}(x) \right\} + \sup_{x}\left\{ \widehat{F}(x) - F_n(x) \right\} \right)$ Computing formula: $V = \sqrt{n}\left(\sup_{j}\left\{ \frac{i}{n} - z_{(j)} \right\} + \sup_{j}\left\{ z_{(j)} - \frac{i-1}{n} \right\} \right)$
AD	$AD = \sqrt{n}\sup_{x}\left\| \frac{F_n(x) - \widehat{F}(x)}{\sqrt{\widehat{F}(x)\left(1 - \widehat{F}(x)\right)}} \right\|$ Computing formula: $AD = \sqrt{n}\max\left\{ \sup_{j}\left\{ \frac{\frac{i}{n} - z_{(j)}}{\sqrt{z_{(j)}\left(1 - z_{(j)}\right)}} \right\}, \; \sup_{j}\left\{ \frac{z_{(j)} - \frac{i-1}{n}}{\sqrt{z_{(j)}\left(1 - z_{(j)}\right)}} \right\} \right\}$
AD^2	$AD^2 = n\int_{-\infty}^{\infty} \frac{\left(F_n(x) - \widehat{F}(x)\right)^2}{\widehat{F}(x)\left(1 - \widehat{F}(x)\right)} d\widehat{F}(x)$ Computing formula: $AD^2 = -n + \frac{1}{n}\sum_{j=1}^{n}(1 - 2j)\log z_{(j)} - \frac{1}{n}\sum_{j=1}^{n}(1 + 2(n - j))\log(1 - z_{(j)})$
AD_{up}	$AD_{up} = \sqrt{n}\sup_{x}\left\| \frac{F_n(x) - \widehat{F}(x)}{1 - \widehat{F}(x)} \right\|$ Computing formula: $AD_{up} = \sqrt{n}\max\left\{ \sup_{j}\left\{ \frac{\frac{i}{n} - z_{(j)}}{1 - z_{(j)}} \right\}, \; \sup_{j}\left\{ \frac{z_{(j)} - \frac{i-1}{n}}{1 - z_{(j)}} \right\} \right\}$
AD_{up}^2	$AD_{up}^2 = n\int_{-\infty}^{\infty} \frac{\left(F_n(x) - \widehat{F}(x)\right)^2}{\left(1 - \widehat{F}(x)\right)^2} d\widehat{F}(x)$ Computing formula: $AD_{up}^2 = \frac{1}{n}\sum_{j=1}^{n}(1 + 2(n - j))\frac{1}{(1 - z_{(j)})} + 2\sum_{j=1}^{n}\log(1 - z_{(j)})$
W^2	$W^2 = n\int_{-\infty}^{\infty}\left(F_n(x) - \widehat{F}(x)\right)^2 d\widehat{F}(x)$ Computing formula: $W^2 = \frac{n}{3} + \frac{1}{n}\sum_{j=1}^{n}(1 - 2j)z_{(j)} + \sum_{j=1}^{n}z_{(j)}^2$

Kuiper Test   A test closely related to the KS test is the Kuiper test. Instead of relying on a single largest distance between $F_n(x)$ and $F(x)$, it gives an equal weight to both D^+ and D^-. The test statistic is calculated as

$$V = \sqrt{n}(D^+ + D^-).$$

The computing formula is

$$V = \sqrt{n}\left(\sup_j \left\{\frac{j}{n} - z_{(j)}\right\} + \sup_j \left\{z_{(j)} - \frac{j-1}{n}\right\}\right).$$

Both the KS test and the Kuiper test tend to put most weight on the center (medium) of the distribution.

Anderson-Darling Test   The Anderson-Darling (AD) tests are of two types: the supremum type and the quadratic type. The supremum class AD statistic is calculated by

$$AD = \sqrt{n} \sup_x \left| \frac{F_n(x) - F(x)}{\sqrt{F(x)(1 - F(x))}} \right|.$$

The computing formula is

$$AD = \sqrt{n} \max\left\{ \sup_j \left\{ \frac{\frac{j}{n} - z_{(j)}}{\sqrt{z_{(j)}(1 - z_{(j)})}} \right\}, \sup_j \left\{ \frac{z_{(j)} - \frac{j-1}{n}}{\sqrt{z_{(j)}(1 - z_{(j)})}} \right\} \right\}.$$

The quadratic class AD statistic is found as

$$AD^2 = n \int_{-\infty}^{+\infty} \frac{(F_n(x) - F(x))^2}{F(x)(1 - F(x))} dF(x).$$

The computing formula is

$$AD^2 = -n + \frac{1}{n}\sum_{j=1}^{n}(1 - 2j)\log z_{(j)} - \frac{1}{n}\sum_{j=1}^{n}(1 + 2(n - j))\log(1 - z_{(j)}).$$

Unlike the KS and Kuiper tests, the AD test tends to put most weight on the tails of the distribution. Thus the AD test becomes important when there is reason to believe that the underlying data are heavy-tailed.

A modified version of the AD test was proposed by Chernobai, Rachev, and Fabozzi (2005). They argue that in many financial applications, including modeling of operational risk, only the upper tail of the distribution is of central concern, while the lower tail is of little importance. The modified version of the AD test, which they call the *upper-tail AD test*, puts most weight on the upper tail, and is useful when one wants to test the goodness-of-fit of the distribution in the upper quantiles of the data sample. The corresponding supremum class and quadratic class test statistics are expressed as

$$AD_{up} = \sqrt{n} \sup_{x} \left| \frac{F_n(x) - F(x)}{1 - F(x)} \right|$$

$$AD_{up}^2 = n \int_{-\infty}^{+\infty} \frac{(F_n(x) - F(x))^2}{(1 - F(x))^2} dF(x).$$

The corresponding computing formulae are

$$AD_{up} = \sqrt{n} \max \left\{ \sup_j \left\{ \frac{\frac{j}{n} - z_{(j)}}{1 - z_{(j)}} \right\}, \sup_j \left\{ \frac{z_{(j)} - \frac{j-1}{n}}{1 - z_{(j)}} \right\} \right\}$$

$$AD_{up}^2 = \frac{1}{n} \sum_{j=1}^{n} (1 + 2(n-j)) \frac{1}{(1 - z_{(j)})} + 2 \sum_{j=1}^{n} \log(1 - z_{(j)}).$$

Cramér-von Mises Test The Cramér–von Mises statistic is defined by

$$W^2 = n \int_{-\infty}^{+\infty} (F_n(x) - F(x))^2 dF(x).$$

The computing formula is

$$W^2 = \frac{n}{3} + \frac{1}{n} \sum_{j=1}^{n} (1 - 2j) z_{(j)} + \sum_{j=1}^{n} z_{(j)}^2.$$

EMPIRICAL STUDY WITH OPERATIONAL LOSS DATA

Many empirical studies with actual operational loss data with reported goodness-of-fit test statistics have been presented in Chapter 6, Chapter 5, and Chapter 7 and therefore will not be repeated here. In this section we present our goodness-of-fit test results.

We performed an exploratory analysis of the 1980–2002 operational loss data from a large European public database.[12] The data consist of five loss types: relationship, human, processes, technology, and external.

Figure 10.3 and Figure 10.4 illustrate the QQ-plots for the five data sets against the exponential and Pareto quantiles, respectively. As is evident from the plots, the light-tailed exponential distribution is a poor model choice, while the Pareto distribution appears to fit the data well. Similar conclusions can be drawn from visual examination of the mean excess plots (see Figure 10.5).

Chernobai, Menn, Rachev, and Trück (2005) further examine the data sets and fit a large class of loss distributions to the loss data. Table 10.2 summarizes the goodness-of-fit test statistics and the corresponding p-values for a composite test. The estimated parameter values can be found in the corresponding study in Chapter 7 and the original source in Chernobai, Menn, Rachev, and Trück (2005).

The results reported in Table 10.2 lead us to conclude the following.

- *Relationship type operational losses.* KS and V (Kuiper) tests indicate (both based on the statistic values and p-values) that the Weibull and log-Weibull models are the most optimal for the data. *AD* tests suggest, based on the p-values, that the symmetric alpha-stable model is the best, followed by log-alpha-stable and log-Weibull. The log-Weibull model is also supported by the W^2 test. However, the AD_{up} and AD_{up}^2 tests are in favor of the lognormal model; AD_{up} also resulted in high p-values for the Pareto, Burr, and symmetric alpha-stable models. It is notable that while we may tend to reject the heavy-tailed Pareto and Burr models based on conventional *KS* test, they are strongly supported by the upper tail tests.

- *"Human" type operational losses.* Conventional *KS* test would reject most of the models, with the p-values barely exceeding 35% for the symmetric alpha-stable and log-alpha-stable models. The symmetric alpha-stable distribution appears to be suitable in the tails of the distribution, as indicated by the *AD* and AD^2 tests. W^2 does not strongly support any of the models. However, based on the *upper-tail*

---

[12] The same database was used in Chernobai, Menn, Rachev, and Trück (2005).

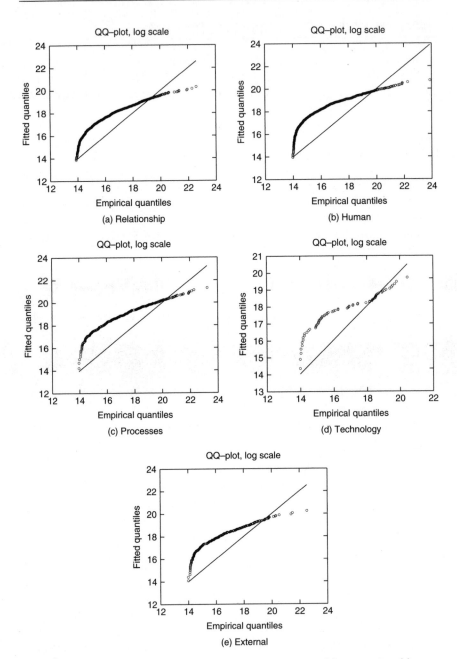

FIGURE 10.3 Exploratory data analysis of 1980 to 2002 public operational loss data: log-transformed QQ-plot against exponential quantiles.

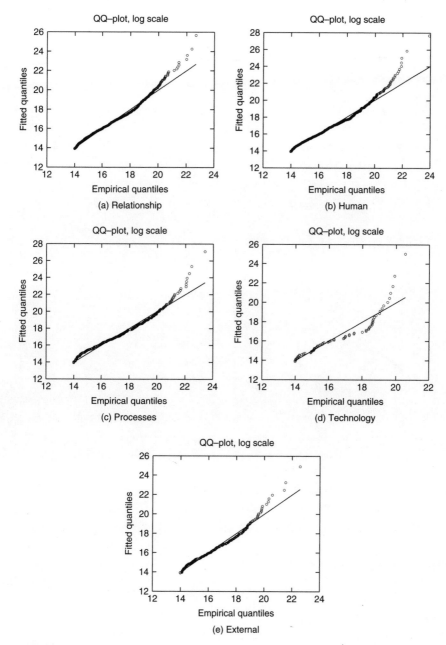

FIGURE 10.4 Exploratory data analysis of 1980 to 2002 public operational loss data: log-transformed QQ-plot against Pareto quantiles.

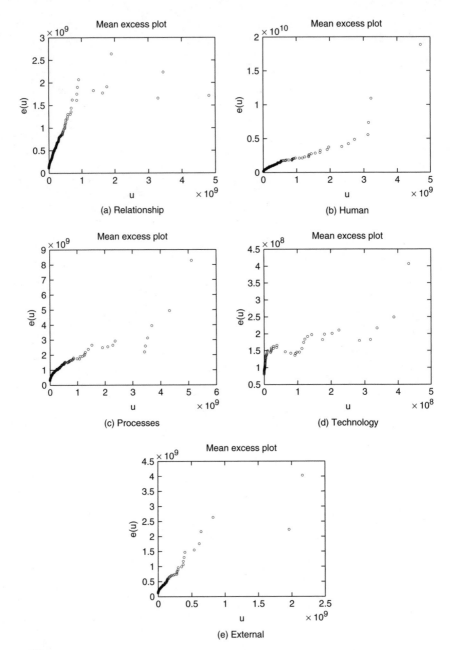

FIGURE 10.5 Exploratory data analysis of 1980–2002 public operational loss data: sample mean excess plot.

TABLE 10.2 Goodness-of-fit test statistics and corresponding p-values (in square brakets) for five loss types in the Chernobai, Menn, Rachev, and Trück study.

	Relationship	Human	Processes	Technology	External
Lognormal					
KS	0.8056 [0.082]	0.8758 [0.032]	0.6854 [0.297]	1.1453 [$\approx$0]	0.6504 [0.326]
V	1.3341 [0.138]	1.5265 [0.039]	1.1262 [0.345]	1.7896 [0.005]	1.2144 [0.266]
AD	2.6094 [0.347]	3.9829 [0.126]	2.0668 [0.508]	2.8456 [0.209]	2.1702 [0.469]
AD_{up}	875.40 [0.593]	1086.2 [0.462]	272.61 [0.768]	41.8359 [0.990]	316.20 [0.459]
AD^2	0.7554 [0.043]	0.7505 [0.044]	0.4624 [0.223]	1.3778 [$\approx$0]	0.5816 [0.120]
AD^2_{up}	4.6122 [0.401]	4.5160 [0.408]	4.0556 [0.367]	6.4213 [0.067]	2.5993 [0.589]
W^2	0.1012 [0.086]	0.0804 [0.166]	0.0603 [0.294]	0.2087 [$\approx$0]	0.0745 [0.210]
Weibull					
KS	0.5553 [0.625]	0.8065 [0.103]	0.6110 [0.455]	1.0922 [$\approx$0]	0.4752 [0.852]
V	1.0821 [0.514]	1.5439 [0.051]	1.0620 [0.532]	1.9004 [$\approx$0]	0.9498 [0.726]
AD	3.8703 [0.138]	4.3544 [0.095]	1.7210 [0.766]	2.6821 [0.216]	2.4314 [0.384]
AD_{up}	2.7×10^4 [0.080]	3.2×10^4 [0.068]	2200.7 [0.192]	52.5269 [0.944]	4382.7 [0.108]
AD^2	0.7073 [0.072]	0.7908 [0.068]	0.2069 [0.875]	1.4536 [$\approx$0]	0.3470 [0.519]
AD^2_{up}	13.8191 [0.081]	8.6610 [0.112]	2.2340 [0.758]	4.8723 [0.087]	5.3662 [0.164]
W^2	0.0716 [0.249]	0.0823 [0.188]	0.0338 [0.755]	0.2281 [$\approx$0]	0.0337 [0.781]
Log-Weibull					
KS	0.5284 [0.699]	0.9030 [0.074]	0.5398 [0.656]	1.1099 [$\approx$0]	0.6893 [0.296]
V	1.0061 [0.628]	1.5771 [0.050]	0.9966 [0.637]	1.9244 [$\approx$0]	1.1020 [0.476]
AD	3.0718 [0.255]	4.1343 [0.115]	1.6238 [0.832]	2.7553 [0.250]	2.2267 [0.481]
AD_{up}	7332.1 [0.186]	1.1×10^4 [0.160]	658.42 [0.343]	49.2373 [0.976]	3130.6 [0.128]
AD^2	0.4682 [0.289]	0.7560 [0.115]	0.1721 [0.945]	1.5355 [$\approx$0]	0.4711 [0.338]
AD^2_{up}	5.2316 [0.282]	4.5125 [0.392]	1.4221 [0.977]	5.2992 [0.114]	4.1429 [0.283]
W^2	0.0479 [0.514]	0.0915 [0.217]	0.0241 [0.918]	0.2379 [$\approx$0]	0.0563 [0.458]
Pareto					
KS	1.4797 [$\approx$0]	1.4022 [$\approx$0]	1.0042 [0.005]	1.2202 [$\approx$0]	0.9708 [0.009]
V	2.6084 [$\approx$0]	2.3920 [$\approx$0]	1.9189 [$\approx$0]	1.8390 [$\approx$0]	1.8814 [$\approx$0]
AD	3.5954 [0.154]	3.6431 [0.167]	4.0380 [0.128]	3.0843 [0.177]	2.7742 [0.284]
AD_{up}	374.68 [$\approx$1]	374.68 [$\approx$1]	148.24 [$\approx$1]	33.4298 [$\approx$1]	151.94 [0.949]
AD^2	3.7165 [$\approx$0]	2.7839 [$\approx$0]	2.6022 [$\approx$0]	1.6182 [$\approx$0]	1.7091 [$\approx$0]
AD^2_{up}	22.1277 [0.048]	23.7015 [0.051]	13.1082 [0.087]	8.8484 [0.067]	8.6771 [0.106]
W^2	0.5209 [$\approx$0]	0.3669 [$\approx$0]	0.3329 [$\approx$0]	0.2408 [$\approx$0]	0.2431 [$\approx$0]
Burr					
KS	1.3673 [0.032]	2.2333 [0.115]	0.5634 [0.598]	1.1188 [0.389]	1.3266 [0.050]
V	2.4165 [$\approx$0]	3.1970 [0.115]	0.9314 [0.800]	0.9374 [0.380]	2.0385 [0.048]
AD	3.3069 [0.309]	4.7780 [0.174]	1.6075 [0.841]	2.6949 [0.521]	2.8775 [0.328]
AD_{up}	371.65 [0.960]	255.91 [$\approx$1]	364.08 [0.429]	28.4827 [$\approx$1]	113.13 [0.989]
AD^2	3.1371 [$\approx$0]	7.0968 [0.115]	0.2639 [0.794]	2.0320 [0.380]	2.8954 [0.048]
AD^2_{up}	22.0374 [0.019]	46.3417 [0.119]	2.0133 [0.844]	10.5469 [0.401]	15.4410 [0.064]
W^2	0.4310 [0.011]	1.2830 [0.115]	0.0323 [0.840]	0.3424 [0.380]	0.5137 [0.048]

(continued)

TABLE 10.2 (*continued*)

Relationship	Human	Processes	Technology	External
Log-alpha-stable				
KS	1.5929 [0.295]	9.5186 [0.319]	0.6931 [0.244]	1.1540 [≈0]	7.3275 [0.396]
V	1.6930 [0.295]	9.5619 [0.324]	1.1490 [0.342]	1.7793 [0.007]	7.4089 [0.458]
AD	3.8184 [0.275]	36.2617 [0.250]	2.0109 [0.534]	2.8728 [0.208]	37.4863 [0.218]
AD_{up}	1075.3 [0.041]	9846.3 [0.354]	272.57 [0.786]	41.7454 [0.995]	4708.7 [0.354]
AD^2	3.8067 [0.290]	304.61 [0.312]	0.4759 [0.202]	1.3646 [≈0]	194.74 [0.284]
AD^2_{up}	10.1990 [0.288]	4198.9 [0.215]	4.0910 [0.361]	6.4919 [0.060]	3132.6 [0.128]
W^2	0.7076 [0.292]	44.5156 [0.315]	0.0660 [0.258]	7.2×10^{10} [≈1]	24.3662 [0.366]
Symmetric alpha-stable				
KS	1.1634 [0.034]	1.1628 [0.352]	1.3949 [0.085]	2.0672 [≈1]	0.7222 [0.586]
V	2.0695 [≈0]	2.1537 [0.026]	1.9537 [0.067]	2.8003 [≈1]	1.4305 [0.339]
AD	1.4×10^5 [≈1]	5.8×10^5 [0.651]	3.3×10^5 [0.931]	2.7×10^5 [≈1]	1.1×10^5 [0.990]
AD_{up}	5.0×10^{16} [0.971]	4.3×10^{17} [0.351]	2.5×10^{17} [0.530]	3.6×10^{16} [≈1]	3.4×10^{16} [0.797]
AD^2	4.4723 [0.992]	11.9320 [0.971]	6.5235 [0.964]	19.6225 [≈1]	1.7804 [0.980]
AD^2_{up}	2.6×10^{14} [≈0]	3.3×10^{11} [0.436]	6.8×10^{14} [0.193]	7.2×10^{10} [≈1]	1.2×10^{10} [0.841]
W^2	0.3630 [≈0]	0.2535 [0.027]	0.3748 [0.102]	1.4411 [0.964]	0.1348 [0.265]

tests, the lognormal, Pareto, Burr, and symmetric alpha-stable assumptions are well supported.

- *Processes type operational losses.* Weibull, log-Weibull, and Burr models fit the data well around the center, as suggested by high *p*-values of the *KS* and *V* tests. All except the exponential and Pareto assumptions result in high *p*-values of the *AD* and AD^2 tests, making judgments regarding the choice of an optimal model complicated; these, combined with the W^2 test results, suggest that the Weibull, log-Weibull, and Burr models are optimal. A look at the *upper-tail* tests gives a slightly different picture, with the Pareto model showing a very good fit, both on the basis of high *p*-value and low statistic value (AD^2_{up} test). In general, the *upper-tail* tests are in favor of very heavy-tailed model assumptions.
- *Technology type operational losses.* The *KS* and *V* tests reject all except the symmetric alpha-stable models. The *AD* test weakly supports the Burr assumption and strongly supports the symmetric alpha-stable assumption; a similar conclusion is drawn from the W^2 test. Judging from the previously mentioned conventional goodness-of-fit tests, the symmetric alpha-stable model seems the only reasonable model. However, the AD_{up} and AD^2_{up} tests also support several other models, making them valid candidates for modeling the losses.
- *External type operational losses.* Weibull model explains the data best around the center, as is evident from the high *p*-values of the *KS* and *V* tests. In the tails, the symmetric alpha-stable model appears the best, while GPD and Burr also appear to fit the data well in the upper tail.

SUMMARY OF KEY CONCEPTS

- Goodness-of-fit tests are necessary to evaluate the validity of a theoretical model. Broadly, they are divided into two groups: in-sample goodness-of-fit tests and out-of-sample (i.e., forecasting or backtesting) tests.
- In-sample goodness-of-fit tests can be visual techniques and formal techniques. Visual tests include the quantile-quantile plot and the mean excess plot. Both tests can be useful as a first step in the model evaluation process and are particularly convenient to evaluate the heaviness in the tail of operational loss distributions.
- Common formal goodness-of-fit tests are the chi-squared type tests and the empirical distribution function-based tests. Chi-squared type tests include the likelihood ratio test and the Pearson's chi-squared test. Empirical distribution function-based tests are the Kolmogorov-Smirnov, Kuiper, Anderson-Darling, and Cramér-von Mises tests. A modified version of the Anderson-Darling test that puts most weight on the upper tail can be of particular importance when modeling heavy-tailed operational losses.
- Goodness-of-fit tests have been used in numerous empirical studies with operational loss data. Some findings suggest that the center and the tail of the loss distribution do not conform to the same law; in particular, the upper tail of the operational loss distribution is heavy and distributions such as Burr, Pareto, and the variations of the alpha-stable may provide a reasonable solution.

APPENDIX: HYPOTHESIS TESTING

A statistical hypothesis makes a statement about a population parameter of interest. The test is commonly formulated in the form of two hypotheses: the *null hypothesis* (denoted by H_0) and the *alternative hypothesis* (denoted by H_1).[13] The goal of a hypothesis test is to determine, based on a sample drawn from this population, which of the two complementary hypotheses is true.

Suppose that Θ_0 and Θ_0^c are the complementary parameter spaces of the population parameter θ, under the null and the alternative hypotheses, respectively. Then, the test is summarized as

$$H_0 : \theta \in \Theta_0 \quad \text{vs.} \quad H_1 : \theta \in \Theta_0^c.$$

---

[13]In many textbooks, the alternative hypothesis is denoted by H_A.

TABLE 10.3 Type I error and Type II error

		Decision	
		Accept H_0	Reject H_0
Truth	H_0	Correct decision	Type I Error
	H_1	Type II Error	Correct decision

A hypothesis test is a rule that specifies for which sample values[14]

1. The decision is made to accept H_0 as true.
2. H_0 is rejected and H_1 is accepted as true.

The subset of the sample space for which H_0 is rejected is called the *rejection region* (or *critical region*), and the remaining subset is called the *acceptance region*.

A hypothesis test can make one the two types of errors:

1. Type I error
2. Type II error

Type I error occurs when one falsely rejects H_0 when H_0 is in fact true. *Type II error* happens when one accepts H_0 when H_0 is false. The *power of the test* is calculated as one minus the Type II error. Table 10.3 summarizes two different types of errors.

A good test would seek to minimize the probability of both errors. However, it is impossible to eliminate both errors completely: a test that always rejects H_0 has a zero probability of the Type II error, while a test that never rejects H_0 has a zero probability of the Type I error. To reconcile the situation, one defines a *level of significance* (denoted by α) that fixes the maximally tolerated probability of committing the Type I error. Among all tests that have the Type I error less than α, the one with the smallest Type II error is selected.

A test statistic is usually calculated and is used as a benchmark to carry out the test. The *p*-value is the probability of exceeding the observed test statistic. The null hypothesis is rejected if the *p*-value is less than α.

There are two types of tests, *simple tests* and *composite tests*, that differ in the specification of the null hypothesis. *Simple tests* specify a concrete

---

[14]See Casella and Berger (2002).

parameter value under the null. For these tests, there exist tables of critical values with which the test statistic values should be compared. *Composite test* do not specify parameter values in the null hypothesis, and only test whether the data belong to the specified class of distributions.

In the composite tests, the distribution of the test statistic is not parameter-free, and one way to compute the *p*-values and the critical values is by means of Monte Carlo simulation, for each hypothesized fitted distribution.[15] Under the procedure, first, the observed value D of the statistic of interest is computed. Then, for a given level α the following algorithm is applied:

1. Generate large number (e.g., $I = 1,000$) of samples from the fitted distribution of size n that is equal to the number of observed data.
2. Fit the distribution to each of the samples and estimate the unknown parameters for each sample $i = 1, 2, \ldots I$.
3. Estimate the goodness-of-fit statistic value D_i for each sample, $i = 1, 2, \ldots I$.
4. Calculate *p*-value as the proportion of times the sample statistic values exceed the observed value D of the original sample.
5. Reject H_0 if the *p*-value is smaller than α.

In the tests for the goodness of fit, a high *p*-value suggests a good fit of the hypothetical model to the data.

REFERENCES

Anderson, T. W., and Darling, D. A. (1952), "Asymptotic Theory of Certain "Goodness of Fit" Criteria Based on Stochastic Processes," *The Annals of Mathematical Statistics* 23(2), pp. 193–212.

Anderson, T. W., and Darling, D. A. (1954), "A Test of Goodness of Fit," *Journal of the American Statistical Association* 49(268), pp. 765–769.

Casella, G., and Berger, R. L. (2002), *Statistical Inference*, 2nd ed., Thomson, Belmont, CA.

Chernobai, A., Menn, C., Rachev, S. T., and Trück, S. (2005), Estimation of Operational Value-at-Risk in the Presence of Minimum Collection Thresholds, *Technical report*, University of California at Santa Barbara.

Chernobai, A., Rachev, S. T., and Fabozzi, F. J. (2005), Composite Goodness-of-Fit Tests for Left-Truncated Loss Samples, *Technical report*, University of California at Santa Barbara.

---

[15] See, for example, Ross (2001) for the discussion of the Monte Carlo approach.

D'Agostino, R., and Stephens, M. (1986), *Goodness-of-Fit Techniques*, Marcel Dekker, Inc., New York and Basel.

Embrechts, P., Klüppelberg, C., and Mikosch, T. (1997), *Modeling Extremal Events for Insurance and Finance*, Springer-Verlag, Berlin.

Ross, S. M. (2001), *Simulation*, 3rd ed., Academic Press, Boston.

Shorack, G. R., and Wellner, J. A. (1986), *Empirical Processes with Applications to Statistics*, John Wiley & Sons, New York.

CHAPTER 11

Value-at-Risk

A financial manager is often concerned with answering a question of the following form: "What is the maximum amount that I can expect to lose with a certain probability over a given horizon?" At the same time, regulators' concern is to ensure that banks hold sufficient quantities of reserves that would cover most of their material losses arising from financial risks. The concerns of both parties can be reconciled by estimating *value-at-risk* (VaR). In the context of operational risk, VaR is, informally speaking, the total one-year amount of capital that would be sufficient to cover all unexpected losses with a high level of confidence.

VaR is a powerful statistical tool that has gained popularity within the financial community and has become a benchmark for measuring and forecasting market, credit, operational, and other risks. This chapter discusses the notion of VaR and its alternatives and its role in quantifying and managing of operational risk.

INTUITIVELY, WHAT IS VaR?

Intuitively, VaR determines the worst possible loss that may occur with a given confidence level and for a given timeframe. $(1 - \alpha) \times 100\%$ VaR is defined as the $(1 - \alpha)$th percentile of the loss distribution over a target time horizon Δt. $1 - \alpha$ is called the confidence level. For example, a one-year 95% VaR is the total amount of loss that may be exceeded by the total of all potential losses that may occur over a one-year period no more than 5% of the time.

Three parameters need to be specified before VaR is computed:

1. Confidence level
2. Forecast horizon
3. Base currency

Confidence level is the probability of loss associated with VaR measurement. The confidence level is typically taken between 95% and 99%. Often, however, practitioners are concerned with forecasting the losses that occur at a confidence level of 99.99%, or even higher. *Forecast horizon* indicates the time interval that is considered for VaR analysis. Since the underlying factors determining the risk structure vary with time, the time interval is usually short. For example, financial managers usually consider a one-day or one-month forecast window, but nonfinancial corporations may apply one quarter or one year. *Base currency* is typically the currency in which a certain institution's capital is recorded. Thus, in the case of operational risk VaR for a U.S. bank, VaR would be calculated in U.S. dollars (USD).

VaR has been a benchmark for risk-based internal models for measuring market and credit risk for a number of years. This basis can be extended for internal measurement of operational risk. In Chapter 3, we discussed that under the Basel II Capital Accord the operational capital charge must be evaluated for a one-year period subject to a high confidence level, such as 99%.[1] The definition of VaR allows us to use it as a proxy for the capital charge under the advanced measurement models. This way, under the loss distribution approach (LDA), VaR can be estimated as a high percentile of the cumulative one-year operational loss distribution.

COMPOUND OPERATIONAL LOSS MODELS AND DERIVATION OF OPERATIONAL VaR

We now review the notion of cumulative (or aggregate) loss distribution. In Chapter 4, we emphasized that both the frequency and severity of operational losses play an important role in the operational risk modeling process. Examples of the frequency distributions were provided in Chapter 5 and examples of common severity distributions were presented in Chapter 6. When the frequency for a particular timeframe is combined with the severity process, one obtains the compound process for this timeframe.

A Simple Actuarial Model

Actuarial-type models are commonly used to aggregate the severity and frequency distributions into one single model. They rely on some assumptions:[2]

---

[1]See Chapter 3 for the discussion of various approaches to estimate the operational capital charge.
[2]For more details, see, for example, Chapter 6 in Klugman, Panjer, and Willmot (2004).

1. Given the total number of loss events, loss amounts are *independent* from each other and are *identically distributed (iid)* positive random variables.
2. Conditional on the given total number of loss events n, the common distribution of the loss amounts is independent from n.
3. The distribution of the total number of loss events does not depend on the loss amounts.

Suppose that for the aggregated operational losses for a particular business line/event type combination, the losses are assumed to follow such actuarial-type model. Denoting loss amounts by X and the number of loss events $N_{\Delta t}$ within a one-year timeframe Δt, the aggregate losses follow the stochastic process of the following form:

$$S_{\Delta t} = X_1 + X_2 + \cdots + X_{N_{\Delta t}}$$

$$= \sum_{k=1}^{N_{\Delta t}} X_k.$$

The cumulative distribution function of this aggregate process can be written as

$$F_{S_{\Delta t}}(s) = P(S_{\Delta t} \le s) = \begin{cases} \sum_{n=1}^{\infty} P(N_{\Delta t} = n) F_X^{n*}(s) & s > 0 \\ P(N_{\Delta t} = 0) & s = 0, \end{cases}$$

where F_X is the distribution function of the random variable X and F_X^{n*} denotes the n-fold convolution of F_X with itself:

$$F_X^{n*}(s) = P\left(\sum_k^n X_k \le s \right).$$

The population mean and variance of $S_{\Delta t}$ are found using

$$\text{mean}(S_{\Delta t}) = \mathbb{E}[N_{\Delta t}]\mathbb{E}[X], \qquad \text{var}(S_{\Delta t}) = \mathbb{E}[N_{\Delta t}]\text{var}(X) + \text{var}(N_{\Delta t})\mathbb{E}^2[X].$$

Figure 11.1 illustrates the mechanism of aggregation of operational loss and frequency distributions. It is notable that a possibly complex dependence structure between operational losses and the frequency is a necessary component to be incorporated into the aggregation model; this aspect is beyond the scope of this book.

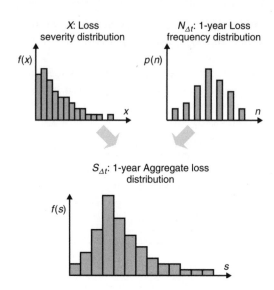

FIGURE 11.1   The mechanism of aggregation of operational loss and frequency distributions.

Computing the Aggregate Loss Distribution

It is notable that the equation for the cumulative distribution function of aggregate losses is nonlinear in X and N. Therefore, except for some simple scenarios, analytic expressions for the compound distribution function do not exist. Thus, the computation of the compound distribution function is not an easy task. We now give a brief overview of some approaches to numerical evaluation of the loss distribution for a general Poisson-type frequency distribution: numerical approximation, direct computation, recursive method, and inversion method.[3]

Monte Carlo Approach   The simplest and most commonly used approach relies on Monte Carlo simulations of loss scenarios. It involves generation of a large number of scenarios using computer software. For a simple example with a simple Poisson frequency distribution with a parameter λ, the algorithm can be summarized as follows:

1. Simulate a large number of Poisson random variates with parameter λ, such as 100,000, and obtain a sequence $n_1, n_2, \ldots, n_{100,000}$ representing scenarios fo the total number of loss events in a one-year period.

---

[3] See discussions of alternative methods in Klugman, Panjer, and Willmot (2004).

2. For each of the scenarios n_k, $1 \leq k \leq 100{,}000$, simulate n_k number of loss amounts from the underlying loss distribution.
3. For each of the scenarios n_k, $1 \leq k \leq 100{,}000$, aggregate the loss amounts generated in the last step to obtain a sequence of the cumulative one-year losses.
4. Sort the sequence obtained in the last step in the increasing order to obtain the desired aggregate loss distribution.

Using this algorithm, VaR can be easily obtained as the $(1 - \alpha)$th empirical percentile of the obtained aggregate loss distribution. Clearly, the precision of the approximation would increase with a larger number of scenarios. This becomes particularly important for heavy-tailed loss distributions, because a large number of simulations is required to generate a sufficient number of the tail events.

Direct Computation Approach The second method to evaluate the cumulative distribution function is direct computation. The $F_X^{n*}(s)$ quantity can be approximated by replacing the continuous loss distribution by its discretized version defined at multiples $0, 1, 2, \ldots$ of some monetary unit such as 1,000 and then calculating

$$F_X^{n*}(s) = \sum_{x=0}^{s} F_X^{(n-1)*}(s - x) f_X(x),$$

where $f_X(x)$ is the corresponding density of the loss distribution. The drawback of this approach is in its computational intensity and a large number of multiplications required to obtain a desired estimate.

Panjer's Recursive Method Panjer's recursive method requires discretizing continuous loss distributions. Suppose that the frequency distribution satisfies property

$$P(N = k) = \left(a + \frac{b}{k}\right) P(N = k - 1), \qquad k = 1, 2, 3, \ldots,$$

where a and b are some constants. Then the density of the cumulative loss distribution function at any point s can be calculated by

$$f_S(s) = \frac{\sum_{y=1}^{s} (a + by/s) f_X(y) f_S(s - y)}{1 - a f_X(0)}.$$

The advantages of the recursive method lie in its significant reduction of computation time; however, the method is limited to certain frequency distributions. It is applicable to the binomial, Poisson, geometric, and negative binomial distributions.[4]

Inversion Method   The inversion method numerically inverts the characteristic function of the aggregate loss distribution. The characteristic function[5] of the aggregate loss process with a Poisson frequency distribution with intensity rate λ can be expressed as

$$\varphi_{S_{\Delta t}}(u) := \mathbb{E}[e^{iuS_{\Delta t}}] = \exp\left(\Delta t \int_{-\infty}^{+\infty}(e^{ius}-1)\lambda dF(s)\right),$$

where $i = \sqrt{-1}$ is a complex number.

The computational part can be implemented using the fast Fourier transform method and the Heckman-Myers inversion method.

Operational VaR

Following earlier discussions, for an actuarial model, the operational VaR is defined as the solution to the following equation:[6]

$$1 - \alpha = F_{S_{\Delta t}}(VaR) = \sum_{n=1}^{\infty} P(N_{\Delta t} = n)F^{n*}(VaR),$$

or, using the inverse of the cumulative distribution function, VaR is expressed as

$$VaR = F_{S_{\Delta t}}^{-1}(1 - \alpha).$$

An example of 99% VaR is illustrated in Figure 11.2 Although an analytic expression of VaR generally does not exist (as was previously

---

[4]For details of Panjer's recursive method, see Panjer and Willmot (1986) and Panjer and Willmot (1992).

[5]See Chapter 7 for the definition of characteristic functions.

[6]In the context of operational risk measurement, VaR was discussed by the Basel Committee (2001–2006) and in works such as Cruz (2002), Alexander (2003), Crouhy, Galai, and Mark (2001), Jorion (2000), Ebnöther, Vanini, McNeil, and Antolinez-Fehr (2001), Frachot, Moudoulaut, and Roncalli (2003), Medova and Kuriacou (2001), Embrechts, Kaufmann, and Samorodnitsky (2004), Chernobai, Menn, Rachev, and Trück (2005a), Chernobai, Menn, Rachev, and Trück (2005b), Rachev, Chernobai, and Menn (2006), and Dutta and Perry (2006).

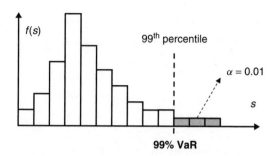

1-year Aggregate Loss
Distribution

FIGURE 11.2 Illustration of operational 99% value-at-risk.

discussed), one exception is a special case in which the loss distributions belong to the class of subexponential distributions. Subexponentiality is a property possessed by heavy-tailed distributions, in which the maximum observation $M_n = max\{X_1, X_2, \ldots, X_n\}$ in a sample of size n "determines" the behavior of the entire sum $S_n = X_1 + X_2 + \ldots + X_n$. For example, one very high observation can dictate the tail behavior of the whole aggregate process: mathematically, for all $n > 2$, as x approaches infinity,

$$P(S_n > x) \approx P(M_n > x).$$

As a consequence, for subexponential loss distributions, the following approximation holds:[7]

$$P(S_{\Delta t} > x) \approx \mathbb{E}[N_{\Delta t}] \cdot \overline{F}_X(x).$$

Combining the last equation with the definition of VaR, we obtain the following important result:

$$VaR \approx F_X^{-1}\left(1 - \frac{\alpha}{\mathbb{E}[N_{\Delta t}]}\right).$$

This equation allows estimation of an approximate amount of VaR for very heavy-tailed loss distributions. As an example, assume losses are measured

---

[7]See, for example, Embrechts, Klüppelberg, and Mikosch (1997) for more detailed treatment of the topic.

in millions of USD and follow a lognormal distribution with parameters $\mu = 5$ and $\sigma = 1$, and the one-year frequency is represented by a Poisson distribution with parameter $\lambda = 100$. Suppose, we wish to estimate 95% VaR and 99% VaR. The corresponding quantities are

$$q_1 = 1 - \frac{0.05}{100} = 0.9995 \quad \text{and} \quad q_2 = 1 - \frac{0.01}{100} = 0.9999,$$

resulting in 95% VaR and 99% VaR estimated to be

$$95\% \ VaR = F^{-1}(0.9999) = \$3,985.9 \ \text{million}$$

and

$$99\% \ VaR = F^{-1}(0.9995) = \$6,118.2 \ \text{million}.$$

VaR SENSITIVITY ANALYSIS

Operational risk managers may be concerned with the sensitivity of VaR to underlying risk factors or parameters of the model. VaR sensitivity factor can be estimated, for example, as

$$\Delta VaR / \Delta \omega,$$

where ω denotes the risk factor or the model parameter and Δ refers to the change in the position.

Sensitivity of VaR to various operational risk factors was discussed in Ebnöther, Vanini, McNeil, and Antolinez-Fehr (2001). In their empirical analysis, they showed that the 10 most important processes out of 103 processes contributing to the risk exposure of the portfolio risk account for 98% of the entire VaR amount. Frachot, Georges, and Roncalli (2001) conducted sensitivity analysis of VaR to the intensity parameter λ of the Poisson distribution of the loss event frequency in the LDA. They calculated $\Delta VaR / \Delta \lambda$ for five event types. For the confidence level of 99%, the sensitivities were in the interval [2/3, 4/5], and for the 99.9% confidence level, the interval became [1/2, 2/3], shorter and lower in magnitude, indicating that the sensitivity of VaR to the λ factor decreases with the increase in the confidence level.

Chernobai, Menn, Rachev, and Trück (2005b) discussed the importance of extreme events on the VaR measure and find that 5% of outlying events account for over 50% of operational VaR. They also emphasized the importance of the operational loss distribution selection on VaR and showed that under heavier-tailed loss distribution assumptions the VaR estimates are dramatically higher than under the assumption of light-tailed loss distributions.

Stress tests are intended to explore the effect of low probability events that lie outside the predictive capacity of any statistical model on VaR. Such events may include natural disasters, wars, changes in risk appetites of investors, and other abnormal events. We discussed stress tests in Chapter 4.

BACKTESTING VaR

Given the increasing importance of VaR estimates to banks and their regulators, evaluating the accuracy of the VaR models is an essential next step. Such check is conducted by *backtesting*. In market risk management, BIS imposes penalties on the financial institutions whose market VaR models do not work well. Whether or not the model for VaR needs to be improved determines whether additional expenses are necessary in this direction. Thus, backtesting helps in this cost-benefit analysis.

Banks usually perform backtesting on the monthly or quarterly basis. BIS suggests using the green, orange, and red zones for the anomalies. A variety of tests can be used to perform backtesting of VaR: Kupiec's Proportion of Failures test, Kupiec's Time Until First Failure test, Lopez' Magnitude Loss Function test, tests for clustering of violations (such as the Mean Cluster Size Method and the Blocks Method), and Crnkovich-Drachman Q-Test.[8] We review below the first two tests.

Kupiec's Proportion of Failures Test

In the Kupiec's proportion of failures test developed by Kupiec (1995), the number of violations (violations occur when the actual loss exceeds the estimate) from the empirical data are compared with the accepted number of exceedances at a given confidence level. Let ϵ_t denote the true total loss at point t and VaR_t be the forecasted VaR. At every point t (such as one day), a score C_t is assigned according to the following rule:

$$C_t = \begin{cases} 1 & \text{if } \epsilon_t > VaR_t \\ 0 & \text{if } \epsilon_t \leq VaR_t. \end{cases}$$

---

[8]See Haas (2001), Jorion (2000), and Cruz (2002) for a more detailed overview of various backtesting techniques.

TABLE 11.1 Number of violations (N) acceptable under Kupiec's proportion of failures test

VaR Confidence Level	255 days (1 year)	510 days (2 years)	1000 days (4 years)
99%	$N < 7$	$1 < N < 11$	$4 < N < 17$
97.5%	$2 < N < 12$	$6 < N < 21$	$15 < N < 36$
95%	$6 < N < 21$	$16 < N < 36$	$37 < N < 65$
92.5%	$11 < N < 28$	$27 < N < 51$	$59 < N < 92$
90%	$16 < N < 36$	$38 < N < 65$	$81 < N < 120$

A sum of T of such Bernoulli trials results in the binomial distribution for the total number of violations (exceedances) of VaR:

$$P(N = x) = \binom{T}{x} p^x (1 - p)^{T-x}, \qquad x = 0, 1, 2, \ldots, T,$$

where T is the total number of days in the testing interval (for example, a one year interval contains $T = 255$ trading days). Kupiec further performs a standard likelihood-ratio (LR) test.

If the null hypothesis postulates that N/T, the empirical probability of a violation, coincides with p, the true probability of observing a violation, then the likelihood-ratio test requires calculating the statistic:

$$\chi^2 = -2 \ln[(1 - p)^{T-N} p^N] + 2 \ln[(1 - N/T)^{T-N} (N/T)^N].$$

Under the null, the quantity is asymptotically distributed chi-squared with one degree of freedom. The test is rejected if $\chi_2 > 3.84$. Table 11.1 reports the 95% confidence intervals for different confidence levels p obtained via this test.

If the actual number of violations falls below the acceptable number of violations, it suggests that the VaR model is overly conservative, while the number of violations in excess of those accepted is an indicator that the VaR is too low or that the probability of large losses is understated under the model.

Lopez's Magnitude Loss Function Test

The Lopez magnitude loss function was proposed by Lopez (1998). It can be viewed as an extension of the Kupiec's proportion of failures test. In addition to counting the number of exceedances of VaR, it accounts for the magnitude of the violation. At every point t, a score C_t is proportional to the magnitude of violation and is assigned according to the following rule:

$$C_t = \begin{cases} 1 + (\epsilon_t - VaR_t)^2 & \text{if } \epsilon_t > VaR_t \\ 0 & \text{if } \epsilon_t \leq VaR_t. \end{cases}$$

The total score increases with the magnitude of the violations and provides additional information on how the underlying VaR model forecasts the upper tail of the cumulative loss distribution. It is notable, however, that the distribution of the total number of exceedances is no longer binomial but is dependent on the underlying distribution of loss amounts.

BENEFITS AND LIMITATIONS OF VaR AND ALTERNATIVE RISK MEASURES

Is VaR an optimal measure to estimate the operational risk capital charge? VaR has been criticized by many researchers. We discuss benefits and limitations of VaR and then proceed to reviewing some alternative risk measures.

Benefits of VaR

VaR can potentially have a practical impact in the following areas of business activities:[9]

- Comparing risk levels
- Determining capital charge
- Providing a risk-reduction incentive
- Measuring performance

We discuss each of these and focus on the last area.

Comparison of various types of risk, such as market risk with credit risk, or external fraud risk with natural disaster risk, becomes possible because it can be conducted via a uniform metric: VaR. The ability to compare risk contributions provides an institution with insight as to which risk factors are more likely to result in a higher downside performance. Hence, banks can use VaR as a yardstick to compare risks across business units.

---

[9] The first two and the last areas are based on Wilson (1998).

Since VaR is measured in currency units, it can be used to estimate the economic capital charge required to cover high magnitude losses. Provided that it is estimated accurately enough to reflect the true exposure to risk—based on historic data and projected to capture future trends—it can serve as a proxy for the minimum capital requirements imposed by the Basel II. Sufficiently high confidence level is necessary to ensure a safe financial system. Although the general idea for calculating VaR is fairly simple and can be applied uniformly to evaluating any kind of risk, financial institutions may apply more sophisticated versions of VaR to estimate the necessary capital charge. The methodologies could vary by the choice of the time horizon or confidence level, or even involve different estimation methods such as parametric and nonparametric methods.

VaR-based capital requirements provide an incentive to banks to reduce risk by rewarding low-risk banks with lower capital charge.

Finally, when banks form decisions on which strategy or investment to undertake or evaluate general performance of a business unit, VaR could serve as a benchmark in risk-adjustment of the return on equity. Many current *risk-adjusted performance measures* (RAPMs) use VaR for this purpose. An example is *risk-adjusted return on capital* (RAROC)—return on capital adjusted for the corresponding VaR amount.[10] Managers use VaR-based RAPMs for evaluating both relative and absolute performance of different businesses. For example, within the scope of credit risk, it becomes possible to compare different returns on two different kinds of loans with the same maturity and counterparty, or comparing the net return from two different business units. In general, RAROC is calculated as

$$\text{RAROC} = \frac{\text{Revenues} - \text{Expected loss}}{\text{Economic capital}}.$$

Economic capital that appears in the denominator is a proxy for risk associated with the investment for which RAROC is calculated. The underlying idea behind RAROC is to ensure that the revenues generated by the investment are sufficient to cover the associated regulatory capital.

In the context of operational risk, *operational RAROC* measures the adjusted revenues generated by taking operational risk relative to operational risk capital. Expected loss (EL) can be measured by the one-year aggregate EL estimated using an actuarial-type model for operational risk. Economic capital is the estimated regulatory capital charge (K), such as

---

[10]The RAROC framework was first developed and applied by Bankers Trust in the late 1970s to assess the potential profitability of a transaction with the bank's commercial borrowers given the risk and the resulting return on capital.

TABLE 11.2   Operational RAROC estimates (in %) in the Chapelle, Crama, Hübner, and Peters (2004) study

	BIA	SA	AMA	AMA Copula
BL1	27.70	34.62	22.58	
BL2	29.46	36.83	23.12	
Total	28.84	36.05	22.91	36.26

Source: Chapelle, Crama, Hübner, and Peters (2004, p. 47, Panel B).

the 99% one-year VaR measure.[11] Chapelle, Crama, Hübner, and Peters (2004) suggest estimating operational RAROC for each individual business line and applying a fixed fraction, such as 5%, of the corresponding gross income (GI) as a measure of operational revenues. Then, for a business line i, operational RAROC becomes

$$RAROC_i^{Op} = \frac{0.05 \times GI_i - EL_i}{K_i}.$$

Chapelle, Crama, Hübner, and Peters (2004) estimate operational RAROC for a sample of operational loss data from a large European banking institution. The data were split into two business lines:

BL1: Asset Management/Private Banking

BL2: Retail Banking

The operating revenues are assumed to be 5% of the gross income of the corresponding business line. Table 11.2 reports the estimated RAROC values for the two business lines for four scenarios: basic indicator approach (BIA), standardized approach (SA), advanced measurement approach (AMA), and the aggregation of risk capital estimated under the AMA approach using the Gaussian copula. The lognormal distribution was used to measure the risk capital under the AMA approach and to measure the expected aggregate loss for each of the three approaches: BIA, SA, and AMA. As is clear from the table, operational RAROC is maximized (36.26%) when the internal loss data are used to measure the risk capital using the AMA and dependence between different business lines is taken into account using a copula to aggregate capital across business lines.

---

[11]Crouhy, Galai, and Mark (2001) propose estimating economic capital as the worst-case loss at the desired confidence level minus the expected loss.

Pitfalls of VaR

We present some general critiques that have emerged in relation to the VaR measure.[12]

- *VaR is a lower bound for high losses.* VaR merely determines the lower bound for extreme losses given the prespecified conditions and is incapable of providing information on the extent of the losses that lie beyond the threshold. For example, a 95% VaR indicates that in 5% cases losses would exceed the estimated VaR level; however, the magnitudes of these exceedances are not indicated.
- *Multivariate risk factors affect VaR.* Since a portfolio is often affected by a vector of risk factors, one needs to account for the possible dependence structure among the risk drivers. This can significantly impact the VaR estimates.
- *VaR is unable to prevent high losses.* Although VaR can certainly be used to predict the magnitude of potentially high losses, it cannot be used to prevent them in practice. Hence, VaR should be supplemented by an individual risk-controlling scheme that should be in force at the management level of each individual institution.
- *VaR may fail the subadditivity property.* This issue is related to subsequent discussion of coherent risk measures.

Coherent Risk Measures

Properties of a coherent risk measures were proposed by Artzner, Delbaen, Eber, and Heath (1999) and have been widely accepted in risk literature. Denote the risk set (such as losses) by $L = \{X, X_1, X_2, \ldots\}$, and let ρ be the risk measure. Then coherent risk measures must satisfy the following four axioms:

1. *Translation invariance*: For all constants $-\infty < a < +\infty$, $\rho(X + a) = \rho(X) - a$. This axiom states that adding (subtracting) the sure initial amount a to the initial position and investing it in the reference instrument decreases (increases) the risk measure by a.
2. *Subadditivity*: $\rho(X_1 + X_2) \leq \rho(X_1) + \rho(X_2)$. This axiom means that "a merger does not create extra risk." For example, diversification of business activities or an absence of firewalls among different units results in the risk measure at most as high as in the case when they are independent.

---

[12]For a detailed discussion of the drawbacks of VaR and its alternatives, see Yamai and Yoshiba (2002a,b,c, and d).

3. *Positive homogeneity*: For all constants $\beta \geq 0$, $\rho(\beta X) = \beta\rho(X)$. This axiom represents a special case of the subadditivity axiom and says that β perfectly correlated portfolios with an identical position constitute risk level equal to β times the risk of one such portfolio.
4. *Monotonicity*: For $X_1 \leq X_2$, $\rho(X_1) \leq \rho(X_2)$. This axiom states that a better-performing portfolio generates a lower level of risk.

VaR may fail the subadditivity axiom, especially in cases when losses are heavy-tailed, and may result in overestimation of the capital charge. Therefore, VaR is not a coherent measure of risk.[13]

Conditional Value-at-Risk and Other Risk Measures

Conditional value-at-risk (CVaR) determines the amount of money one is expected to lose if an event in the right tail of the distribution beyond VaR takes place. Formally, for a given confidence level $1 - \alpha$ and a prespecified time horizon Δt, CVaR is defined as:[14]

$$CVaR = \mathbb{E}\left[S_{\Delta t} | S_{\Delta t} > VaR\right].$$

Figure 11.3 illustrates the notion of CVaR for an $\alpha = 0.01$ example. Unlike VaR, that may fail the subadditivity property, CVaR is a subadditive measure.

Relevance of CVaR as an appropriate risk measure becomes increasingly important when the choice of the right model becomes dependent on extreme events. The last two decades have witnessed a considerable increase in fat-tailedness, high kurtosis, and skewness of returns for individual assets, portfolios, and market indices. Operational risk is not an exception. Extreme events are the consequence of the increased kurtosis. Although VaR may be a fairly good model for capturing the worst of the ordinary financial losses, the potential of CVaR is superior to VaR in that CVaR better captures the tail events and can provide insight as to how heavy the upper tail of the loss distribution is. Up to now, VaR has become a popular risk management tool in financial world. Meanwhile, only few institutions have demonstrated the systematic ability to deal with the unusual or extreme events that take place more frequently than what conventional VaR models suggest. Therefore,

---

[13] See relevant discussions in RiskMetrics (2001), Embrechts, Resnick, and Samorodnitsky (1999), and Embrechts, McNeil, and Straumann (2002) and some examples in Embrechts (2004) and Neslehová, Embrechts, and Chavez-Demoulin (2006).
[14] In related literature, CVaR is also referred to as expected tail loss (ETL), expected shortfall (ES), tail VaR, mean excess loss, and tail conditional expectation.

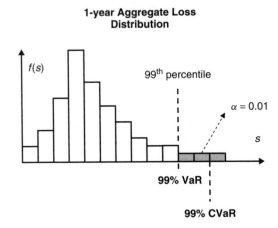

FIGURE 11.3 Illustration of operational 99% conditional value-at-risk.

although CVaR provides a more conservative risk estimate, it appears more appropriate when one is concerned with extreme risk.[15]

Clearly, the right measure for tail risk should be combined with the right distribution. For example, Rachev, Martin, Racheva-Iotova, and Stoyanov (2006) showed that by using a Gaussian model, the estimates for VaR and CVaR are nearly identical, while the alpha-stable VaR and CVaR are by far more conservative and reasonable. The underlying distribution of operational losses becomes crucial for an accurate determination of VaR and CVaR. Studies have shown that the frequency distribution is of lesser importance.

It may be possible that the body of the cumulative loss distribution and the tail may not belong to the same class of distributions. One possibility to measure CVaR is to use a combination of a semiparametric procedure with Extreme Value Theory. A distributional form of the upper tail of the aggregate loss distribution can be taken to follow the generalized Pareto distribution (GPD). GPD has been used to model high magnitude losses that lie above a certain high threshold.[16]

One drawback of CVaR is that the underlying expectation structure of the measure is not robust and can be therefore highly volatile in the

---

[15]See extensive discussions of CVaR in Rachev and Mittnik (2000), as well as discussions in relation to operational risk in Rachev, Menn, and Fabozzi (2005), Berkowitz and O'Brien (2002), Uryasev (2000), and Rockafellar and Uryasev (2002).
[16]For a discussion of extreme value theory, see Chapter 8.

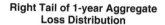

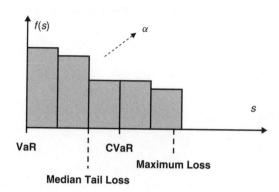

FIGURE 11.4   Illustration of alternative risk measures.

presence of outliers.[17] In addition, with very heavy-tailed loss distributions, estimations may produce infeasible (very high) CVaR values making CVaR impractical. A compromise between VaR and CVaR could be *median tail loss*, which is defined as the median of the tail beyond VaR:

$$\text{Median tail loss} = \text{median}\left[S_{\Delta t}|S_{\Delta t} > VaR\right].$$

For heavy-tailed loss distribution, median tail loss would result in a more optimistic measure of risk than CVaR and more conservative than VaR. Research in this direction remains very limited.[18]

In the context of market risk, RiskMetrics (2001) also proposes using *maximum loss* for the measure of risk.[19] Figure 11.4 illustrates the relationship between alternative risk measures.

EMPIRICAL STUDIES WITH OPERATIONAL LOSS DATA

In the operational risk literature, studies with simulated data dominate; studies that use actual loss data are in the minority. In this section, we present

---

[17]See discussion of robust methods in Chapter 12.
[18]Note that median tail loss may fail the subadditivity property.
[19]See also Studer (1999) for a discussion of using the maximum loss measure.

results of some empirical studies performed with actual operational loss data
and refer the reader to Chapter 8 and Chapter 9 for discussion of other
studies that report VaR estimates. Studies presented in Chapter 8 involve
modeling operational losses with extreme value theory. The empirical part
of Chapter 9 reports some studies of operational VaR and CVaR for the
situations in which loss data are subject to truncation from below and hence
the modeling requires a nonstandard approach.

De Fontnouvelle, Rosengren, and Jordan Study of 2002 LDCE Data

De Fontnouvelle, Rosengren, and Jordan (2005) explore the data collected
by the Risk Management Group (RMG) of the Basel Committee in June
2002's Operational Risk Loss Data Collection Exercise (LDCE). Original
data included 47,269 operational loss events reported by 89 banks from 19
countries in Europe, America, Asia, and Australasia. The authors limited
their analysis to the data collected from six banks, and performed the analysis on a bank-by-bank basis. Three models for the frequency distribution
were considered:

Model 1. Poisson distribution with fixed parameter λ.

Model 2. Poisson distribution with parameter λ being a linear function
of each bank's asset size.

Model 3. Negative binomial distribution with parameter being a linear
function of each bank's asset size.

Table 11.3 reports the estimated high percentiles of the cumulative
distribution function for the three models. To preserve the confidentiality of
the banks, each percentile was rescaled for each bank by that bank's assets.
The table reports the median for each percentile. According to the Basel
Committee, a reasonable level of the overall operational risk capital charge
constitutes about 12% of minimum regulatory capital, which is about 0.6%
of the total value of assets. Figures in Table 11.3 suggest that a simple
Poisson assumption (Model 1) together with a Pareto distribution of losses
result in an estimate (0.468%) that is rather close to the desired 6%. The
authors point out, however, that the obtained estimates are based entirely
on the internal data, not supplemented by external data, and inclusion of
external data into the model would increase the estimate, bringing it closer
to the desired level. Model 2 produced very optimistic estimates for the
capital charge, while Model 3 produced the highest estimates overall. It is
also evident that the Pareto assumption for the loss distribution seems the
most appropriate among the three considered.

TABLE 11.3 Estimates of the operational capital charge as percentage of the total value of assets, for a medium firm, under various distributional assumptions in the de Fontnouvelle, Rosengren, and Jordan study

Loss Distribution	Percentile	Model 1	Model 2	Model 3
Pareto	95%	0.066%	0.106%	0.166%
	99%	0.117%	0.148%	0.237%
	99.9%	0.468%	0.362%	0.400%
Lognormal	95%	0.047%	0.089%	0.143%
	99%	0.056%	0.101%	0.198%
	99.9%	0.070%	0.121%	0.273%
Empirical	95%	0.047%	0.086%	0.146%
	99%	0.053%	0.093%	0.202%
	99.9%	0.058%	0.102%	0.273%

Source: de Fontnouvelle, Rosengren, and Jordan (2005, p. 38), with modifications.

Chapelle, Crama, Hübner, and Peters Study with European Loss Data

Chapelle, Crama, Hübner, and Peters (2005) examine a sample of operational loss data obtained from a large banking institution in Europe, whose data collection process has been carried out in compliance with the Basel II definition of business lines and event types for the adoption of the AMA. To preserve confidentiality of the data, all data points were rescaled and were measured in units rather than in monetary terms. A total of 3,000 points were used for the study.

They estimate VaR for the Retail Banking business line and Clients, Products and Business Practices event type combination. The sample of 235 observations was split into regular and extreme losses by examining the mean excess plot.[20] Gamma, Weibull, and lognormal distributions were considered for the regular losses. Among the three, the lognormal distribution resulted in the best fit based on the Kolmogorov-Smirnov, Anderson-Darling, and Cramér-von Mises tests, with parameters $\mu = 0.94$ and $\sigma = 2.74$. The extreme losses were modeled above the threshold $u = 544$ with the GPD yielding parameters $\xi = 0.736$ and $\beta = 522$. The complete internal loss distribution was then taken to be a mixture of the lognormal distribution and the GPD. A simple Poisson distribution was assumed to model the loss frequency.

---

[20]See Chapter 8, in which we discuss the mean excess function.

TABLE 11.4   Operational VaR estimates (in units) for European loss data in the Chapelle, Crama, Hübner, and Peters study

Real total loss	41,747
Median	63,876
Mean	81,504
95% VaR	167,443
95% VaR	375,584
99.5% VaR	539,823
99.9% VaR	1,439,834
99.95% VaR	1,866,989

Source: Chapelle, Crama, Hübner, and Peters (2005, p. 18), with modifications.

Further, Monte Carlo simulations approach was used to determine VaR at the 95%, 99%, 99.5%, 99.9%, and 99.95% confidence levels. Table 11.4 presents a summary of the results. It is notable how rapidly VaR increases with a small increase in the confidence level.

For further details of this study, with other business line/event type combinations and further modeling considerations, see Chapelle, Crama, Hübner, and Peters (2005). In the empirical part of Chapter 9 we provided an extension to this study and demonstrate the effect of mixing internal data with external data on the resulting capital charge.

SUMMARY OF KEY CONCEPTS

- Value-at-risk (VaR) is an important benchmark for measuring the operational risk capital charge in the advanced measurement approaches. It is a monetary metric that determines the maximum amount of loss that is expected to occur over a prespecified time horizon at a prespecified confidence level.
- Operational VaR is based on the inversion of the compound one-year loss distribution. Actuarial models can be used to aggregate the loss and frequency distributions. Computation of the aggregate distribution can be performed using one of the several algorithms: the Monte Carlo approach, direct computation approach, recursive method, and inversion method.
- VaR sensitivity analysis and backtesting are important elements of a sound VaR model. Backtesting procedures look for violations of VaR and may be performed using Kupiec's proportion of failures test, Lopez's magnitude loss function test, tests for clustering of violations, and Crnkovich-Drachman Q-test, among others.

- VaR can be useful in comparing risk levels, determining capital charge, providing a risk-reduction incentive, and measuring performance.
- Coherent risk measures should satisfy four properties: translation invariance, subadditivity, positive homogeneity, and monotonicity. VaR may fail to fulfill the subadditivity property.
- Conditional value-at-risk (CVaR) may be used as an alternative to VaR. CVaR is defined as the expected value of total loss, given that it exceeds VaR. CVaR satisfies the subadditivity property and can be more appropriate in capturing the heaviness of the right tail of the loss distribution.
- Empirical studies with operational loss data demonstrate that VaR is highly dependent on the choice of the loss and frequency distributions. Small changes in the confidence level may result in substantial changes in VaR.

REFERENCES

Alexander, C., ed. (2003), *Operational Risk: Regulation, Analysis and Management*, Prentice Hall, Upper Saddle River, New Jersey.

Artzner, P., Delbaen, F., Eber, J., and Heath, D. (1999), "Coherent Measures of Risk," *Mathematical Finance* 9, pp. 203–228.

Berkowitz, J. and O'Brien, J. (2002), "How Accurate are Value-at-Risk Models at Commercial Banks?," *Journal of Finance* 57, pp. 1093–1112.

Chapelle, A., Crama, Y., Hübner, G. and Peters, J. (2004), Basel II and Operational Risk: Implications for Risk Measurement and Management in the Financial Sector, Technical report, National Bank of Belgium.

Chapelle, A., Crama, Y., Hübner, G., and Peters, J. (2005), Measuring and Managing Operational Risk in the Financial Sector: An Integrated Framework, Technical report, National Bank of Belgium.

Chernobai, A., Menn, C., Rachev, S. T., and Trück, S. (2005a), "A Note on the Estimation of the Frequency and Severity Distribution of Operational Losses," *Mathematical Scientist* 30(2), pp. 87–97.

Chernobai, A., Menn, C., Rachev, S. T., and Trück, S. (2005b), Estimation of Operational Value-at-Risk in the Presence of Minimum Collection Thresholds, Technical report, University of California at Santa Barbara.

Crouhy, M., Galai, D., and Mark, R. (2001), *Risk Management*, McGraw-Hill, New York.

Cruz, M. G. (2002), *Modeling, Measuring and Hedging Operational Risk*, John Wiley & Sons, New York, Chichester.

de Fontnouvelle, P., Rosengren, E., and Jordan, J. (2005), Implications of Alternative Operational Risk Modelling Techniques, Technical report, Federal Reserve Bank of Boston and Fitch Risk.

Dutta, K., and Perry, J. (2006), A Tale of Tails: An Empirical Analysis of Loss Distribution Models for Estimating Operational Risk Capital, Technical Report 06-13, Federal Reserve Bank of Boston.

Ebnöther, S., Vanini, P., McNeil, A. J., and Antolinez-Fehr, P. (2001), Modelling Operational Risk, Technical report, ETH Zürich.

Embrechts, P. (2004), "Extremes in Economics and Economics of Extremes," in B. Finkenstädt and H. Rootzén, eds., *Extreme Values in Finance, Telecommunications and the Environment*, Chapman & Hall, London, pp. 169–183.

Embrechts, P., Kaufmann, P., and Samorodnitsky, G. (2004), "Ruin Theory Revisited: Stochastic Models for Operational Risk," in C. Bernadell, P. Cardon, J. Coche, F. X. Diebold, and S. Manganelli, eds., *Risk Management for Central Bank Foreign Reserves*, European Central Bank, Frankfurt, pp. 243–261.

Embrechts, P., Klüppelberg, C., and Mikosch, T. (1997), *Modeling Extremal Events for Insurance and Finance*, Springer-Verlag, Berlin.

Embrechts, P., McNeil, A., and Straumann, D. (2002), "Correlation and Dependence in Risk Management: Properties and Pitfalls," in M. A. H. Dempster, ed., *Risk Management: Value-at-Risk and Beyond*, Cambridge University Press, Cambridge, pp. 176–223.

Embrechts, P., Resnick, S. I., and Samorodnitsky, G. (1999), "Extreme Value Theory as a Risk Management Tool," *North American Actuarial Journal* 3, 30–41.

Frachot, A., Georges, P., and Roncalli, T. (2001), Loss distribution approach for operational risk, Technical report, Crédit Lyonnais, Groupe de Recherche Opérationnelle.

Frachot, A., Moudoulaut, O., and Roncalli, T. (2003), Loss Distribution Approach in Practice, Technical report, Crédit Lyonnais, Groupe de Recherche Opérationnelle, France.

Haas, M. (2001), "New methods in backtesting," *Preprint CAESAR*.

Jorion, P. (2000), *Value-at-Risk: The New Benchmark for Managing Financial Risk*, 2nd ed., McGraw-Hill, New York.

Klugman, S. A., Panjer, H. H., and Willmot, G. E. (2004), *Loss Models: From Data to Decisions*, 2nd ed., John Wiley & Sons, Hoboken, New Jersey.

Kupiec, P. (1995), "Techniques for verifying the accuracy of risk measurement models," *Journal of Derivatives* 6, pp. 7–24.

Lopez, J. A. (1998), Methods for evaluating value-at-risk estimates, Technical Report 9802, Federal Reserve Bank of New York.

Medova, E. A., and Kuriacou, M. N. (2001), Extremes in Operational Risk Management, Technical report, Center for Financial Research, University of Cambridge.

Neslehová, J., Embrechts, P., and Chavez-Demoulin, V. (2006), Infinite Mean Models and the LDA for Operational Risk, Technical report, ETH Zürich.

Panjer, H., and Willmot, G. (1986), "Computational aspects of recursive evaluation of compound distributions," *Insurance: Mathematics and Economics 5*.

Panjer, H., and Willmot, G. (1992), *Insurance Risk Models*, Society of Actuaries, Chicago.

Rachev, S., Martin, D., Racheva-Iotova, B., and Stoyanov, S. (2006), Stable ETL optimal portfolios and extreme risk management, Technical report, University of California at Santa Barbara.

Rachev, S. T., Chernobai, A., and Menn, C. (2006), "Empirical examination of operational loss distribution," in M. M. et al., ed., *Perspectives on Operational Research*, Deutscher Unversitäts Verlag/GWV Fachverlage GmbH, Wiesbaden, Germany, pp. 379–402.

Rachev, S. T., Menn, C., and Fabozzi, F. J. (2005), *Fat-Tailed and Skewed Asset Return Distributions: Implications for Risk Management, Portfolio Selection, and Option Pricing*, John Wiley & Sons, Hoboken, NJ.

Rachev, S. T. and Mittnik, S. (2000), *Stable Paretian Models in Finance*, John Wiley & Sons, New York.

RiskMetrics (2001), "Return to RiskMetrics: The Evolution of a Standard," http://www.riskmetrics.com.

Rockafellar, R. T., and Uryasev, S. (2002), "Conditional Value-at-Risk for General Loss Distributions," *Journal of Banking and Finance* 26, pp. 1443–1471.

Studer, G. (1999), "Market risk computation for nonlinear portfolios," *Journal of Risk* 1(4).

Uryasev, S. (2000), "Conditional Value-at-Risk: Optimization Algorithms and Applications," *Financial Engineering News* 14, pp. 1–5.

Wilson, T. (1998), "Value-at-Risk," in C. Alexander, ed., *Risk Management and Analysis—Volume I*, John Wiley & Sons, Chichester, England.

Yamai Y., and Yoshiba, T. (2002a), "Comparative Analyses of Expected Shortfall and value-at-Risk (2): Expected Utility Maximization and Tail Risk," *Monetary and Econmic Studies*, 2002, pp. 95–115.

Yamai Y., and Yoshiba, T. (2002b), "Comparative Analyses of Expected Shortfall and value-at-Risk (2): Their Validity under Market Stress," *Monetary and Econmic Studies*, October, pp. 181–237.

Yamai Y., and Yoshiba, T. (2002c), "Comparative Analyses of Expected Shortfall and value-at-Risk: Their Estimation, Decomposition, and Optimization," *Monetary and Econmic Studies*, January, pp. 87–121.

Yamai Y., and Yoshiba, T. (2002d), "On the Validity of Value-at-Risk: Comparative Analyses with Expected Shortfall," *Manetary and Econmic Studies*, January, pp. 57–85.

CHAPTER 12

Robust Modeling

An actuarial-type model dominates statistical models for operational risk under the advanced measurement approach.[1] The Basel II Capital Accord requires that a quantitative model for operational risk must have the capacity to accommodate peculiarities of the loss distribution: high kurtosis, severe right-skewness, and excessive heavy-tailedness. Model selection is complicated by scarcity of the available data along with the presence of *tail events*, the so-called low frequency/high severity losses, that contribute to the heaviness of the upper tail of the loss distribution. Some critics of the Basel II framework argue that the standards required for the calculation of regulatory capital are such that the amount of the capital charge might even exceed the economic capital,[2] leaving decreased availability of funds required for financial needs and investments.[3] This may be well due to misspecification in the model. In this chapter, we propose an approach that can provide a solution to this dilemma.

In 2001, the Basel Committee made the following recommendation:

> *Data will need to be collected and robust estimation techniques (for event impact, frequency, and aggregate operational loss) will need to be developed. (BIS, 2001, Annex 6, p. 26)*

The notion of *robustness* can be given different interpretations. One interpretation would be the distributional robustness—robustness of the assumed model to minor departures from the model assumptions. *Outlier-resistant* or *distributionally robust* (so-called robust) statistics methods aim at constructing statistical procedures that are stable (robust) even when the underlying model is not perfectly satisfied by the available data

---

[1] See Chapter 11 where these models are discussed.
[2] See, for example, Currie (2005).
[3] See Financial Guardian Group (2005).

set. An example of departure from the assumed model is the presence of outliers—observations that are very different from the rest of the data.

In this chapter we review the basic concepts of robust statistics and examine potentia applications to operational loss data.[4]

OUTLIERS IN OPERATIONAL LOSS DATA

Existing empirical evidence suggests that the general pattern of operational loss severity data is characterized by high kurtosis, severe right-skewness, and a very heavy right tail created by several outlying events.[5] Figure 12.1 portrays an illustrative example of operational loss severity data.

As discussed in Chapter 6, one approach to calibrate operational losses is to fit a parametric family of common loss distributions such as lognormal, Weibull, gamma, Pareto, and so on. One drawback of using these distributions is that they may not be optimal in fitting well both the

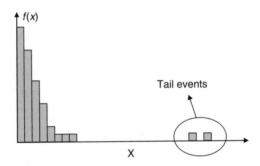

FIGURE 12.1   An example of a histogram of operational loss data.
Source: Chernobai and Rachev (2006, p. 30). Reprinted with permission.

---

[4]In recent years, the methods of robust statistics have been applied to tackle important issues in finance. Knez and Ready (1997) use robust statistics to empirically demonstrate that some of the factors in the well-known three-factor Fama-French model (1992) are not significant once outliers are eliminated. Kim and White (2003) apply robust estimators to examine the properties of the S&P500 index returns. Bassett, Gerber, and Rocco (2004) investigate the performance of portfolio return distribution using robust statistic and and conclude that the resulting forecasts outperform those under a conventional classical analysis. Perret-Gentil and Victoria-Feser (2005) use robust estimates for mean and the covariance matrix in the mean-variance portfolio selection problem. See also Dell'Aquila and Embrechts (2006) for a discussion of robust methods applied to operational risk.
[5]See Chapter 6.

center and the tails.[6] In this case, mixture distributions may be considered. An alternative approach, discussed in Chapter 8, is to use extreme value theory (EVT) to fit a generalized Pareto distribution (GPD) to extreme losses exceeding a high prespecified threshold. A drawback of this approach is that the parameters of the GPD distribution obtained under the EVT approach are highly sensitive to the choice of threshold and additional extreme observations.

The biggest problem of both approaches—fitting a common loss distribution or applying EVT—is that they almost always result in parameter estimates that produce an infinite mean and variance and unreasonably high estimates for the capital charge. Classical estimators that assign equal importance to all available data are highly sensitive to extreme losses and in the presence of just a few such losses can produce arbitrarily large estimates of the mean, variance, and other vital statistics. For example, high mean and standard deviation values for operational loss data do not provide an indication as to whether this is due to generally large values of observations or just one high-scale event, and it may be difficult to give the right interpretation to such result.

The presence of low frequency/high severity events in the operational loss data creates the following paradox. On the one hand, the tail events correspond to the losses that are infrequent but often are the most destructive for an institution. In this sense, tail events cannot be ignored as they convey important information regarding the loss generation process and may signal important flaws in the system. On the other hand, as stated earlier, recent empirical findings suggest that classical methods will frequently fit neither the bulk of the operational loss data nor the tail events well, and the center and the tails of the data appear to conform to different laws. Then we say that the tail events possess the properties of outliers. In this light, applying classical methods that use all available data may not be the best approach, and using robust methods that focus on the dominant portion of the data may be a better one. Robust methods take into account the underlying structure of the data and separate the bulk of the data from outlying events, thereby avoiding the upward bias in the vital statistics and forecasts.

Due to this paradox, the classical model and the robust model are not competitors and both models can be used as important complements to each other. The results from both approaches are not expected to be the same, as they explain different phenomena dictated by the original data: the general tendency (the robust method) and the conservative view (the classical method). According to Hampel (1973),

---

[6]See, for example, discussion in Chernobai, Menn, Rachev, and Trück (2005).

robust methods, in one form or another (and be it a glance at the data), are necessary; those who still don't use them are either careless or ignorant.

SOME DANGERS OF USING THE CLASSICAL APPROACH

There are dangers of using only the classical approach in modeling operational risk. Here we provide two examples.

In the first scenario, a risk expert calculates risk capital based on the sum of the aggregate expected loss (EL) and unexpected loss (UL). Suppose he constructs a one-quarter-ahead forecast of the total operational loss based on the historic data of his institution. Further, assume the data include the events of the order of magnitude of *9/11* or Hurricane Andrew (1992) and the Hurricane Katrina (2005). Would his forecast be robust? Most likely, his forecasts would indicate that his bank will have little reserves left if it decides to cover the potential loss.

In the second scenario, the EL amount is excluded from the total estimated capital charge (e.g., VaR or CVaR) and the charge is set on the basis of the marginal UL.[7] Suppose, a risk analyst fits a heavy-tailed loss distribution to full data, which include several low frequency/high severity data points. The estimate of the aggregate expected loss (EL) is likely to be very high. In particular, if the fitted distribution is very heavy-tailed, such as some cases of Pareto or alpha-stable, he may get an infinite mean and infinite second and higher moments' estimates. Occasionally, EL may even exceed VaR. The danger of treating outliers equally with the rest of the data is that the resulting UL-only-based capital charge may appear insufficient to cover the true exposure to the risk.

OVERVIEW OF ROBUST STATISTICS METHODOLOGY

Robust statistics is the generalization of the classical theory: It takes into account the possibility of model misspecification, and the inferences remain valid not only at the parametric model but also in the neighborhood.[8] The objectives of robust statistics are as follows:[9]

---

[7]BIS defines UL as VaR−EL. The most recent Basel II guidelines suggest excluding EL from total risk capital, provided that the bank can demonstrate its ability to effectively monitor expected operational losses. See BIS (2005) and BIS (2006).

[8]The pioneering work on robust statistics is due to Huber (1964) and Hampel (1968).

[9]These objectives of robust statistics are adopted from Chapter 1 in Hampel, Ronchetti, Rousseeuw, and Stahel (1986).

- To describe the structure best fitting the bulk of the data
- To identify deviating data points (outliers) or deviating substructures for further treatment, if desired
- To identify and give a warning about highly influential data points ("leverage points")
- To deal with unsuspected serial correlations, or more generally, with deviations from the assumed correlation structures

According to Hampel (1973), 5% to 10 % of wrong values in the data appear to be the rule rather than the exception. Outliers may appear in data due to (a) gross errors; (b) wrong classification of the data (outlying observations may not belong to the model followed by the bulk of the data); (c) grouping; and (d) correlation in the data.[10]

Formal Model for Robust Statistics

We now present a formal framework for robust statistics. Let $(1 - \epsilon)$ be the probability of well-behaved data, and ϵ be the probability of data being contaminated by bad observations. If $H(x)$ is an arbitrary distribution defining a neighborhood of the parametric model F_γ, then G is the two-point mixture of the parametric model and the contamination distribution:

$$G(x) = (1 - \varepsilon)F_\gamma(x) + \varepsilon H(x).$$

Traditional Methods of Outlier Detection

Under traditional robust models, outliers are exogenously detected and excluded from the dataset, and the classical analysis is performed on the "cleaned" data. Data editing, screening, truncation, censoring, Winsorizing, and trimming are various methods for data cleaning. Such procedures for outlier detection are referred to in the literature as *forwards-stepping rejection*, or *outside-in rejection* of outliers.[11]

Outlier detection methods in the forwards-stepping rejection procedure can be of two types: informal and formal. The former approach is rather subjective: a visual inspection of the database may be performed by a risk expert, and data points that clearly do not follow the rule of the majority are excluded. A risk expert may further conduct a background analysis of extreme losses, analyze whether they follow a pattern, and decide whether they are likely to repeat in the future. Which losses and how many to exclude is left up to his subjective judgment. For example, Moscadelli

---

[10] See Hampel, Ronchetti, Rousseeuw, and Stahel (1986).

[11] See, for example, Simonoff (1987a,b).

(2004) examines the operational loss data[12] and excludes one outlier from the Retail Brokerage loss data (that consists of a total of 3,267 observations) and five outliers from the Commercial Banking loss database (that consists of a total of 3,414 observations).

Formal approaches to discriminate outliers include trimming and Winsorizing data. For example, $(\delta, 1 - \gamma)$-trimmed data have the lowest δ and the highest γ fractions of the original data removed. For symmetrically contaminated data, $\delta = \gamma$. In the context of operational risk, contamination is asymmetric (on the right) and $\delta = 0$. For an original sample x, $x = x_1, x_2, \ldots, x_n$ of size n, define $L_n = \lfloor n\delta \rfloor$ and $U_n = \lfloor n\gamma \rfloor$, where $\lfloor a \rfloor$ denotes the floor of a, and let $x_{(k)}$ denote the kth order statistic such that $x_{(1)} \leq \ldots \leq x_{(n)}$. Winsorizing data is more efficient than trimming: the lowest $\lfloor n\delta \rfloor$ observations in the original dataset are set equal to the lowest observation in the "cleaned" data, and the highest observations are set equal to the greatest observation in the cleaned data. The Winsorized sample points y_j, $j = 1, \ldots, n$ are thus obtained by transforming x_j, $j = 1, \ldots, n$ in the following way:

$$
y_j = \begin{cases}
x_{(L_n+1)} & j \leq L_n \\
x_{(j)} & L_n + 1 \leq j \leq U_n, \quad j = 1, \ldots, n \\
x_{(U_n)} & j \geq U_n + 1.
\end{cases}
$$

Other outlier rejection principles are based on kurtosis, largest Studentized residual, Studentized range, Shapiro-Wilk statistic, and Dixon's rule. A variety of outlier rejection methods have been discussed by Hampel (1973, 1985), Hampel, Ronchetti, Rousseeuw, and Stahel (1986), Simonoff (1987a,b), Stigler (1973), and David (1981), to name a few. The main criticism of the outlier rejection approach is that information is lost due to discarding several data points. One possibility is to choose to allow a fixed efficiency loss of, say, 5% or 10%.[13] Hampel (1985) also showed that outside-in outlier rejection procedures possess low *breakdown points*.[14] Estimators can be severely affected by a relatively small number of extreme observations, which means that estimators are not robust to heavy contamination. Nevertheless, despite the criticism, "any way of treating outliers which is not totally inappropriate, prevents the worst" (Hampel 1973).

---

[12] The data are taken from the second Loss Data Collection Exercise (Quantitative Impact Study 3); see also BIS (2003).

[13] See Hampel, Ronchetti, Rousseeuw, and Stahel (1986).

[14] The breakdown of an estimator is the maximum fraction of outliers that an estimator can tolerate.

Examples of Nonrobust versus Robust Estimators

Examples of nonrobust estimators include the arithmetic mean, standard deviation, mean deviation and range, covariance and correlation, and *ordinary least squares*. Robust measures of center include median, trimmed mean, and Winsorized mean. Robust measures of spread include *interquartile range*, *median absolute deviation*, mean absolute deviation, and Winsorized standard deviation. More estimators of scale were proposed by Rousseeuw and Croux (1993). Robust estimators of skewness were studied by Kendall and Stuart (1977), Bowley (1920), Hinkley (1975), and Groeneveld and Meeden (1984). Robust estimators of kurtosis for heavy-tailed distributions were proposed by Hogg (1972, 1974); others are due to Moors (1988), Hogg (1972, 1974), and Groeneveld and Meeden (1984).

Outlier Detection Approach Based on Influence Functions

Under more modern robust models, outliers are given a further treatment rather than being simply discarded. Outliers can be detected and rejected using a "backwards-stepping" or "inside-out" rejection procedure. One approach is based on the *influence functions* (IF), proposed by Hampel (1968, 1974).[15] IF measures the differential effect of an infinitesimal amount of contamination (for example, one additional observation) in an uncontaminated sample on the value of the estimator T at a point x, standardized by the amount of contamination:

$$\text{IF}(x; T, F_\gamma) = \lim_{\varepsilon \searrow 0} \frac{T(G) - T(F_\gamma)}{\varepsilon}.$$

IF can be used to measure the *gross-error sensitivity* (GES)—the worst (approximate) influence which a small amount of contamination of fixed size can have on the value of the estimator T:[16]

$$\text{GES}(T, F_\gamma) = \sup_x |\text{IF}(x; T, F_\gamma)|.$$

GES can be used as a tool to detect the observations having a large influence on the value of the estimator. *Inside-out* outlier rejection rules have high breakdown points, and the estimators can tolerate up to 50% of contamination according to Simonoff (1987a).[17]

---

[15] See also Hampel, Ronchetti, Rousseeuw, and Stahel (1986).
[16] See Hampel, Ronchetti, Rousseeuw, and Stahel (1986).
[17] Further discussion on IF and "inside-out" outlier treatment procedures can be found in Huber (1981) and Simonoff (1987a,b). Other references on robust statistics

Advantages of Robust Statistics

We have previously argued that outliers are *bad data* in the sense that they deviate from the pattern set by the majority of the data.[18] Hence, they tend to obscure the data's generic flow and may lack explanatory and predictive power regarding the generic portion of the data. Classical models use all available data in the analysis, giving an equal weight to every observation, while robust models focus on the statistical properties of the bulk of the data without being distracted by outliers.

Performing robust or classical analysis of the data is a trade-off between safety and efficiency: Although some information may be lost while discarding or diminishing the contribution of the outlying events, one can significantly improve forecasts and produce more reliable estimates by applying a robust methodology.

An important application of robust statistics is using them as a *diagnostic technique* for evaluating the sensitivity of the inference conducted under the classical model to the rare events and to reveal their possible economic role.[19] Such analysis can be performed by comparing the results obtained under the classical and robust procedures.

Outlier Rejection Approach and Stress Tests

There is a parallel between data trimming and stress tests that are widely applied in the operational risk modeling. The idea of stress tests is to add several extreme observations to the data set. By doing so, a risk analyst seeks to examine the incremental effect of potentially hazardous events on VaR and other risk measures. With the robust methodology, instead of adding potential events, already existing but potentially improbable events are excluded from the database. The purpose is to investigate the fundamental properties of the main subset of the data in the absence of these unlikely events, as well as to study their incremental impact on risk measures.

Decisions about whether to include (stress tests) or exclude high-magnitude events (robust method), or whether to perform both tests, as well as how many points and of what magnitudes to include or exclude, can be left up to the subjective judgment of the risk expert or can be performed using one of the formal (objective) procedures discussed earlier.

---

include Rousseeuw and Leroy (1987), Martin and Simin (2003), Kim and White (2003), Aucremanne, Brys, Hubert, Rousseeuw, and Struyf (2004), Hubert, Pison, Struyf, and van Aelst (2004), and Olive (2005).
[18] See Huber (1981) and Hampel, Ronchetti, Rousseeuw, and Stahel (1986).
[19] See Knez and Ready (1997).

APPLICATION OF ROBUST METHODS TO OPERATIONAL LOSS DATA

In this section, we apply the simple data-trimming technique to historic operational loss data.[20] The purpose of the application is to investigate the impact of outlying tail events on the performance of EL, VaR, and CVaR.

The data set used in the study was obtained from a major European operational public loss data provider.[21] The database is composed of operational loss events throughout the world. The data set used for the analysis covers losses in U.S. dollars exceeding $1,000,000 for the time period between 1980 and 2002. Our analysis is restricted to the data of loss type *external* that includes events related to natural and man-made disasters and external fraud.

Contamination of the data is located in the far right tail of the loss distribution. In this sense, the contamination is of a nonsymmetric nature. We trim the original data by cutting off the *highest* 5% of losses. These correspond to 12 observations. Table 12.1 summarizes the descriptive statistics of the full and cleaned data. A dramatic change in the statistics is evident when the robust methodology is applied: the mean and the standard deviation have decreased to roughly one-third and one-seventh of the initial values, respectively; the skewness coefficient has dropped four times, and the kurtosis coefficient has decreased roughly 14 times. Note that the robust measures of center and spread—median and median absolute deviation (MAD), respectively—remain practically unchanged.

In the next step, we fit loss distributions to both complete and trimmed datasets.[22] Table 12.2 exhibits parameter estimates, mean, and standard deviation[23] for the lognormal and Weibull distributions. Outlier rejection

---

[20]Another application can be found in Chernobai, Burneçki, Rachev, Trück, and Weron (2006), where the robust methodology was applied to the U.S. natural catastrophe claims data. Results presented here are partially reproduced from Chernobai, Menn, Rachev, and Trück (2005).

[21]The same dataset was examined in Chapter 9.

[22]To account for the reporting bias, left-truncated loss distributions were fitted using the method of maximizing the restricted likelihood function. See Chapter 9 for a detailed description of the methodology, its theoretical implication on the estimates of the loss and frequency distribution parameters and the capital charge, and the empirical application to operational loss data.

[23]Note that in Table (12.1) the estimates of location and spread are based on the observed data that exceed $1,000,000. In Table (12.2) the population estimates of location and spread are extrapolated to correspond to complete data.

TABLE 12.1 Descriptive sample statistics of full and top-5%-trimmed operational loss data

		Classical	Robust
n		233	221
min	($ '000,000)	1.1	1.1
max	($ '000,000)	6,384	364.80
mean	($ '000,000)	103.35	39.7515
median	($ '000,000)	12.89	11.40
st. dev.	($ '000,000)	470.24	63.84
MAD	($ '000,000)	11.17	9.64
skewness		11.0320	2.5635
kurtosis		140.8799	10.0539

Source: Chernobai and Rachev (2006, p. 36). Reprinted with permission.

TABLE 12.2 Estimated parameters, mean, and standard deviation for loss distributions fitted to the full and top-5%-trimmed operational loss data

	Lognormal			Weibull	
	Classical	Robust		Classical	Robust
μ	15.7125	15.8095	β	0.0108	0.0012
σ	2.3639	1.9705	α	0.2933	0.4178
mean	$1.09 \cdot 10^8$	$0.51 \cdot 10^8$	mean	$5.21 \cdot 10^7$	$2.90 \cdot 10^7$
st. dev.	$1.78 \cdot 10^9$	$0.35 \cdot 10^9$	st. dev.	$2.96 \cdot 10^8$	$0.85 \cdot 10^8$

Source: Chernobai and Rachev (2006, p. 37). Reprinted with permission.

has resulted in significantly decreased mean and the standard deviation estimates.

Next, we examine the aggregated one-year EL, 95% VaR, 99% VaR, 95% CVaR, and 99% CVaR. The estimates are based on out-of-sample one-year ahead forecast. For the frequency distribution, a Cox process with a nonhomogeneous intensity rate function was used. We omit the estimated parameter values of the frequency distribution from this paper—see Chernobai, Menn, Rachev, and Trück (2005) for the details. We note, however, that robust methods have a negligible effect on the parameters of the frequency distribution. Table 12.3 reports the findings. The estimates of the risk measures are considerably lower under the robust method in all cases. Hence, robust methods can prevent overestimation of the capital charge.

TABLE 12.3 Estimated one-year EL, VaR, and CVaR values ($\times 10^{10}$) for the full and top-5%-trimmed operational loss data, and incremental effect (Δ) of the highest 5% losses

	Lognormal			Weibull		
	Classical	Robust	Δ	Classical	Robust	Δ
EL	0.0327	0.0154	53%	0.0208	0.0088	58%
95% VaR	0.1126	0.0580	48%	0.0885	0.0354	60%
99% VaR	0.4257	0.1642	61%	0.2494	0.0715	71%
95% CVaR	0.3962	0.1397	65%	0.2025	0.0599	70%
99% CVaR	1.1617	0.3334	71%	0.4509	0.1066	76%

Source: Chernobai and Rachev (2006, p. 37).

Finally, we examine the incremental effect inflicted on these measures by the top 5% observations. The marginal impact was computed by

$$\Delta = \frac{T_{classical} - T_{robust}}{T_{classical}} \times 100\%,$$

with T being the appropriate measure—one of EL, VaR, and CVaR. Table 12.3 demonstrates that the 12 extreme data points account for up to 58% of the total EL, and up to 76% of the total operational risk capital charge (VaR or CVaR) for the data sample under consideration.

The magnitude of the impact of extreme events on the operational risk capital charge can serve as an important guideline for a bank to decide whether and at what price it should use insurance against extreme losses.

SUMMARY OF KEY CONCEPTS

- Mathematically elegant classical estimation procedures may behave poorly under minor departures in the data from the model assumptions. In the presence of outliers classical procedures may produce biased estimates of the model parameters and vital statistics.
- Low frequency/high severity events are an important characteristic of the operational loss data but possess the properties of outliers. A nondiscriminant treatment of the bulk of the data together with these extreme events would drive the estimates of the mean and scale of the loss distribution upward, and the resulting estimates of the value-at-risk and conditional value-at-risk measures would be unreasonably overstated

(whenever these are estimated on the basis of both expected and unexpected aggregate losses).

- Robust statistics approach focuses on the key characteristics of the generic stream of the data. Robust methods use a subjective or a formal routine to reject outliers or diminish the effect of outlying events. Employing robust methods may signal important flaws in the models, such as outliers, poor classification of loss events, or failure of the assumption on no correlation between loss events.
- Applying robust methods enables a risk analyst to investigate the marginal contribution of extreme low-frequency events to various risk measures. Application of robust methods to operational loss data has demonstrated that the incremental contribution of extreme events that account for the highest 5% of data, stands at roughly 58% to 76% of the annual aggregate expected loss and the operational risk regulatory capital charge.

REFERENCES

Aucremanne, L., Brys, G., Hubert, M., Rousseeuw, P. J., and Struyf, A. (2004), "A Study of Belgian Inflation, Relative Prices and Nominal Rigidities Using New Robust Measures of Skewness and Tail Weight," in Hubert et al. (2004), pp. 13–25.

Bassett, G., Gerber, G., and Rocco, P. (2004), "Robust Strategies for Quantitative Investment Management," in Hubert et al. (2004), pp. 27–37.

BIS (2001), "Consultative Document: Operational Risk," www.BIS.org.

BIS (2003), "The 2002 Loss Data Collection Exercise for Operational Risk: Summary of the Data Collected," www.BIS.org.

BIS (2005), "The Treatment of Expected Losses by Banks Using the AMA Under the Basel II Framework," www.BIS.org.

BIS (2006), "International Convergence of Capital Measurement and Capital Standards," www.BIS.org.

Bowley, A. L. (1920), Elements of Statistics, Charles Scribner's Sons, New York.

Chernobai, A., Burneçki, K., Rachev, S. T., Trück, S., and Weron, R. (2006), "Modeling Catastrophe Claims with Left-Truncated Severity Distributions," Computational Statistics 21(3), pp. 537–555.

Chernobai, A., Menn, C., Rachev, S. T., and Trück, S. (2005), Estimation of Operational Value-at-Risk in the Presence of Minimum Collection Thresholds, Technical report, University of California at Santa Barbara.

Chernobai, A., and Rachev, S. T. (2006), "Applying Robust Methods to Operational Risk Modeling," Journal of Operational Risk 1(1), pp. 27–42.

Currie, C. (2005), A Test of the Strategic Effect of Basel II Operational Risk Requirements for Banks, Technical Report 141, University of Technology, Sydney.

David, H. A. (1981), Order Statistics, 2nd ed., John Wiley & Sons, New York.

Dell'Aquila, R., and Embrechts, P. (2006), "Extremes and Robustness: A Contradiction?," *Financial Markets and Portfolio Management* 20, pp. 103–118.

Financial Guardian Group (2005), The Risk of Operational Risk-Based Capital: Why Cost and Competitive Implications Make Basel II's Requirement Ill-Advised in the United States, Technical report, Financial Guardian Group.

Groeneveld, R. A., and Meeden, G. (1984), "Measuring Skewness and Kurtosis," *The Statistician* 33, pp. 391–399.

Hampel, F. R. (1968), Contribution to the Theory of Robust Estimation, PhD thesis, University of California at Berkeley.

Hampel, F. R. (1973), "Robust Estimation: A Condensed Partial Survey," *Z. Wahrscheinlichkeitstheorie verw. Gebiete* 27, pp. 87–104.

Hampel, F. R. (1974), "The Influence Curve and Its Role in Robust Estimationy," *Journal of the American Statistical Association* 69, pp. 383–393.

Hampel, F. R. (1985), "The Breakdown Points of the Mean Combined with Some Rejection Rules," *Technometrics* 27, pp. 95–107.

Hampel, F. R., Ronchetti, E. M., Rousseeuw, R. J., and Stahel, W. A. (1986), *Robust Statistics: The Approach Based on Influence Functions*, John Wiley & Sons, New York.

Hinkley, D. V. (1975), "On Power Transformations to Symmetry," *Biometrika* 62, pp. 101–111.

Hogg, R. V. (1972), "More Light on the Kurtosis and Related Statistics," *Journal of the American Statistical Association* 67, pp. 422–424.

Hogg, R. V. (1974), "Adaptive Robust Procedures: A Partial Review and Some Suggestions for Future Applications and Theory," *Journal of the American Statistical Association* 69, pp. 909–923.

Huber, P. J. (1964), "Robust Estimation of a Location Parameter," *Annals of Mathematical Statistics* 35, pp. 73–101.

Huber, P. J. (1981), *Robust Statistics*, John Wiley & Sons, New York.

Hubert, M., Pison, G., Struyf, A., and van Aelst, S., eds. (2004), *Theory and Applications of Recent Robust Methods*, Birkhäuser, Basel.

Kendall, M. G., and Stuart, A. (1977), *The Advanced Theory of Statistics*, vol. 1, Charles Griffin and Co., London.

Kim, T.-H., and White, H. (2003), On More Robust Estimation of Skewness and Kurtosis: Simulation and Application to the S&P500 Index, Technical report, University of California at San Diego.

Knez, P. J., and Ready, M. J. (1997), "On the Robustness of Size and Book-to-Market in Cross-Sectional Regressions," *Journal of Finance* 52, 1355–1382.

Martin, R. D., and Simin, T. T. (2003), "Outlier Resistant Estimates of Beta," *Financial Analysts Journal* 59, pp. 56–69.

Moors, J. J. A. (1988), "A Quantile Alternative for Kurtosis," *The Statistician* 37, 25–32.

Moscadelli, M. (2004), The Modeling of Operational Risk: Experience with the Analysis of the Data Collected by the Basel Committee, Technical report, Bank of Italy.

Olive, D. J. (2005), *Applied Robust Statistics*, Southern Illinois University.

Perret-Gentil, C., and Victoria-Feser, M. (2005), Robust Mean-Variance Portfolio Selection, Technical Report 140, International Center for Financial Asset Management and Engineering.

Rousseeuw, P. J., and Croux, C. (1993), Alternatives to the Median Absolute Deviation, *Journal of American Statistics Association* 88, pp. 1273–1283.

Rousseeuw, P. J., and Leroy, A. M. (1987), *Robust Regression and Outlier Detection*, John Wiley & Sons, New York.

Simonoff, J. S. (1987a), "The Breakdown and Influence Properties of Outlier-Rejection-Plus-Mean Procedures," *Communications in Statistics: Theory and Methods* 16, pp. 1749–1769.

Simonoff, J. S. (1987b), Outlier Detection and Robust Estimation of Scale, *Journal of Statistical Computation and Simulation* 27, pp. 79–92.

Stigler, S. M. (1973), Simon Newcomb, Percy Daniell, and the History of Robust Estimation 1885–1920, *Journal of the American Statistical Association* 68, pp. 872–878.

CHAPTER 13

Modeling Dependence

I n earlier chapters we talked about modeling operational risk data that belongs to a particular business line and a particular loss type combination. If a typical internationally active bank has eight business lines and seven event types,[1] then there are a total of 56 such combinations. The question is how to aggregate these risks (e.g., measured by value-at-risk) to produce a consolidated capital charge amount. Would a simple summation of the risk measures be the right solution?[2] But this implies a perfect correlation across groups and suggests that all losses are driven by one single source of randomness instead of multiple independent sources for each of the 56 business line/event type combinations. If this is not the case (and generally, one would expect there to be a certain degree of dependence among groups), then a simple summation would yield an overstated measure of aggregate risk. In this case, one should account for dependence across different business line/event type combinations. According to Chapelle, Crama, Hübner, and Peters (2004), taking dependence into account may substantially reduce the required capital charge, by a factor ranging from 30% to 40%.

Under the recent Basel II guidelines, the *advanced measurement approaches* (AMA) to measuring the operational risk capital charge are allowed to account for the correlations:

Risk measures for different operational risk estimates must be added for purposes of calculating the regulatory minimum capital requirement. However, the bank may be permitted to use internally determined correlations in operational risk losses across individual operational risk estimates, provided it can demonstrate to the

---

[1]Such classification was proposed by the Basel Committee; see the discussion in Chapter 3.
[2]In fact, such solution was initially proposed by the Basel II Capital Accord; see BIS (2001).

satisfaction of the national supervisor that its systems for deter-mining correlations are sound, implemented with integrity, and take into account the uncertainty surrounding any such correlation estimates (particularly in periods of stress). The bank must vali-date its correlation assumptions using appropriate quantitative and qualitative techniques. (BIS, 2006, p. 152)

This chapter focuses on the discussion of various dependence concepts. Note that we discuss dependence between groups rather than the dependence of losses (frequency and/or severity) within a group. There are two types of dependence structures: linear dependence and nonlinear dependence. Linear correlation is the common measure of linear dependence, while copulas can be used to capture nonlinear dependence. We review the notion of correlation and then discuss copulas.

THREE TYPES OF DEPENDENCE IN OPERATIONAL RISK

In operational risk, one can identify three types of dependence:[3]

1. Frequency dependence
2. Loss (severity) dependence
3. Aggregate loss dependence

Frequency dependence may be present in the data when frequencies across groups are dependent on common factors, such as the business size or economic cycle. Empirically, frequency dependence may be measured by computing the historical correlation between events belonging to different business lines or event types.

Severity dependence may be observed when, for example, high losses within one group tend to be accompanied by high losses in another group.

Aggregate loss dependence refers to the dependence between the aggre-gate loss amounts over a particular time period. In other words, aggregate loss dependence is the joint effect of frequency dependence and loss depen-dence. In operational risk, while frequency dependence is expected to be strong, the level of loss dependence is generally low. Moreover, since the loss dependence effects are dominant, it is expected that the aggregate loss dependence would be small.[4] This would be particularly true for

---

[3] See Frachot, Roncalli, and Salomon (2004).

[4] See the discussion of this issue in Frachot, Roncalli, and Salomon (2004). See also Chavez-Demoulin, Embrechts, and Nešlehová (2005), who discuss modeling dependent Poisson processes of operational loss data with copulas.

heavy-tailed loss distributions.[5] Nevertheless, the following subadditivity principle is expected to hold:

$$\sum_{i}^{8}\sum_{j}^{7} VaR(L_{ij}) \geq VaR\left(\sum_{i}^{8}\sum_{j}^{7} L_{ij}\right),$$

where VaR is a shortcut for value-at-risk and L_{ij} denotes a business line/event type combination for business lines $i = 1, 2, \ldots, 8$ and event types $j = 1, 2, \ldots, 7$. Thus, a simple sum of VaR measures, which refers to the scenario of perfect positive correlation (or full positive correlation), is an upper bound for the estimate of a bank's total VaR. In fact, if the correlation effects between groups are very small, this would strongly favor diversification of business activities for an institution.

According to Frachot, Roncalli, and Salomon (2004), the dependence considered by the Basel Committee is most likely to be the aggregate loss dependence, since the form of the dependence structure becomes important primarily at the stage when capital charges from different groups are to be aggregated. In the rest of this chapter we concentrate on the discussion of the aggregate loss dependence.

LINEAR CORRELATION

We explain the notion of correlation using an example of two random variables. Let X and Y be the two random variables with respective finite variances $var(X) > 0$ and $var(Y) > 0$ and respective means $mean(X)$ and $mean(Y)$.

Covariance and Its Properties

Covariance between X and Y is measured as

$$cov(X, Y) = \mathbb{E}\left[(X - mean(X))(Y - mean(Y))\right]$$
$$= \mathbb{E}[XY] - mean(X)mean(Y).$$

Covariance can be positive or negative. Positive covariance indicates that large values of X tend to be observed with large values of Y, and small values of X tend to be observed with small values of Y. In contrast, negative

---

[5]See Frachot, Roncalli, and Salomon (2004).

covariance indicates that the movements in X and Y tend to occur in opposite directions.

Some properties of covariance are as follows:

- $cov(X, X) = \mathrm{var}(X)$
- $cov(aX, Y) = a\, cov(X, Y)$ for a constant a
- $cov(X, Y + Z) = cov(X, Y) + cov(X, Z)$

Correlation and Its Properties

The magnitude of the estimated covariance measure may be difficult to interpret. For example, a covariance equal to 528 does not in itself give us a clear picture as to whether the strength of the relationship between the two variables is strong or weak because there is no standardized benchmark to compare the estimate against. One way to standardize the measure is to divide it by the product of the standard deviations of the two variables. The *correlation coefficient*[6] is calculated as

$$\rho(X, Y) = \frac{cov(X, Y)}{\sqrt{\mathrm{var}(X)}\sqrt{\mathrm{var}(Y)}}.$$

Correlation coefficient can be positive or negative and lies within the bounds $[-1, +1]$, i.e., $-1 \le \rho \le +1$. Therefore, a correlation coefficient contains the information on both the sign and the strength of the dependence relationship. For example, a correlation coefficient equal to $+1$ indicates a perfect positive correlation (or perfect correlation), and a correlation coefficient of -1 indicates a perfect negative correlation. $\rho = 0$ suggests no correlation. It is notable that if X and Y are independent, then $\rho = 0$; however, the converse is not always true.[7] Illustrative examples of negatively and positively correlated random variables are provided in Figure 13.1.

Linear correlation satisfies the following linearity property:

$$\rho(aX + b, cY + d) = \mathrm{sign}(ac)\rho(X, Y),$$

where a, b, c and d are some constants and $\mathrm{sign}(ac)$ equals -1 if $ac < 0$, 0 if $ac = 0$, and 1 if $ac > 0$. This property says that linear correlation is easily handled under positive (i.e., strictly increasing) linear operations.

---

[6]In literature, correlation coefficient is also called Pearson's correlation coefficient.
[7]Consider the following example. Let X and $Y = X^2$ be two random variables, and X follows a normal distribution with mean 0 and variance 1. The covariance is equal to $cov(X, Y) = \mathrm{E}[(X - 0)(X^2 - 1)] = \mathrm{E}[X^3 - X] = 0$, since $\mathrm{E}[X^3] = 0$ (symmetry). Nevertheless, X and Y are not independent by the construction of Y.

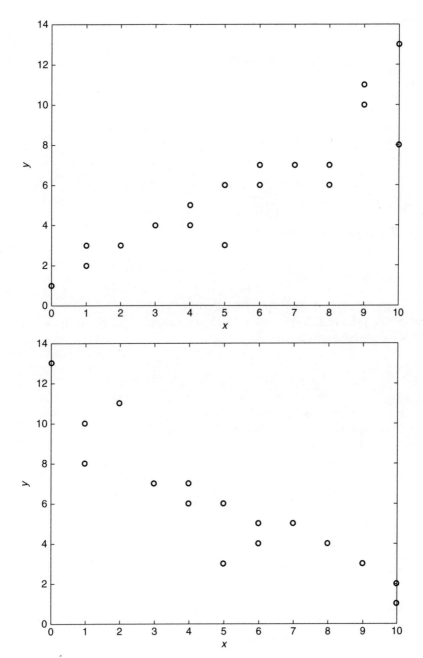

FIGURE 13.1 Illustration of positive correlation (top) and negative correlation (bottom).

Aggregate Loss Correlation When Only Frequencies Are Dependent

Frachot, Roncalli, and Salomon (2004) discuss the situation when only operational frequency distributions are correlated while operational loss distributions are not.[8] Suppose we have two groups (for example, corresponding to two business line/event type combinations) so that their aggregate losses are represented as compound Poisson processes with respective intensity rates λ_1 and λ_2:

$$L_1 = \sum_{i=1}^{N_1} X_{1i}, \qquad L_2 = \sum_{i=1}^{N_2} X_{2i}.$$

The covariance between L_1 and L_2 is

$$cov(L_1, L_2) = \mathbb{E}[L_1 L_2] - \mathbb{E}[L_1]\mathbb{E}[L_2]$$
$$= (\mathbb{E}[N_1 N_2] - \lambda_1 \lambda_2)\, \mathbb{E}X_1 \mathbb{E}X_2,$$

where $E[X_1]$ and $E[X_2]$ are mean(X_1) and mean(X_2), respectively, resulting in the correlation equal to[9]

$$\rho(L_1, L_2) = \rho(N_1, N_2) \frac{\mathbb{E}[X_1]\mathbb{E}[X_2]}{\sqrt{\mathbb{E}[X_1^2]\mathbb{E}[X_2^2]}}.$$

For example, when X_1 and X_2 follow the lognormal distribution with corresponding parameters μ_1, μ_2 and σ_1, σ_2, the aggregate correlation would be:[10]

$$\rho(L_1, L_2) = \rho(N_1, N_2) \exp\left\{ -\frac{\sigma_1^2}{2} - \frac{\sigma_2^2}{2} \right\}.$$

The correlation is clearly dependent on the correlation between the frequencies and the scale parameters of the loss distributions. Frachot, Roncalli,

---

[8]For a related literature, see also Lindskog and McNeil (2003) for a discussion of common Poisson shock models with applications to financial loss modeling and Bäuerle and Grübel (2005) for a discussion of multivariate counting processes.
[9]The same result was obtained by Chavez-Demoulin, Embrechts, and Nešlehová (2005).
[10]See Frachot, Roncalli, and Salomon (2004).

and Salomon (2004) tested the model on Crédit Lyonnais operational loss data: for all severity distributions the scale parameter of the lognormal distribution was above 1.5, which resulted in aggregate correlation between any two business lines/event type combinations below 4%.

Drawbacks of Linear Correlation

There are several reasons for which linear correlation may not be an optimal measure of dependence between risks:

- The major drawback is that linear correlation is a measure of linear dependence. Linear correlation is not invariant under nonlinear strictly increasing transformations. Linear dependence is used in elliptical distributions, such as the multivariate normal and multivariate *t*-distribution. However, random variables may not be jointly elliptically distributed.
- When distributions are very heavy-tailed (as in the case of an alpha-stable distribution), they may not possess a finite second moment. However, finite variance is a necessary requirement for the covariance between two variables to be defined.
- As was explained earlier, independence of two random variables implies zero correlation (i.e., linear correlation equals zero). However, the converse is generally not true, and only holds for elliptical distributions (both marginal and joint).

ALTERNATIVE DEPENDENCE MEASURE: RANK CORRELATION

One of the alternative dependence measures to correlation is *Spearman's rank correlation*. It is defined by

$$\rho_S(X, Y) = \rho(F_X(X), F_Y(Y)),$$

where ρ is the usual linear correlation. The second measure is *Kendall's rank correlation* defined by

$$\rho_K(X, Y) = P((X_1 - X_2)(Y_1 - Y_2) > 0)$$
$$- P((X_1 - X_2)(Y_1 - Y_2) < 0),$$

where (X_1, Y_1) and (X_2, Y_2) are two independent pairs of random variables drawn from a distribution function F. F_X, F_Y, and F above are generally assumed to be continuous.

Just like ρ, ρ_S and ρ_K measure the degree of dependence between random variables X and Y. The main advantage of rank correlation over correlation is the invariance under monotonic transformations. In other words, while ρ_S and ρ_K measure monotonic dependence, ρ only captures the linear dependence. ρ_S and ρ_K are commonly used to measure the unknown parameter in the expression of copulas (see the discussion of copulas to follow). A drawback of rank correlation is that it may be difficult to calculate.

COPULAS

Copulas constitute a generalization of correlation and can be used to model advanced dependence structures beyond linear. Copulas also allow studying the tail dependence and hence are useful to model the dependence between extreme values.[11]

Definition of Copula

Intuitively, a *copula* is a multidimensional function that allows for coupling the marginal distribution functions of two or more random variables with their dependence scheme. Let $F(x_1, x_2, \ldots, x_d)$ be the joint distribution of d $(d \geq 2)$ random variables $X_1, X_2, \ldots, X_d$ evaluated at $(x_1, x_2, \ldots, x_d)$, and $F_1(x_1) = P(X_1 \leq x_1)$, $F_2(x_2) = P(X_2 \leq x_2)$, $\ldots$, and $F_d(x_d) = P(X_d \leq x_d)$ be their respective marginal distribution functions. The copula is a d-dimensional distribution function C on $[0, 1]^d$ such that

$$F(x_1, x_2, \ldots, x_d) = P(X_1 \leq x_1, X_2 \leq x_2, \ldots, X_d \leq x_d)$$
$$= C\left(F_1(x_1), F_2(x_2), \ldots, F_d(x_d)\right).$$

Clearly, the joint distribution function becomes decomposed into the marginal distribution functions and the copula that captures the nature of their dependence. We say that C is an d-dimensional copula, or simply a d-copula. Furthermore, if $F_1, F_2, \ldots, F_d$ are continuous, then C is unique.[12]

---

[11] For more information on copulas, see Nelsen (1999), Sklar (1996), and Joe (1997). Simulation techniques for copulas can be found in Cherubini, Luciano, and Vecchiato (2004) and Embrechts, McNeil, and Straumann (2002). See also Chavez-Demoulin, Embrechts, and Nešlehová (2005) for a discussion of the generation of dependent Poisson processes using copulas.

[12] This definition of copula is a result of Sklar's theorem that states that any multivariate distribution with continuous marginal distributions can be transformed into a multivariate uniform distribution. See Sklar (1959).

The concept of copula can also be represented in terms of the joint density $f(x_1, x_2, \ldots, x_d)$ rather than the joint distribution function $F(x_1, x_2, \ldots, x_d)$. For a two-dimensional example,

$$f(x_1, x_2) = f_X(x)f_Y(y)\frac{\partial^2 C(F_1(x_1), F_2(x_2))}{\partial F_1(x_1)\partial F_2(x_2)}.$$

Examples of Copulas

We present some examples of copulas for a bivariate case.

1. Suppose X and Y are two independent random variables. Then the bivariate copula that explains their dependence is the *independence copula*:

$$C(u, v) = u \cdot v.$$

2. Elliptical copulas:
   a. *Gaussian copula*:

$$C(u, v) = \int_{-\infty}^{\Phi^{-1}(u)} \int_{-\infty}^{\Phi^{-1}(v)} \frac{1}{2\pi\sqrt{1-\rho^2}} \exp\left\{-\frac{s^2 - 2\rho st + t^2}{2(1-\rho^2)}\right\} ds\, dt,$$

   where ρ is simply the linear correlation coefficient. Gaussian copulas do not have upper tail and lower tail dependence and therefore cannot capture joint extreme observations that are possibly present in the operational risk data.[13] Figure 13.2 provides an illustration of a Gaussian copula.
   b. *t-copula*:

$$C(u, v) = \int_{-\infty}^{t_d^{-1}(u)} \int_{-\infty}^{t_d^{-1}(v)} \frac{1}{2\pi\sqrt{1-\rho^2}} \left(1 + \frac{s^2 - 2\rho st + t^2}{d(1-\rho^2)}\right)^{-\frac{d+2}{2}},$$

---

[13]Let X and Y be random variables with continuous distribution functions F_X and F_Y. The coefficient of upper-tail dependence is calculated as $\lambda = \lim_{\alpha \to 1} P\left(Y > F_Y^{-1}(\alpha)|X > F_X^{-1}(\alpha)\right)$. λ ranges between 0 and 1. For example, if $\lambda = 0$, then X and Y are asymptotically independent. See Embrechts, McNeil, and Straumann (2002) for details.

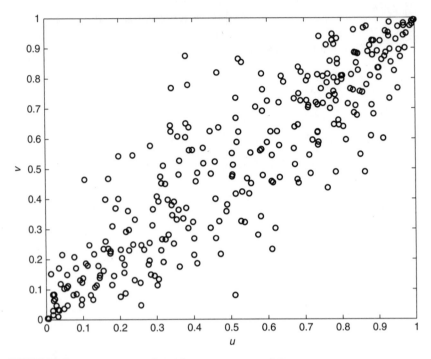

FIGURE 13.2 Gaussian copula with parameter $\rho = 0.9$.

where ρ is simply the linear correlation coefficient, and d is the degrees of freedom such that $d > 2$. t-copula has upper and lower tail dependence that is decreasing in d and is therefore useful for modeling tail dependence. An illustration of tail dependence is provided in Figure 13.3.

3. Archimedean copulas:
   a. *Gumbel copula*:

$$C(u,v) = \exp\left\{-\left((-\ln u)^{\theta} + (-\ln v)^{\theta}\right)^{1/\theta}\right\},$$

where the parameter θ is greater or equal to one and controls the amount of dependence: for example, $\theta = 1$ refers to the case of independence. Gumbel copula has an upper tail dependence and can be used to model extremes. See Figure 13.4 for an illustration.

   b. *Clayton copula*:

$$C(u,v) = (u^{-\theta} + v^{-\theta} - 1)^{-\frac{1}{\theta}},$$

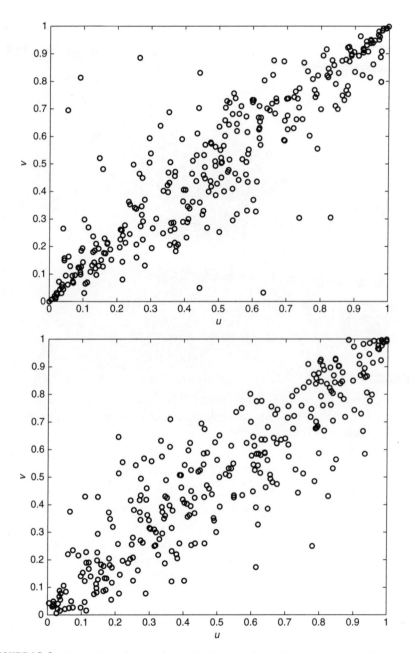

FIGURE 13.3 Examples of *t*-copulas and tail dependence. Top: *t*-copula with parameters $\rho = 0.9$ and $d = 2$; bottom: *t*-copula with parameters $\rho = 0.9$ $d = 30$. Tail dependence decreases when d increases.

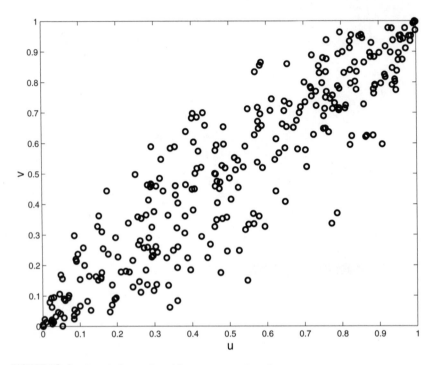

FIGURE 13.4   Gumbel copula with parameter $\theta = 5$.

where the parameter θ is greater than zero. Clayton copula has lower tail dependence. An example of a Clayton copula is illustrated in Figure 13.5.

c. *Frank copula:*

$$C(u,v) = -\frac{1}{\theta} \ln\left(1 + \frac{(e^{-\theta u} - 1)(e^{-\theta v} - 1)}{e^{-\theta} - 1}\right),$$

where the parameter θ is between $-\infty$ and $+\infty$. If the two variables are independent, then $\theta = 0$; positive dependence refers to the case when $\theta > 0$, and perfect negative dependence refers to the case when $\theta < 0$. Frank copula has neither upper nor lower tail dependence. See the illustration of a Frank copula in Figure 13.6.

Other examples include the Lévy copula, which is particularly useful for modeling extreme operational losses. It is defined on $[0, \infty]$ rather than $[0, 1]$. For details, see Böcker and Klüppelberg (2006). For other examples of copulas and constructing them, see Joe (1997).

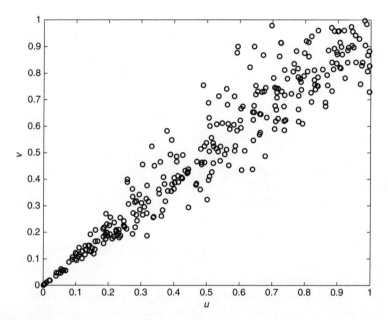

FIGURE 13.5 Clayton copula with parameter $\theta = 10$.

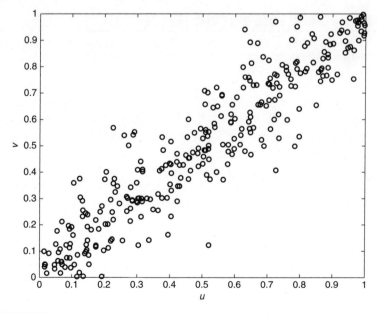

FIGURE 13.6 Frank copula with parameter $\theta = 15$.

USING COPULAS TO AGGREGATE CREDIT, MARKET, AND OPERATIONAL RISKS

The ultimate goal of risk managers is to measure and manage all financial risks simultaneously in a consolidated framework, as opposed to measuring and managing each of the risks in isolation, and to develop a single measure of riskiness (such as risk capital) of a bank. This single measure of riskiness can be useful for investors to compare the overall level of risk of different firms. Before taking any managerial action, banks need to address the total uncertainty and examine how risks correlate, aggregate, and affect each other and how they affect the bank.

It is easy to see that all types of banking risk are related to each other. For example, market volatility affects the value of collateral which in turn has an impact on a banks credit risk. Similarly, market volatility can drive transaction volumes, which in turn has an impact on a banks operational risk exposure. Similarly, large banking losses caused by, for example, operational risk, can inflict severe reputational damage, hence exposing a bank to reputational risk.[14]

Just as copulas provide a solution to aggregating operational risk across various business units, they can also be useful for aggregation of various types of financial risks.

EMPIRICAL STUDIES WITH OPERATIONAL LOSS DATA

In this section we give an overview of related empirical studies.[15] We classify these empirical studies in two groups: (1) those that focus on the dependence of operational risk across various business units or business line/event type combinations; and (2) those that examine the dependence between credit, market, and operational risks on the global level. The first two studies belong to the first group, and the last two to the second group.

Chapelle, Crama, Hübner, and Peters Study

Chapelle, Crama, Hübner and Peters (2004) examine a set of operational loss data from a large European banking institution, whose data collection

---

[14]See also Chapter 2 for further discussion of relation between various risks.
[15]Other studies include Powojowski et al. (2002), Di Clemente and Romano (2004), Reshetar (2005), Embrechts and Puccetti (2005), Chavez-Demoulin, Embrechts, and Nešlehoá (2005) and Böcker and Klüppelberg (2006).

has been carried out in compliance with the Basel II definition of business lines and event types for the adoption of the AMA. Loss data were rescaled to preserve confidentiality.[16]

They argue that most of the correlation in operational loss data comes from the correlated frequency distributions rather than severity distributions. They estimate the Spearman's rank correlation coefficient between frequencies belonging to different business lines. The estimates are summarized in Table 13.1 for six business lines.[17] The reported values are relatively low suggesting that the perfect correlation assumption would be highly misleading for these data (numbers in parentheses indicate the number of sample points).

BL1: Trading and Sales (61)

BL2: Retail Banking (2,033)

BL3: Commercial Banking (23)

BL4: Payment and Settlement (66)

BL5: Agency Services (118)

BL6: Asset Management and Private Banking (693)

They further estimate the aggregate VaR for the bank. They perform the analysis by considering both the correlation effects between business lines

TABLE 13.1 Estimates for Spearman's rank correlation coefficient between various business lines in Chapelle, Crama, Hübner, and Peters study

	BL1	BL2	BL3	BL4	BL5	BL6
BL1	1.000					
BL2	0.162	1.000				
BL3	0.000	0.084	1.000			
BL4	0.299	0.253	0.197	1.000		
BL5	0.293	0.156	0.565	0.423	1.000	
BL6	0.063	0.155	0.269	0.187	0.291	1.000

Source: Chapelle, Crama, Hübner, and Peters (2004, p. 43).

---

[16]Detailed descriptive statistics of the data can be found in Chapelle, Crama, Hübner, and Peters (2004).

[17]A table of this type is often called a correlation matrix.

TABLE 13.2   Estimates for VaR in Chapelle, Crama, Hübner, and Peters study

	Full Positive Dependence	Dependence between BL	Dependence between All Cells	Independence
95% VaR	2,139,472	1,947,965	1,811,360	1,781,489
99% VaR	4,106,013	3,320,426	3,032,034	2,868,935
99.9% VaR	7,908,790	5,379,562	4,487,290	4,192,533
99.95% VaR	9,184,315	6,098,291	4,863,845	4,390,021

Source: Chapelle, Crama, Hübner, and Peters (2004, p. 44).

only and the correlation effects between all cells corresponding to different business line/event type combinations. For the dependence scheme, they consider the Gaussian copula with the Spearman's correlation coefficient of $\rho_S = 0.155$ and the Frank copula with the estimated coefficient of 0.97. Table 13.2 summarizes the VaR estimates at different confidence levels and four scenarios: (1) full positive dependence; (2) dependence between business lines only; (3) dependence between all business line/event type cells; and (4) independence.

Clearly, full positive dependence assumption results in a severe overestimation of VaR, with the magnitude of overestimation increasing to nearly 2 times as the confidence level increases. When the Frank copula was used for the analysis, the capital charge was estimated to be slightly higher: when only the correlation between business lines was considered, the capital charge was estimated to be 4.55 million (after taking into account insurance effects) versus 4.53 million under the Gaussian copula. From the empirical results it is also evident that the independence assumption results in only slightly lower VaR estimates than under the cross-cell dependence scheme, evidence that losses across groups are not strongly dependent.

Finally, Chapelle, Crama, Hübner, and Peters estimate and compare the capital charge amounts (K) for the three Basel II approaches: the basic indicator approach (BIA), the standardized approach (SA), and the advanced measurement approach (AMA) with the Gaussian copula. See Table 13.3. For example, the value of 49 in the sixth row and third column means that the AMA-based capital charge, after accounting for all cell dependence, is only 49% of the capital charge estimated using the BIA.

Dalla Valle, Fantazzini, and Giudici Study

Dalla Valle, Fantazzini, and Giudici (2005) examine operational loss data from a bank whose name was not disclosed. The data set consists of monthly

TABLE 13.3 Comparison of operational capital charge estimates for different estimation approaches in Chapelle, Crama, Hübner, and Peters study

	K	$\frac{K}{K_{BIA}} \times 100$	$\frac{K}{K_{SA}} \times 100$	$\frac{K}{K_{AMA-fulldep.}} \times 100$
BIA	7,470,036	100	106	125
SA	5,976,029	80	100	85
AMA full dependence	7,053,381	94	118	100
AMA BL dependence	4,533,046	61	76	64
AMA cell dependence	3,634,030	49	61	52
AMA independence	3,343,393	45	56	47

Source: Chapelle, Crama, Hübner, and Peters (2004, p. 45).

TABLE 13.4 Descriptive statistics of operational loss data sample in Dalla Valle, Fantazzini, and Giudici study

	Amount (in euro)
Minimum	0
Maximum	4,570,852
Monthly average	202,158

observations collected over the January 1999 to December 2004 timeframe. There are 407 loss events classified into two business lines and four event types, forming a total of eight business line/event type combinations. The cells are labeled cell 1, 2 , ... , 8, respectively. Table 13.4 summarizes some descriptive statistics of the data set.

They further fit Poisson and negative binomial distributions to the frequency data and exponential, gamma, and Pareto distributions to the loss severity data. Table 13.5 summarizes the parameters for each cell estimated using the method of moments.

Next, Dalla Valle, Fantazzini, and Giudici (2005) fit the Gaussian and t-copulas to the aggregate losses within each cell. Table 13.6 provides the estimates of the ρ coefficient for the Gaussian copula. The estimates suggest that the degree of dependence is very small (around zero) and is often negative, that is consistent with the results described in the Chapelle, Crama, Hübner, and Peters study.

Table 13.7 summarizes the estimates for 95% and 99% VaR and CVaR (in euro) for three scenarios: (1) full positive dependence, (2) Gaussian copula, and (3) t-copula. $d = 9$ degrees of freedom were used for the t-copula. It is evident from Table 13.7 that the perfect positive correlation

TABLE 13.5 Frequency and severity distributions parameter estimates for every business line/event type combination in Dalla Valle, Fantazzini, and Giudici study

| | Frequency | | | Severity | | | | |
| | Poisson | Neg. Binomial | | Expon. | Gamma | | Pareto | |
	λ	p	θ	α	α	β	α	β
Cell 1	1.40	0.59	2.01	9,844	0.15	64,848	2.36	13,368
Cell 2	2.19	0.40	1.49	21,721	0.20	109,321	2.50	32,494
Cell 3	0.08	0.80	0.33	153,304	0.20	759,717	2.51	230,817
Cell 4	0.46	0.92	5.26	206,162	0.11	1,827,627	2.25	258,588
Cell 5	0.10	0.84	0.52	96,873	0.20	495,701	2.49	143,933
Cell 6	0.63	0.33	0.31	7,596	0.38	19,734	3.25	17,105
Cell 7	0.68	0.42	0.49	12,623	0.06	211,098	2.13	14,229
Cell 8	0.11	0.88	0.80	35,678	0.26	135,643	2.71	61,146

Source: Dalla Valle, Fantazzini, and Giudici (2005, pp. 11 and 12).

TABLE 13.6 Correlation coefficient estimates for every business line/event type combination in Dalla Valle, Fantazzini, and Giudici study

	Cell 1	Cell 2	Cell 3	Cell 4	Cell 5	Cell 6	Cell 7	Cell 8
Cell 1	1.000							
Cell 2	−0.050	1.000						
Cell 3	−0.142	−0.009	1.000					
Cell 4	0.051	0.055	0.139	1.000				
Cell 5	−0.204	0.023	−0.082	−0.008	1.000			
Cell 6	0.252	0.115	−0.187	0.004	0.118	1.000		
Cell 7	0.140	0.061	−0.193	−0.073	−0.102	−0.043	1.000	
Cell 8	−0.155	0.048	−0.090	−0.045	−0.099	0.078	−0.035	1.000

Source: Dalla Valle, Fantazzini, and Giudici (2005, p. 13).

assumption results in much higher estimates of the capital charge than under the assumptions of a copula-type dependence scheme: using copulas results in savings for the bank ranging between 30% and 50%.

The authors then carry out extensive backtesting for the models. In particular, they conclude that the exponential distribution is a poor fit to the loss data, and gamma appears to provide the best fit. On the other hand, a choice of the frequency distribution (Poisson or negative binomial) played a minor role on the estimates of VaR and CVaR. (For more details on the study, see the original paper.)

TABLE 13.7 Estimates of VaR and CVaR (in euro) under different dependence structures for every business line/event type combination in the Dalla Valle, Fantazzini, and Giudici study

Frequency	Severity	Dependence	95% VaR ('000,000)	99% VaR ('000,000)	95% VaR ('000,000)	99% VaR ('000,000)
Poisson	Expon.	Full dependence	0.925	1.940	1.557	2.557
		Gaussian copula	0.656	1.087	0.920	1.341
		t-copula	0.634	1.125	0.955	1.415
	Gamma	Full dependence	0.861	3.695	2.640	6.253
		Gaussian copula	0.767	2.246	1.719	3.522
		t-copula	0.789	2.337	1.810	3.798
	Pareto	Full dependence	0.860	2.389	2.016	4.662
		Gaussian copula	0.637	1.506	1.295	2.786
		t-copula	0.673	1.591	1.329	2.814
Negative Binomial	Expon.	Full dependence	0.965	2.120	1.676	2.810
		Gaussian copula	0.672	1.110	0.942	1.360
		t-copula	0.687	1.136	0.976	1.458
	Gamma	Full dependence	0.907	3.832	2.766	6.506
		Gaussian copula	0.784	2.339	1.770	3.644
		t-copula	0.806	2.452	1.848	3.845
	Pareto	Full dependence	0.860	2.487	2.028	4.540
		Gaussian copula	0.673	1.547	1.312	2.732
		t-copula	0.694	1.567	1.329	2.750

Source: Dalla Valle, Fantazzini, and Giudici (2005, p. 13).

Kuritzkes, Schuermann, and Weiner Study

Kuritzkes, Schuermann, and Weiner (2003) examine the implications of the risk structure for capital adequacy. In particular, they study diversification effects of taking various risks on a financial institution's risk capital. For the purpose of illustrating the diversification effects, they make a simplifying assumption that all risks are jointly normally distributed. The diversification benefit is then calculated as the ratio in which the numerator is the difference between the sum of standalone economic capital estimates and the true total economic capital after the diversification effects, and the denominator is the sum of stand-alone economic capital estimates.

They suggest aggregating risks at three different levels:

Level I: Aggregating risks within a single risk factor within a single business line.

Level II: Aggregating risks across different risk factors within a single business line.

Level III: Aggregating risks across different business lines.

TABLE 13.8 Correlation matrix between various risk types in the Kuritzkes, Schuermann, and Weiner study

	Credit risk	Market/ALM risk	Operational & other risks
Credit risk	1.0		
Market/ALM risk	0.8	1.0	
Operational & other risks	0.4	0.4	1.0

Source: Kuritzkes, Schuermann, and Weiner (2003, p. 27), with modifications.

They find that the diversification effects decrease as the level increases. For example, at level I, over 50% reduction in economic capital for credit risk can be achieved from diversifying the credit risk on an equally weighted commercial loan portfolio internationally. At level II, 15% to 28% diversification benefits can be achieved for a typical bank when correlations between credit, market, operational, and other risks are considered. Table 13.8 presents an example of correlations across the three main risk types: credit risk, market and *asset-liability management* (ALM) risk, and operational and other risks.[18] At level III, the diversification benefit is only 0% to 12%.

Rosenberg and Schuermann Study

Rosenberg and Schuermann (2004) carry out a comprehensive study of banks' returns driven by credit, market, and operational risks. They propose a copula-based methodology to integrate a bank's distributions of credit, market, and operational risk-driven returns. Finally, they compute VaR and CVaR measures for a bank's aggregate returns.

The general model considers a case of a bank's portfolio return generated by three sources of risk: credit, market, and operational. The mean of such portfolio is

$$\mu_p = w_x\mu_x + w_y\mu_y + w_z\mu_z,$$

where w_i and μ_i, $i = x, y, z$ represent the weights and the means corresponding to the three sources of risk.

---

[18]In the original study, they presented three versions of interrisk correlation coefficients.

Rosenberg and Schuermann consider four cases for a bank's return-based VaR, depending on the dependence structure and marginal distributions of individual risk returns. For the first three cases they assume that the individual returns' distributions and the portfolio return distribution belong to the same distribution family.

1. *Normal VaR*. It assumes that the risk distribution is multivariate normal (which assumes that each of the marginal risk return distributions are also normal).
2. *Additive VaR*. It assumes perfect correlation (i.e., the correlation coefficient equals unity) between risks.
3. *Hybrid VaR*. No further assumptions are made.
4. *Copula VaR*. Return distributions are dependent via a Gaussian or t − copula scheme.

For their empirical study Rosenberg and Schuermann use quarterly data from the first quarter of 1994 to the fourth quarter of 2002 for 10 bank holding companies. They determine the weights of market, credit, and operational risks to be 4.1%, 26.4%, and 69.5%, respectively. Due to the small sample size of the data used for the analysis, they identify a set of observable relevant risk factors affecting each of the market and credit risk-related returns, and then generate a large sample (200,000) of returns based on the regression estimates. The proxy for market returns is trading revenue obtained from regulatory reports divided by the sum of trading assets and liabilities, rescaled to reflect annualized returns. Credit risk-driven returns are captured by a ratio with the numerator being net interest income minus provisions and denominator being the amount of lending assets. Operational risk-related returns are obtained by simulating 200,000 operational losses and dividing them by the total value of assets. The one-year aggregate losses are simulated based on the Pareto loss distribution with parameter $\alpha = 0.65$ and the average number of large losses (in excess of $1 million) of 65 losses per year.

Once the annualized returns were obtained for all three sources of risk, distributions were fitted to the market and credit returns. They used the t-distribution (with 11 degrees of freedom) and Weibull distribution for the market and credit returns, respectively. A cubic spline (rather than a parametric distribution) was fitted to the simulated operational returns. Table 13.9 reports sample descriptive statistics for the simulated bank's returns. Market risk has the highest volatility, followed by credit risk and operational risk. Operational risk has the thickest tails, while market risk has the thinnest tails. Operational risk also appears significantly skewed.

TABLE 13.9 Sample descriptive statistics for simulated 200,000 returns in the Rosenberg and Schuermann study

	Market Risk	Credit Risk	Operational Risk
Mean	0.26%	0.18%	0.02%
St. deviation	0.64%	0.41%	0.04%
Skewness	0.0	−1.1	−4.5
Kurtosis	3.9	5.2	35.3

Source: Rosenberg and Schuermann (2004, p. 44).

TABLE 13.10 Correlation matrix for a benchmark institution, used in the Rosenberg and Schuermann study

	Market Risk	Credit Risk	Operational Risk
Market risk	1.0		
Credit risk	0.5	1.0	
Operational risk	0.2	0.2	1.0

The three risks were then aggregated using the four scenarios outlined earlier. For the copula VaR approach, the normal copula and t-copula were considered to estimate the 99% VaR.[19] Correlation estimates between the three risks are reported in Table 13.10. Additive VaR was the lowest estimate of VaR (below zero but highest in absolute magnitude), followed by hybrid VaR, copula VaR, and finally normal VaR.

While Rosenberg and Schuermann further experimented with changing the portfolio weights and examining the impact on VaR estimates, the relative results remained unchanged. For example, with equal shares of market risk and credit risk and 69.5% share of operational risk out of total risk, the 99% VaR was roughly −1% for additive VaR, −0.7% for hybrid VaR, −0.6% for copula VaR, and −0.4% for normal VaR. Increasing the operational risk share resulted in a slight increase the VaR estimates (i.e., VaR became closer to zero). In addition, increasing correlation between market and credit risks, while keeping their correlations with operational risk unchanged, resulted in a slight decrease in VaR. Increasing correlations of the two risks with operational risk while keeping the correlation

[19]The VaR estimates were below zero, because the aggregate returns distribution ranged from positive to negative values.

between credit and market risks unchanged, resulted in a more pronounced decrease in total VaR. Comparable results were obtained by considering CVaR instead of VaR and by using *t*-copula instead of the Gaussian one. Interestingly, the hybrid approach resulted in the VaR estimates surprisingly close to those under the *t*-copula and therefore appears to capture well the tail dependence between various sources of risk.

SUMMARY OF KEY CONCEPTS

- Dependence in operational loss data can be of three different types: frequency dependence, severity dependence, and aggregate loss dependence. Under the Basel II Capital Accord, the aggregate loss dependence is central in the advanced measurement approaches and becomes essential when risk capital measures need to be aggregated across all business line/event type combinations. If a perfect positive correlation is assumed, then the total risk capital for a bank is a simple sum of all individual risk capital measures.
- Three basic dependence principles include linear correlation, rank correlation, and copulas. Linear correlation, though easy to manipulate, suffers from major drawbacks: it is a measure of linear dependence, it requires a finite second moment, and zero correlation does not necessarily imply independence.
- Copulas provide a good alternative to linear correlation and extend the nature of dependence to nonlinear cases. A copula couples the marginal distribution functions of two or more random variables with their dependence scheme. Examples of copulas include the Gaussian, *t*, Gumbel, Clayton, Frank, and Lévy copulas. Of particular interest in operational risk modeling are the copulas that have an upper-tail dependence, such as the *t*, Gumbel, and Lévy copulas.
- Empirical studies with operational loss data provide a strong evidence that there is a near-zero (often negative) degree of dependence among different business line/event type combinations. This rules out the case of perfect positive dependence scheme. Studies suggest that diversification of business units provides a favorable situation for a financial institution in that it allows for a reduction in the risk capital.
- Other empirical studies focus on modeling dependence between different risks—credit, market, and operational. Taking into account the correlation effects produces a smaller estimate for a bank's aggregate level of risk, thus supporting the idea that diversification results in reduction of risk.

REFERENCES

Bäuerle, N. and Grübel, R. (2005), *Multivariate Counting Processes: Copulas and Beyond*, University of Hannover, preprint.

BIS (2001), "Consultative Document: Operational Risk", www.BIS.org.

BIS (2006), "International Convergence of Capital Measurement and Capital Standards", www.BIS.org.

Böcker, K. and Klüppelberg, K. (2006), Multivariate Models for Operational Risk, Technical report, Munich University of Technology.

Chapelle, A., Crama, Y., Hübner, G., and Peters, J. (2004), Basel II and Operational Risk: Implications for Risk Measurement and Management in the Financial Sector, Technical report, National Bank of Belgium.

Chavez-Demoulin, V., Embrechts, P., and Nešlehová, J. (2005), Quantitative Models for Operational Risk: Extremes, Dependence, and Aggregation, Technical report, ETH Zürich.

Cherubini, U., Luciano, E., and Vecchiato, W. (2004), *Copula Methods in Finance*, John Wiley & Sons, Chichester.

Dalla Valle, L., Fantazzini, D. and Giudici, P. (2005), Copulae and Operational Risks, Technical report, University of Pavia.

Di Clemente, A. and Romano, C. (2004), "A Copula-Extreme Value Theory Approach for Modelling Operational Risk," in M. G. Cruz, ed., *Operational Risk Modelling and Analysis. Theory and Practice*, RISK Books, London, pp. 189–208.

Embrechts, P., McNeil, A., and Straumann, D. (2002), "Correlation and Dependence in Risk Management: Properties and Pitfalls," in M. A. H. Dempster, ed., *Risk Management: Value-at-Risk and Beyond*, Cambridge University Press, Cambridge, pp. 176–223.

Embrechts, P. and Puccetti, G. (2005), Aggregating Risk Capital, with an Application to Operational Risk, Technical report, ETH Zurich.

Frachot, A., Roncalli, T., and Salomon, E. (2004), The Correlation Problem in Operational Risk, Technical report, Groupe de Recherche Opérationnelle, Crédit Lyonnais, France.

Joe, H. (1997), *Multivariate Models and Dependence Concepts*, Chapman & Hall, London.

Kuritzkes, A., Schuermann, T., and Weiner, S. M. (2003), Risk Measurement, Risk Management, and Capital Adequacy in Financial Conglomerates, Technical report, Federal Reserve Bank of New York.

Lindskog, F. and McNeil, A. (2003), "Common poisson shock models: Application to insurance and credit risk modelling," *ASTIN Bulletin* 33, pp. 209–238.

Nelsen, R. (1999), *An Introduction to Copulas*, Springer, New York.

Powojowski, M. R., Reynolds, D. and Tuenter, H. J. H. (2002), "Dependent events and operational risk," *Algo Research Quarterly* 5(2), pp. 68–73.

Reshetar, A. (2005), Operational Risk and the Effect of Diversification on Capital Charge, Technical Report, Universität Zurich.

Rosenberg, J. V., and Schuermann, T. (2004), A General Approach to Integrated Risk Management with Skewed, Fat-Tailed Risks, Technical report, Federal Reserve Bank of New York.

Sklar, A. (1959), "Fonctions de répartition à n dimensions et leurs marges," *Publications de l'Institut de Statistique de l'Université de Paris* 8, pp. 229–231.

Sklar, A. (1996), "Random Variables, Distribution Functions, and Copulas—A Personal Look Backward and Forward," in L. Rüschendorff, B. Schweizer and M. Taylor, eds, *Distributions with Fixed Marginals and Related Topics*, Institute of Mathematical Statistics, Hayward, CA, pp. 1–14.

Index

busliness line/event type combination
  correlation coefficient estimates. *See*
    Operational loss data
  frequency/severity distributions parameter
    estimates. *See* Operational loss data
  Spearman's rank correlation coefficient,
    estimation. *See* Operational loss data

Cantor Fitzgerald, employee loss, 10
Capital
  adequacy, risk structure implications
    (Kuritzkes-Schuermann-Weiner study),
    277–278
  allocation. *See* Credit risk; Market risk;
    Operational risk
  calculation, 59
  charge
    determination, 231
    estimates. *See* Crédit Lyonnais loss data
  decomposition, 37–38
  levels (fall), supervisory intervention (timeliness),
    48
  requirements
    guidelines, 63
    increase, 62–63
  structure, 18
  Capital Accord. *See* Basel Capital Accord
  Capital adequacy principles, 47–48
Capital Asset Pricing Model (CAPM), 69–70
Capital Markets Company (CapCo) study. *See*
    Hedge fund failures
Capital Task Force (CTF), responsibility, 36
CAPM. *See* Capital Asset Pricing Model
Catastrophe (cat)
  bonds, 58–59
  options, 58
Catastrophic loss, 39
  absorption, 53
Causal models, 72. *See also* Multifactor causal
    models
CB. *See* Commercial Banking
Chapelle, Crama, Hübner, and Peters study,
    197–199. *See also* European loss data;
    Operational loss data
  mean estimates, 199t
  median estimates, 199t
  VaR estimates, 199t
Characteristic functions. *See* Continuous
    distributions; Discrete distributions
  approach. *See* Alpha-stable distributions

definition, 159–160
properties, 160
Chavez-Demoulin and Embrechts study. *See*
    Operational loss data
Chernobai, Burnecki, Rachev, and Trück-Weron
    study. *See* Insurance; U.S. natural catastrophe
    insurance claims data
Chernobai, Menn, Rachev, and Trück study. *See*
    Public loss data; Public operational loss data
Chernobai and Rachev study. *See* Public loss data;
    Public operational loss data
Chicago Board of Trade (CBOT), cat bonds
    trading, 58
Chi-squared test, 205–206
  disadvantage, 205
  grouping, 204
  usage. *See* Goodness of fit
Chi-square test statistic, 205
Citigroup, information loss, 9
Citron, Robert, 5
Class action suit, 71
Clayton copula, 268, 270
Clayton copula, illustration, 271f
Closed-form densities, 149
Commercial Banking (CB), capital charge, 42
Compliance loss, 20t
Compound operational loss models, 222–226
Conditional approach, 185. *See also* Operational
    risk
  comparison, 188–191
  usage, 191t
Conditional excess distribution
  function, 164
  illustration, 165f
Conditional value-at-risk (CVaR)
  estimates, 176t, 191
  expected aggregate operational loss, impact, 192f
  illustration. *See* Operational 99% conditional
    value-at-risk
  relevance, 235
  risk measure, 235–237
  usage, 196t
  values, estimation. *See* Full operational loss data;
    Top-5%-trimmed operational loss data
Constrained maximum likelihood function
    approach, 187
Continuous distribution
  characteristic function, 159t
  relevance, 112–113
  right tail, illustration, 140f